The Gay Science

Friedrich Nietzsche, The Gay Science, 1882.

Paperback Edition June 2020

Friedrich Nietzsche 1844– 1900

The Gay Science

Friedrich Nietzsche

ÉDITIONS DUCOURT

Contents

EDITORIAL NOTE

"The Joyful Wisdom," written in 1882, just before "Zarathustra," is rightly judged to be one of Nietzsche's best books. Here the essentially grave and masculine face of the poet-philosopher is seen to light up and suddenly break into a delightful smile. The warmth and kindness that beam from his features will astonish those hasty psychologists who have never divined that behind the destroyer is the creator, and behind the blasphemer the lover of life. In the retrospective valuation of his work which appears in "Ecce Homo" the author himself observes with truth that the fourth book, "Sanctus Januarius," deserves especial attention: "The whole book is a gift from the Saint, and the introductory verses express my gratitude for the most wonderful month of January that I have ever spent." Book fifth "We Fearless Ones," the Appendix "Songs of Prince Free-as-a-Bird," and the Preface, were added to the second edition in 1887.

The translation of Nietzsche's poetry has proved[Pg viii] to be a more embarrassing problem than that of his prose. Not only has there been a difficulty in finding adequate translators—a difficulty overcome, it is hoped, by the choice of Miss Petre and Mr Cohn,—but it cannot be denied that even in the original the poems are of unequal merit. By the side of such masterpieces as "To the Mistral" are several verses of comparatively little value. The Editor, however, did not feel justified in making a selection, as it was intended that the edition should be complete. The heading, "Jest, Ruse and Revenge," of the "Prelude in Rhyme" is borrowed from Goethe.

PREFACE TO THE SECOND EDITION.

1.

Perhaps more than one preface would be necessary for this book; and after all it might still be doubtful whether any one could be brought nearer to the *experiences* in it by means of prefaces, without having himself experienced something similar. It seems to be written in the language of the thawing-wind: there is wantonness, restlessness, contradiction and April-weather in it; so that one is as constantly reminded of the proximity of winter as of the *victory* over it: the victory which is coming, which must come, which has perhaps already come... Gratitude continually flows forth, as if the most unexpected thing had happened, the gratitude of a convalescent—for *convalescence* was this most unexpected thing. "Joyful Wisdom": that implies the Saturnalia of a spirit which has patiently withstood a long, frightful pressure—patiently, strenuously, impassionately, without submitting, but without hope—and which is now suddenly o'erpowered with hope, the hope of health, the *intoxication* of convalescence. What wonder that much that is unreasonable and foolish thereby comes to light: much wanton tenderness expended even on problems which have a prickly hide, and are not therefore fit to be fondled and allured. The whole book is really nothing but a revel after long privation and impotence: the frolicking of returning energy, of newly awakened belief in a to-morrow and after-to-morrow; of sudden sentience and prescience of a future, of near adventures, of seas open once more, and aims once more permitted and believed in. And what was now all behind me! This track of desert, exhaustion, unbelief, and frigidity in the midst of youth, this advent of grey hairs at the wrong time, this tyranny of pain, surpassed, however, by the tyranny of pride which repudiated the *consequences* of pain—and consequences are comforts,—this radical isolation, as defence against the contempt of mankind become morbidly clairvoyant, this restriction upon principle to all that is bitter, sharp, and painful in knowledge, as prescribed by the *disgust* which had gradually resulted from imprudent spiritual diet and pampering—it is called Romanticism,—oh, who could realise all those feelings of mine! He, however, who could do so would certainly forgive me everything, and more than a little folly, boisterousness and "Joyful Wisdom"—for example, the handful of songs which are given along with the book on this occasion,—songs in which a poet makes merry over all poets in a way not easily pardoned.—Alas, it is not only on the poets and their fine "lyrical sentiments" that this reconvalescent must vent his malignity: who knows what kind of victim he seeks, what kind of monster of material for parody will allure him ere long? *Incipit tragœdia*, it is said at the conclusion of this seriously frivolous book; let people be on their guard! Something or other extraordinarily bad and wicked announces itself: *incipit parodia*, there is no doubt...

2.

—But let us leave Herr Nietzsche; what does it matter to people that Herr Nietzsche has got well again?... A psychologist knows few questions so attractive as those concerning the relations of health to philosophy, and in the case when he himself falls sick, he carries with him all his scientific curiosity into his sickness. For, granting that one is a person, one has necessarily also the philosophy of one's personality; there is, however, an important distinction here. With the one it is his defects which philosophise, with the other it is his riches and powers. The former *requires* his philosophy, whether it be as support, sedative, or medicine, as salvation, elevation, or self-alienation; with the latter it is merely a fine luxury, at best the voluptuousness of a triumphant gratitude, which must inscribe itself ultimately in cosmic capitals on the heaven of ideas. In the other more usual case, however, when states of distress occupy themselves with philosophy (as is the case with all sickly thinkers—and perhaps the sickly thinkers preponderate in the history of philosophy), what will happen to the thought itself which is brought under the *pressure* of sickness? This is the important question for psychologists: and here experiment is possible. We philosophers do just like a traveller who resolves to awake at a given hour, and then quietly yields himself to sleep: we surrender ourselves temporarily, body and soul, to the sickness, supposing we become ill—we shut, as it were, our eyes on ourselves. And as the traveller knows that something *does not* sleep, that something counts the hours and will awake him, we also know that the critical moment will find us awake—that then something will spring forward and surprise the spirit *in the very act,* I mean in weakness, or reversion, or submission, or obduracy, or obscurity, or whatever the morbid conditions are called, which in times of good health have the *pride* of the spirit opposed to them (for it is as in the old rhyme: "The spirit proud, peacock and horse are the three proudest things of earthly source"). After such self-questioning and self-testing, one learns to look with a sharper eye at all that has hitherto been philosophised; one divines better than before the arbitrary by-ways, side-streets, resting-places, and *sunny* places of thought, to which suffering thinkers, precisely as sufferers, are led and misled: one knows now in what direction the sickly *body* and its requirements unconsciously press, push, and allure the spirit—towards the sun, stillness, gentleness, patience, medicine, refreshment in any sense whatever. Every philosophy which puts peace higher than war, every ethic with a negative grasp of the idea of happiness, every metaphysic and physic that knows a *finale,* an ultimate condition of any kind whatever, every predominating, æsthetic or religious longing for an aside, a beyond, an outside, an above—all these permit one to ask whether sickness has not been the motive which inspired the philosopher. The unconscious disguising of physiological requirements under the cloak of the objective, the ideal, the purely spiritual, is carried on to an alarming extent,—and I have often enough asked myself, whether on the whole philosophy hitherto has not generally been merely, an interpretation of the body, and a *misunderstanding of the body.* Behind the loftiest estimates of value by which the history of thought has hitherto been governed, misunderstandings of the bodily constitution, either of individuals, classes, or entire races are concealed. One may always primarily consider these audacious freaks of metaphysic, and especially its answers to the question of the *worth* of existence, as symptoms of certain bodily constitutions; and if, on the whole, when scientifically determined, not a particle of significance attaches to such affirmations and denials of the world, they nevertheless furnish the historian and psychologist with hints so much the more valuable (as we have said) as symptoms of the bodily constitution, its good or bad condition, its fullness, powerfulness, and sovereignty in history; or else of its obstructions, exhaustions, and impoverishments, its premonition of the end, its will to the end. I still expect that a philosophical *physician*, in the exceptional sense of the word—one who applies himself to the problem of the collective health of peoples, periods, races, and mankind generally—will some day have the courage to follow out my suspicion to its ultimate conclusions, and to venture on the judgment that in all philosophising it has not hitherto been a question of "truth" at all, but of something else,—namely, of health, futurity, growth, power, life...

3.

It will be surmised that I should not like to take leave ungratefully of that period of severe sickness, the advantage of which is not even yet exhausted in me: for I am sufficiently conscious of what I have in advance of the spiritually robust generally, in my changeful state of health. A philosopher who has made the tour of many states of health, and always makes it anew, has also gone through just as many philosophies: he really *cannot* do otherwise than transform his condition on every occasion into the most ingenious posture and position,—this art of transfiguration *is* just philosophy. We philosophers are not at liberty to separate soul and body, as the people separate them; and we are still less at liberty to separate soul and spirit. We are not thinking frogs, we are not objectifying and registering apparatuses with cold entrails,—our thoughts must be continually born to us out of our pain, and we must, motherlike, share with them all that we have in us of blood, heart, ardour, joy, passion, pang, conscience, fate and fatality. Life—that means for us to transform constantly into light and flame all that we are, and also all that we meet with; we *cannot* possibly do otherwise. And as regards sickness, should we not be almost tempted to ask whether we could in general dispense with it? It is great pain only which is the ultimate emancipator of the spirit; for it is the teacher of the *strong suspicion* which makes an X out of every U[1], a true, correct X, *i.e.*, the ante-penultimate letter... It is great pain only, the long slow pain which takes time, by which we are burned as it were with green wood, that compels us philosophers to descend into our ultimate depths, and divest ourselves of all trust, all good-nature, veiling, gentleness, and

[1]This poem is a parody of the "Chorus Mysticus" which concludes the second part of Goethe's "Faust." Bayard Taylor's translation of the passage in "Faust" runs as follows:—

averageness, wherein we have perhaps formerly installed our humanity. I doubt whether such pain "improves" us; but I know that it *deepens* us. Be it that we learn to confront it with our pride, our scorn, our strength of will, doing like the Indian who, however sorely tortured, revenges himself on his tormentor with his bitter tongue; be it that we withdraw from the pain into the oriental nothingness—it is called Nirvana,—into mute, benumbed, deaf self-surrender, self-forgetfulness, and self-effacement: one emerges from such long, dangerous exercises in self-mastery as another being, with several additional notes of interrogation, and above all, with the *will* to question more than ever, more profoundly, more strictly, more sternly, more wickedly, more quietly than has ever been questioned hitherto. Confidence in life is gone: life itself has become a *problem.*—Let it not be imagined that one has necessarily become a hypochondriac thereby! Even love of life is still possible—only one loves differently. It is the love of a woman of whom one is doubtful... The charm, however, of all that is problematic, the delight in the X, is too great in those more spiritual and more spiritualised men, not to spread itself again and again like a clear glow over all the trouble of the problematic, over all the danger of uncertainty, and even over the jealousy of the lover. We know a new happiness...

4.

Finally (that the most essential may not remain unsaid), one comes back out of such abysses, out of such severe sickness, and out of the sickness of strong suspicion—*new-born,* with the skin cast; more sensitive, more wicked, with a finer taste for joy, with a more delicate tongue for all good things, with a merrier disposition, with a second and more dangerous innocence in joy; more childish at the same time, and a hundred times more refined than ever before. Oh, how repugnant to us now is pleasure, coarse, dull, drab pleasure, as the pleasure-seekers, our "cultured" classes, our rich and ruling classes, usually understand it! How malignantly we now listen to the great holiday-hubbub with which "cultured people" and city-men at present allow themselves to be forced to "spiritual enjoyment" by art, books, and music, with the help of spirituous liquors! How the theatrical cry of passion now pains our ear, how strange to our taste has all the romantic riot and sensuous bustle which the cultured populace love become (together with their aspirations after the exalted, the elevated, and the intricate)! No, if we convalescents need an art at all, it is *another* art—a mocking, light, volatile, divinely serene, divinely ingenious art, which blazes up like a clear flame, into a cloudless heaven! Above all, an art for artists, only for artists! We at last know better what is first of all necessary *for it*—namely, cheerfulness, *every* kind of cheerfulness, my friends! also as artists:—I should like to prove it. We now know something too well, we men of knowledge: oh, how well we are now learning to forget and *not* know, as artists! And as to our future, we are not likely to be found again in the tracks of those Egyptian youths who at night make the temples unsafe, embrace statues, and would fain unveil, uncover, and put in clear light, everything which for good reasons is kept concealed[2]. No, we have got disgusted with this bad taste, this will to truth, to "truth at all costs," this youthful madness in the love of truth: we are now too experienced, too serious, too joyful, too singed, too profound for that... We no longer believe that truth remains truth when the veil is withdrawn from it: we have lived long enough to believe this. At present we regard it as a matter of propriety not to be anxious either to see everything naked, or to be present at everything, or to understand and "know" everything. "Is it true that the good God is everywhere present?" asked a little girl of her mother: "I think that is indecent":—a hint to philosophers! One should have more reverence for the *shame-facedness* with which nature has concealed herself behind enigmas and motley uncertainties. Perhaps truth is a woman who has reasons for not showing her reasons? Perhaps her name is Baubo, to speak in Greek?... Oh, those Greeks! They knew how *to live:* for that purpose it is necessary to keep bravely to the surface, the fold and the skin; to worship appearance, to believe in forms, tones, and words, in the whole Olympus of appearance! Those Greeks were superficial—*from profundity!* And are we not coming back precisely to this point, we dare-devils of the spirit, who have scaled the highest and most dangerous peak of contemporary thought, and have looked around us from it, have *looked down* from it? Are we not precisely in this respect—Greeks? Worshippers of forms, of tones, and of words? And precisely on that account—artists?

RUTA, near GENOA
>*Autumn,* 1886.

JEST, RUSE AND REVENGE. A PRELUDE IN RHYME.

1.

Invitation.
Venture, comrades, I implore you,

---

[2]Translated by Miss M. D. Petre. Inserted by permission of the editor of the *Nation*, in which it appeared on April 17, 1909.

On the fare I set before you,
You will like it more to-morrow,
Better still the following day:
If yet more you're then requiring,
Old success I'll find inspiring,
And fresh courage thence will borrow
Novel dainties to display.

2.

My Good Luck.

Weary of Seeking had I grown,
So taught myself the way to Find:
Back by the storm I once was blown,
But follow now, where drives the wind.

3.

Undismayed.

Where you're standing, dig, dig out:
Down below's the Well:
Let them that walk in darkness shout:
"Down below—there's Hell!"

4.

Dialogue.

A. Was I ill? and is it ended?
Pray, by what physician tended?
I recall no pain endured!
B. Now I know your trouble's ended:
He that can forget, is cured.

5.

To the Virtuous.

Let our virtues be easy and nimble-footed in
motion,
Like unto Homer's verse ought they to come *and
to go.*

6.

Worldly Wisdom.

Stay not on level plain,
Climb not the mount too high.

But half-way up remain—
The world you'll best descry!

7.

Vademecum—Vadetecum.

Attracted by my style and talk
You'd follow, in my footsteps walk?
Follow yourself unswervingly,
So—careful!—shall you follow me.

8.

The Third Sloughing

My skin bursts, breaks for fresh rebirth,
And new desires come thronging:
Much I've devoured, yet for more earth
The serpent in me's longing.
'Twixt stone and grass I crawl once more,
Hungry, by crooked ways,
To eat the food I ate before,
Earth-fare all serpents praise!

9.

My Roses.

My luck's good—I'd make yours fairer,
(Good luck ever needs a sharer),
Will you stop and pluck my roses?
Oft mid rocks and thorns you'll linger,
Hide and stoop, suck bleeding finger—
Will you stop and pluck my roses?
For my good luck's a trifle vicious,
Fond of teasing, tricks malicious—
Will you stop and pluck my roses?

10.

The Scorner.

Many drops I waste and spill,
So my scornful mood you curse:
Who to brim his cup doth fill,
Many drops *must* waste and spill—
Yet he thinks the wine no worse.

11.

The Proverb Speaks.

Harsh and gentle, fine and mean,
Quite rare and common, dirty and clean,
The fools' and the sages' go-between:
All this I will be, this have been,
Dove and serpent and swine, I ween!

12.

To a Lover of Light.

That eye and sense be not fordone
E'en in the shade pursue the sun!

13.

For Dancers.

Smoothest ice,
A paradise
To him who is a dancer nice.

14.

The Brave Man.

A feud that knows not flaw nor break,
Rather then patched-up friendship, take.

15.

Rust.

Rust's needed: keenness will not satisfy!
"He is too young!" the rabble loves to cry.

16.

Excelsior.

"How shall I reach the top?" No time
For thus reflecting! Start to climb!

17.

The Man of Power Speaks.

Ask never! Cease that whining, pray!
Take without asking, take alway!

18.

Narrow Souls.

Narrow souls hate I like the devil,
Souls wherein grows nor good nor evil.

19.

Accidentally a Seducer[3]

He shot an empty word
Into the empty blue;
But on the way it met
A woman whom it slew.

20.

For Consideration.

A twofold pain is easier far to bear
Than one: so now to suffer wilt thou dare?

21.

Against Pride.

Brother, to puff thyself up ne'er be quick:
For burst thou shalt be by a tiny prick!

22.

Man and Woman.

"The woman seize, who to thy heart appeals!"
Man's motto: woman seizes not, but steals.

23.

Interpretation.

If I explain my wisdom, surely
'Tis but entangled more securely,
I can't expound myself aright:
But he that's boldly up and doing,
His own unaided course pursuing,
Upon my image casts more light!

24.

A Cure for Pessimism.

Those old capricious fancies, friend!
You say your palate naught can please,
I hear you bluster, spit and wheeze,
My love, my patience soon will end!
Pluck up your courage, follow me—
Here's a fat toad! Now then, don't blink,

---

[3]This poem is a parody of the "Chorus Mysticus" which concludes the second part of Goethe's "Faust." Bayard Taylor's translation of the passage in "Faust" runs as follows:—

Swallow it whole, nor pause to think!
From your dyspepsia you'll be free!
25.
A Request.
Many men's minds I know full well,
Yet what mine own is, cannot tell.
I cannot see—my eye's too near—
And falsely to myself appear.
'Twould be to me a benefit
Far from myself if I could sit,
Less distant than my enemy,
And yet my nearest friend's too nigh—
'Twixt him and me, just in the middle!
What do I ask for? Guess my riddle.
26.
My Cruelty.
I must ascend an hundred stairs,
I must ascend: the herd declares
I'm cruel: "Are we made of stone?"
I must ascend an hundred stairs:
All men the part of stair disown.
27.
The Wanderer.
"No longer path! Abyss and silence chilling!"
Thy fault! To leave the path thou wast too willing!
Now comes the test! Keep cool—eyes bright and clear!
Thou'rt lost for sure, if thou permittest—fear.
28.
Encouragement for Beginners.
See the infant, helpless creeping—
Swine around it grunt swine-talk—
Weeping always, naught but weeping,
Will it ever learn to walk?
Never fear! Just wait, I swear it
Soon to dance will be inclined,
And this babe, when two legs bear it,

Standing on its head you'll find.
29.
Planet Egoism.
Did I not turn, a rolling cask,
Ever about myself, I ask,
How could I without burning run
Close on the track of the hot sun?
30.
The Neighbour.
Too nigh, my friend my joy doth mar,
I'd have him high above and far,
Or how can he become my star?
31.
The Disguised Saint.
Lest we for thy bliss should slay thee,
In devil's wiles thou dost array thee,
Devil's wit and devil's dress.
But in vain! Thy looks betray thee
And proclaim thy holiness.
32.
The Slave.
A. He stands and listens: whence his pain?
What smote his ears? Some far refrain?
Why is his heart with anguish torn?
B. Like all that fetters once have worn,
He always hears the clinking—chain!
33.
The Lone One.
I hate to follow and I hate to lead.
Obedience? no! and ruling? no, indeed!
Wouldst fearful be in others' sight?
Then e'en *thyself* thou must affright:
The people but the Terror's guidance heed.
I hate to guide myself, I hate the fray.
Like the wild beasts I'll wander far afield.
In Error's pleasing toils I'll roam

Awhile, then lure myself back home,
Back home, and—to my self-seduction yield.

34.

Seneca et hoc Genus omne.

They write and write (quite maddening me)
Their "sapient" twaddle airy,
As if 'twere *primum scribere,*
Deinde philosophari.

35.

Ice.

Yes! I manufacture ice:
Ice may help you to digest:
If you *had* much to digest,
How you would enjoy my ice!

36.

Youthful Writings.

My wisdom's A and final O
Was then the sound that smote mine ear.
Yet now it rings no longer so,
My youth's eternal Ah! and Oh!
Is now the only sound I hear.[4]

37.

Foresight.

In yonder region travelling, take good care!
An hast thou wit, then be thou doubly ware!
They'll smile and lure thee; then thy limbs they'll tear:
Fanatics' country this where wits are rare!

38.

The Pious One Speaks.

God loves us, *for* he made us, sent us here!—
"Man hath made God!" ye subtle ones reply.
His handiwork he must hold dear,
And *what he made* shall he deny?
There sounds the devil's halting hoof, I fear.

---

[4]Translated by Miss M. D. Petre. Inserted by permission of the editor of the *Nation*, in which it appeared on April 17, 1909.

39.

In Summer.

In sweat of face, so runs the screed,
We e'er must eat our bread,
Yet wise physicians if we heed
"Eat naught in sweat," 'tis said.
The dog-star's blinking: what's his need?
What tells his blazing sign?
In sweat of face (so runs *his* screed)
We're meant to drink our wine!

40.

Without Envy.

His look betrays no envy: and ye laud him?
He cares not, asks not if your throng applaud him!
He has the eagle's eye for distance far,
He sees you not, he sees but star on star!

41.

Heraclitism.

Brethren, war's the origin
Of happiness on earth:
Powder-smoke and battle-din
Witness friendship's birth!
Friendship means three things, you know,—
Kinship in luckless plight,
Equality before the foe
Freedom—in death's sight!

42.

Maxim of the Over-refined.

"Rather on your toes stand high
Than crawl upon all fours,
Rather through the keyhole spy
Than through the open doors!"

43.

Exhortation.

Renown you're quite resolved to earn?
My thought about it

Is this: you need not fame, must learn
To do without it!

44.

Thorough.

I an inquirer? No, that's not my calling
Only *I weigh a lot*—I'm such a lump!—
And through the waters I keep falling, falling,
Till on the ocean's deepest bed I bump.

45.

The Immortals.

"To-day is meet for me, I come to-day,"
Such is the speech of men foredoomed to stay.
"Thou art too soon," they cry, "thou art too late,"
What care the Immortals what the rabble say?

46.

Verdicts of the Weary.

The weary shun the glaring sun, afraid,
And only care for trees to gain the shade.

47.

Descent.

"He sinks, he falls," your scornful looks portend:
The truth is, to your level he'll descend.
His Too Much Joy is turned to weariness,
His Too Much Light will in your darkness end.

48.

Nature Silenced[5]

Around my neck, on chain of hair,
The timepiece hangs—a sign of care.
For me the starry course is o'er,
No sun and shadow as before,
No cockcrow summons at the door,
For nature tells the time no more!
Too many clocks her voice have drowned,
And droning law has dulled her sound.

---

[5]Translated by Miss M. D. Petre. Inserted by permission of the editor of the *Nation,* in which it appeared on May 15, 1909.

49.
The Sage Speaks.
Strange to the crowd, yet useful to the crowd,
I still pursue my path, now sun, now cloud,
But always pass above the crowd!

50.
He lost his Head...
She now has wit—how did it come her way?
A man through her his reason lost, they say.
His head, though wise ere to this pastime lent,
Straight to the devil—no, to woman went!

51.
A Pious Wish.
"Oh, might all keys be lost! 'Twere better so
And in all keyholes might the pick-lock go!"
Who thus reflects ye may as—picklock know.

52.
Foot Writing.
I write not with the hand alone,
My foot would write, my foot that capers,
Firm, free and bold, it's marching on
Now through the fields, now through the papers.

53.
"Human, All-too-Human." ...
Shy, gloomy, when your looks are backward thrust,
Trusting the future where yourself you trust,
Are you an eagle, mid the nobler fowl,
Or are you like Minerva's darling owl?

54.
To my Reader.
Good teeth and a digestion good
I wish you—these you need, be sure!
And, certes, if my book you've stood,
Me with good humour you'll endure.

55.
The Realistic Painter.

"To nature true, complete!" so he begins.
Who complete Nature to his canvas *wins?*
Her tiniest fragment's endless, no constraint
Can know: he paints just what his *fancy* pins:
What does his fancy pin? What he *can* paint!
56.

Poets' Vanity.

Glue, only glue to me dispense,
The wood I'll find myself, don't fear!
To give four senseless verses sense—
That's an achievement I revere!
57.

Taste in Choosing.

If to choose my niche precise
Freedom I could win from fate,
I'd be in midst of Paradise—
Or, sooner still—before the gate!
58.

The Crooked Nose.

Wide blow your nostrils, and across
The land your nose holds haughty sway:
So you, unhorned rhinoceros,
Proud mannikin, fall forward aye!
The one trait with the other goes:
A straight pride and a crooked nose.
59.

The Pen is Scratching…

The pen is scratching: hang the pen!
To scratching I'm condemned to sink!
I grasp the inkstand fiercely then
And write in floods of flowing ink.
How broad, how full the stream's career!
What luck my labours doth requite!
'Tis true, the writing's none too clear—
What then? Who reads the stuff I write?
60.

Loftier Spirits.

This man's climbing up—let us praise him—
But that other we love
From aloft doth eternally move,
So above even praise let us raise him,
He *comes* from above!

61.

The Sceptic Speaks.

Your life is half-way o'er;
The clock-hand moves; your soul is thrilled with fear,
It roamed to distant shore
And sought and found not, yet you—linger here!
Your life is half-way o'er;
That hour by hour was pain and error sheer:
Why stay? What seek you more?
"That's what I'm seeking—reasons why I'm here!"

62.

Ecce Homo.

Yes, I know where I'm related,
Like the flame, unquenched, unsated,
I consume myself and glow:
All's turned to light I lay my hand on,
All to coal that I abandon,
Yes, I am a flame, I know!

63.

Star Morality[6]

Foredoomed to spaces vast and far,
What matters darkness to the star?
Roll calmly on, let time go by,
Let sorrows pass thee—nations die!
Compassion would but dim the light
That distant worlds will gladly sight.
To thee one law—be pure and bright!

---

[6]Title of the well-known poem of Uhland.—TR.

BOOK FIRST

1.

The Teachers of the Object of Existence.—Whether I look with a good or an evil eye upon men, I find them always at one problem, each and all of them: to do that which conduces to the conservation of the human species. And certainly not out of any sentiment of love for this species, but simply because nothing in them is older, stronger, more inexorable and more unconquerable than that instinct,—because it is precisely *the essence* of our race and herd. Although we are accustomed readily enough, with our usual short-sightedness, to separate our neighbours precisely into useful and hurtful, into good and evil men, yet when we make a general calculation, and reflect longer on the whole question, we become distrustful of this defining and separating, and finally leave it alone. Even the most hurtful man is still perhaps, in respect to the conservation of the race, the most useful of all; for he conserves in himself, or by his effect on others, impulses without which mankind might long ago have languished or decayed. Hatred, delight in mischief, rapacity and ambition, and whatever else is called evil—belong to the marvellous economy of the conservation of the race; to be sure a costly, lavish, and on the whole very foolish economy:—which has, however, hitherto preserved our race, *as is demonstrated to us.* I no longer know, my dear fellow-man and neighbour, if thou *canst* at all live to the disadvantage of the race, and therefore, "unreasonably" and "badly"; that which could have injured the race has perhaps died out many millenniums ago, and now belongs to the things which are no longer possible even to God. Indulge thy best or thy worst desires, and above all, go to wreck!—in either case thou art still probably the furtherer and benefactor of mankind in some way or other, and in that respect thou mayest have thy panegyrists—and similarly thy mockers! But thou wilt never find him who would be quite qualified to mock at thee, the individual, at thy best, who could bring home to thy conscience its limitless, buzzing and croaking wretchedness so as to be in accord with truth! To laugh at oneself as one would have to laugh in order to laugh *out of the veriest truth,*—to do this, the best have not hitherto had enough of the sense of truth, and the most endowed have had far too little genius! There is perhaps still a future even for laughter! When the maxim, "The race is all, the individual is nothing,"—has incorporated itself in humanity, and when access stands open to every one at all times to this ultimate emancipation and irresponsibility.—Perhaps then laughter will have united with wisdom, perhaps then there will be only "joyful wisdom." Meanwhile, however, it is quite otherwise, meanwhile the comedy of existence has not yet "become conscious" of itself, meanwhile it is still the period of tragedy, the period of morals and religions. What does the ever new appearing of founders of morals and religions, of instigators of struggles for moral valuations, of teachers of remorse of conscience and religious war, imply? What do these heroes on this stage imply? For they have hitherto been the heroes of it, and all else, though solely visible for the time being, and too close to one, has served only as preparation for these heroes, whether as machinery and coulisse, or in the rôle of confidants and valets. (The poets, for example, have always been the valets of some morality or other.)—It is obvious of itself that these tragedians also work in the interest of the *race*, though they may believe that they work in the interest of God, and as emissaries of God. They also further the life of the species, *in that they further the belief in life.* "It is worthwhile to live"—each of them calls out,—"there is something of importance in this life; life has something behind it and under it; take care!" That impulse, which rules equally in the noblest and the ignoblest, the impulse to the conservation of the species, breaks forth from time to time as reason and passion of spirit; it has then a brilliant train of motives about it, and tries with all its power to make us forget that fundamentally it is just impulse, instinct, folly and baselessness. Life *should* beloved, for...! Man *should* benefit himself and his neighbour, *for*...! And whatever all these *shoulds* and *fors* imply, and may imply in future! In order that that which necessarily and always happens of itself and without design, may henceforth appear to be done by design, and may appeal to men as reason and ultimate command,—for that purpose the ethiculturist comes forward as the teacher of design in existence; for that purpose he devises a second and different existence, and by means of this new mechanism he lifts the old common existence off its old common hinges. No! he does not at all want us to *laugh* at existence, nor even at ourselves—nor at himself; to him an individual is always an individual, something first and last and immense, to him there are no species, no sums, no noughts. However foolish and fanatical his inventions and valuations may be, however much he may misunderstand the course of nature and deny its conditions—and all systems of ethics hitherto have been foolish and anti-natural to such a degree that mankind would have been ruined by any one of them had it got the upper hand,—at any rate, every time that "the hero" came upon the stage something new was attained: the frightful counterpart of laughter, the profound convulsion of many individuals at the thought, "Yes, it is worth while to live! yes, I am worthy to live!"—life, and thou, and I, and all of us together became for a while *interesting* to ourselves once more.—It is not to be denied that hitherto laughter and reason and nature have *in the long run* got the upper hand of all the great teachers of design: in the end the short tragedy always passed over once more into the eternal comedy of existence; and the "waves of innumerable laughters"—to use the expression of Æschylus—must also in the end beat over the greatest of these tragedies. But with all this corrective laughter, human nature has on the whole been changed by the ever new appearance of those teachers of the design of existence,—human nature has now an additional requirement, the very requirement of the ever new appearance of such teachers and doctrines of "design." Man has gradually become a visionary animal, who has to fulfil one more condition of existence than the other animals: man *must* from time to time believe that he knows *why* he exists; his species cannot flourish without periodically confiding in life! Without the belief in *reason in life!* And always from time to time will the human race decree anew that "there is something which really may not be laughed at." And the most clairvoyant philanthropist will add that "not only laughing and joyful wisdom, but also the tragic with all its sublime irrationality, counts among the means and necessities for the conservation of the race!"—And consequently! Consequently! Consequently! Do you understand me, oh my brothers? Do you understand this new law of ebb and flow? We also shall have our time!

2.

The Intellectual Conscience.—I have always the same experience over again, and always make a new effort against it; for although it is evident to me I do not want to believe it: *in the greater number of men the intellectual conscience is lacking;* indeed, it would often seem to me that in demanding such a thing, one is as solitary in the largest cities as in the desert. Everyone looks at you with strange eyes and continues to make use of his scales, calling this good and that bad; and no one blushes for shame when you remark that these weights are not the full amount,—there is also no indignation against you; perhaps they laugh at your doubt. I mean to say that *the greater number of people* do not find it contemptible to believe this or that, and live according to it, *without* having been previously aware of the ultimate and surest reasons for and against it, and without even giving themselves any trouble about such reasons afterwards,—the most Sifted men and the noblest women still belong to this "greater number." But what is kind-heartedness, refinement and genius to me, if he who has these virtues harbours indolent sentiments in belief and judgment, if *the longing for certainty* does not rule in him, as his innermost desire and profoundest need—as that which separates higher from lower men! In certain pious people I have found a hatred of reason, and have been favourably disposed to them for it: their bad intellectual conscience at least still betrayed itself in this manner! But to stand in the midst of this *rerum concordia discors* and all the marvellous uncertainty and ambiguity of existence, *and not to question*, not to tremble with desire and delight in questioning, not even to hate the questioner—perhaps even to make merry over him to the extent of weariness—that is what I regard as *contemptible,* and it is this sentiment which I first of all search for in every one—some folly or other always persuades me anew that every man has this sentiment, as man. This is my special kind of unrighteousness.

3.

Noble and Ignoble.—To ignoble natures all noble, magnanimous sentiments appear inexpedient, and on that account first and foremost, as incredible: they blink with their eyes when they hear of such matters, and seem inclined to say," there will, no doubt, be some advantage therefrom, one cannot see through all walls;"—they are jealous of the noble person, as if he sought advantage by back-stair methods. When they are all too plainly convinced of the absence of selfish intentions and emoluments, the noble person is regarded by them as a kind of fool: they despise him in his gladness, and laugh at the lustre of his eye. "How can a person rejoice at being at a disadvantage, how can a person with open eyes want to meet with disadvantage! It must be a disease of the reason with which the noble affection is associated";—so they think, and they look depreciatingly thereon; just as they depreciate the joy which the lunatic derives from his fixed idea. The ignoble nature is distinguished by the fact that it keeps its advantage steadily in view, and that this thought of the end and advantage is even stronger than its strongest impulse: not to be tempted to inexpedient activities by its impulses—that is its wisdom and inspiration. In comparison with the ignoble nature the higher nature is *more irrational:*—for the noble, magnanimous, and self-sacrificing person succumbs in fact to his impulses, and in his best moments his reason *lapses* altogether. An animal, which at the risk of life protects its young, or in the pairing season follows the female where it meets with death, does not think of the risk and the death; its reason pauses likewise, because its delight in its young, or in the female, and the fear of being deprived of this delight, dominate it exclusively; it becomes stupider than at other times, like the noble and magnanimous person. He possesses feelings of pleasure and pain of such intensity that the intellect must either be silent before them, or yield itself to their service: his heart then goes into his head, and one henceforth speaks of "passions." (Here and there to be sure, the antithesis to this, and as it were the "reverse of passion," presents itself; for example in Fontenelle, to whom some one once laid the hand on the heart with the words, "What you have there, my dearest friend, is brain also.") It is the unreason, or perverse reason of passion, which the ignoble man despises in the noble individual, especially when it concentrates upon objects whose value appears to him to be altogether fantastic and arbitrary. He is offended at him who succumbs to the passion of the belly, but he understands the allurement which here plays the tyrant; but he does not understand, for example, how a person out of love of knowledge can stake his health and honour on the game. The taste of the higher nature devotes itself to exceptional matters, to things which usually do not affect people, and seem to have no sweetness; the higher nature has a singular standard of value. Yet it is mostly of the belief that it has *not* a singular standard of value in its idiosyncrasies of taste; it rather sets up its values and non-values as the generally valid values and non-values, and thus becomes incomprehensible and impracticable. It is very rarely that a higher nature has so much reason over and above as to understand and deal with everyday men as such; for the most part it believes in its passion as if it were the concealed passion of every one, and precisely in this belief it is full of ardour and eloquence. If then such exceptional men do not perceive themselves as exceptions, how can they ever understand the ignoble natures and estimate average men fairly! Thus it is that they also speak of the folly, inexpediency and fantasy of mankind, full of astonishment at the madness of the world, and that it will not recognise the "one thing needful for it."—This is the eternal unrighteousness of noble natures.

4.

That which Preserves the Species.—The strongest and most evil spirits have hitherto advanced mankind the most: they always rekindled the sleeping passions—all orderly arranged society lulls the passions to sleep; they always reawakened the sense of comparison, of contradiction, of delight in the new, the adventurous, the untried; they compelled men to set opinion against opinion, ideal plan against ideal plan. By means of arms, by upsetting boundary-stones, by violations of piety most of all: but also by new religions and morals! The same kind of "wickedness" is in every teacher and preacher of the *new*—which makes a conqueror infamous, although it expresses itself more refinedly, and does not immediately set the muscles in motion (and just on that account does not make so infamous!) The new, however, is under all circumstances the *evil*, as that which wants to conquer, which tries to upset the old boundary-stones and the old piety; only the old is the good! The good men of every age are those who go to the roots of the old thoughts and bear fruit with them, the agriculturists of the spirit. But every soil becomes finally exhausted, and the ploughshare of evil must always come once more.—There is at present a fundamentally erroneous theory of morals which is much celebrated, especially in England: according to it the judgments "good" and "evil" are the accumulation of the experiences of that which is "expedient" and "inexpedient"; according to this theory, that which is called good is conservative of the species, what is called evil, however, is detrimental to it. But in reality the evil impulses are just in as high a degree expedient, indispensable, and conservative of the species as the good:—only, their function is different.

5.

Unconditional Duties.—All men who feel that they need the strongest words and intonations, the most eloquent gestures and attitudes, in order to operate *at all*—revolutionary politicians, socialists, preachers of repentance with or without Christianity, with all of whom there must be no mere half-success,—all these speak of "duties," and indeed, always of duties, which have the character of being unconditional—without such they would have no right to their excessive pathos: they know that right well! They grasp, therefore, at philosophies of morality which preach some kind of categorical imperative, or they assimilate a good lump of religion, as, for example, Mazzini did. Because they want to be trusted unconditionally, it is first of all necessary for them to trust themselves unconditionally, on the basis of some ultimate, undebatable command, sublime in itself, as the ministers and instruments of which, they would fain feel and announce themselves. Here we have the most natural, and for the most part, very influential opponents of moral enlightenment and scepticism: but they are rare. On the other hand, there is always a very numerous class of those opponents wherever interest teaches subjection, while repute and honour seem to forbid it. He who feels himself dishonoured at the thought of being the *instrument* of a prince, or of a party and sect, or even of wealthy power (for example, as the descendant of a proud, ancient family), but wishes just to be this instrument, or must be so before himself and before the public—such a person has need of pathetic principles which can at all times be appealed to:—principles of an unconditional *ought*, to which a person can subject himself without shame, and can show himself subjected. All more refined servility holds fast to the categorical imperative, and is the mortal enemy of those who want to take away the unconditional character of duty: propriety demands this from them, and not only propriety.

6.

Loss of Dignity.—Meditation has lost all its dignity of form; the ceremonial and solemn bearing of the meditative person have been made a mockery, and one would no longer endure a wise man of the old style. We think too hastily and on the way and while walking and in the midst of business of all kinds, even when we think on the most serious matters; we require little preparation, even little quiet:—it is as if each of us carried about an unceasingly revolving machine in his head, which still works, even under the most unfavourable circumstances. Formerly it was perceived in a person that on some occasion he wanted to think—it was perhaps the exception!—that he now wanted to become wiser and collected his mind on a thought: he put on a long face for it, as for a prayer, and arrested his step-nay, stood still for hours on the street when the thought "came"—on one or on two legs. It was thus "worthy of the affair"!

7.

Something for the Laborious.—He who at present wants to make moral questions a subject of study has an immense field of labour before him. All kinds of passions must be thought about singly, and followed singly throughout periods, peoples, great and insignificant individuals; all their rationality, all their valuations and elucidations of things, ought to come to light! Hitherto all that has given colour to existence has lacked a history: where would one find a history of love, of avance, of envy, of conscience, of piety, of cruelty? Even a comparative history of law, as also of punishment, has hitherto been completely lacking. Have the different divisions of the day, the consequences of a regular appointment of the times for labour, feast, and repose, ever been made the object of investigation? Do we know the moral effects of the alimentary substances? Is there a philosophy of nutrition? (The ever-recurring outcry for and against vegetarianism proves that as yet there is no such philosophy!) Have the experiences with regard to communal living, for example, in monasteries, been collected? Has the dialectic of marriage and friendship been set forth? The customs of the learned, of trades-people, of artists, and of mechanics—have they already found their thinkers? There is so much to think of thereon! All that up till now has been considered as the "conditions of existence," of human beings, and all reason, passion and superstition in this consideration—have they been investigated to the end? The observation alone of the different degrees of development which the human impulses have attained, and could yet attain, according to the different moral climates, would furnish too much work for the most laborious; whole generations, and regular co-operating generations of the learned, would be needed in order to exhaust the points of view and the material here furnished. The same is true of the determining of the reasons for the differences of the moral climates ("*on what account* does this sun of a fundamental moral judgment and standard of highest value shine here—and that sun there?"). And there is again a new labour which points out the erroneousness of all these reasons, and determines the entire essence of the moral judgments hitherto made. Supposing all these labours to be accomplished, the most critical of all questions would then come into the foreground: whether science is in a position to *furnish* goals for human action, after it has proved that it can take them away and annihilate them—and then would be the time for a process of experimenting, in which every kind of heroism could satisfy itself, an experimenting for centuries, which would put into the shade all the great labours and sacrifices of previous history. Science has not hitherto built its Cyclopic structures; for that also the time will come.

8.

Unconscious Virtues.—All qualities in a man of which he is conscious—and especially when he presumes that they are visible and evident to his environment also—are subject to quite other laws of development than those qualities which are unknown to him, or imperfectly known, which by their subtlety can also conceal themselves from the subtlest observer, and hide as it were behind nothing—as in the case of the delicate sculptures on the scales of reptiles (it would be an error to suppose them an adornment or a defence—for one sees them only with the microscope; consequently, with an eye artificially strengthened to an extent of vision which similar animals, to which they might perhaps have meant adornment or defence, do not possess!). Our visible moral qualities, and especially our moral qualities *believed to be* visible, follow their own course,—and our invisible qualities of similar name, which in relation to others neither serve for adornment nor defence, *also follow their own course:* quite a different course probably, and with lines and refinements, and sculptures, which might perhaps give pleasure to a God with a divine microscope. We have, for example, our diligence, our ambition, our acuteness: all the world knows about them,—and besides, we have probably once more *our* diligence, *our* ambition, *our* acuteness; but for these—our reptile scales—the microscope has not yet been invented!—And here the adherents of instinctive morality will say, "Bravo! He at least regards unconscious virtues as possible—that suffices us!"—Oh, ye unexacting creatures!

9.

Our Eruptions.—Numberless things which humanity acquired in its earlier stages, but so weakly and embryonically that it could not be noticed that they were acquired, are thrust suddenly into light long afterwards, perhaps after the lapse of centuries: they have in the interval become strong and mature. In some ages this or that talent, this or that virtue seems to be entirely lacking, as it—is in some men; but let us wait only for the grandchildren and grandchildren's children, if we have time to wait,—they bring the interior of their grandfathers into the sun, that interior of which the grandfathers themselves were unconscious. The son, indeed, is often the betrayer of his father; the latter understands himself better since he has got his son. We have all hidden gardens and plantations in us; and by another simile, we are all growing volcanoes, which will have their hours of eruption:—how near or how distant this is, nobody of course knows, not even the good God.

10.

A Species of Atavism.—I like best to think of the rare men of an age as suddenly emerging after-shoots of past cultures, and of their persistent strength: like the atavism of a people and its civilisation—there is thus still something in them to *think of!* They now seem strange, rare, and extraordinary: and he who feels these forces in himself has to foster them in face of a different, opposing world; he has to defend them, honour them, and rear them to maturity: and he either becomes a great man thereby, or a deranged and eccentric person, if he does not altogether break down betimes. Formerly these rare qualities were usual, and were consequently regarded as common: they did not distinguish people. Perhaps they were demanded and presupposed; it was impossible to become great with them, for indeed there was also no danger of becoming insane and solitary with them.—It is principally in the *old-established* families and castes of a people that such after-effects of old impulses present themselves, while there is no probability of such atavism where races, habits, and valuations change too rapidly. For the *tempo* of the evolutional forces in peoples implies just as much as in music; for our case an *andante* of evolution is absolutely necessary, as the *tempo* of a passionate and slow spirit:—and the spirit of conserving families is certainly of *that* sort.

11.

Consciousness.—Consciousness is the last and latest development of the organic, and consequently also the most unfinished and least powerful of these developments. Innumerable mistakes originate out of consciousness, which, "in spite of fate," as Homer says, cause an animal or a man to break down earlier than might be necessary. If the conserving bond of the instincts were not very much more powerful, it would not generally serve as a regulator: by perverse judging and dreaming with open eyes, by superficiality and credulity, in short, just by consciousness, mankind would necessarily have broken down: or rather, without the former there would long ago have been nothing more of the latter! Before a function is fully formed and matured, it is a danger to the organism: all the better if it be then thoroughly tyrannised over! Consciousness is thus thoroughly tyrannised over—and not least by the pride in it! It is thought that here is *the quintessence* of man; that which is enduring, eternal, ultimate, and most original in him! Consciousness is regarded as a fixed, given magnitude! Its growth and intermittences are denied! It is accepted as the "unity of the organism"!—This ludicrous overvaluation and misconception of consciousness has as its result the great utility that a too rapid maturing of it has thereby been *hindered.* Because men believed that they already possessed consciousness, they gave themselves very little trouble to acquire it—and even now it is not otherwise! It is still an entirely new *problem* just dawning on the human eye, and hardly yet plainly recognisable: *to embody knowledge in ourselves* and make it instinctive,—a problem which is only seen by those who have grasped the fact that hitherto our *errors* alone have been embodied in us, and that all our consciousness is relative to errors!

12.

The Goal of Science.—What? The ultimate goal of science is to create the most pleasure possible to man, and the least possible pain? But what if pleasure and pain should be so closely connected that he who *wants* the greatest possible amount of the one *must* also have the greatest possible amount of the other,—that he who wants to experience the "heavenly high jubilation,"[7] must also be ready to be "sorrowful unto death"?[8] And it is so, perhaps! The Stoics at least believed it was so, and they were consistent when they wished to have the least possible pleasure, in order to have the least possible pain from life. (When one uses the expression: "The virtuous man is the happiest," it is as much the sign-board of the school for the masses, as a casuistic subtlety for the subtle.) At present also ye have still the choice: either the *least possible pain*, in short painlessness—and after all, socialists and politicians of all parties could not honourably promise more to their people,—or the *greatest possible amount of pain*, as the price of the growth of a fullness of refined delights and enjoyments rarely tasted hitherto! If ye decide for the former, if ye therefore want to depress and minimise man's capacity for pain, well, ye must also depress and minimise his *capacity for enjoyment.* In fact, one can further the one as well as the other goal *by science!* Perhaps science is as yet best known by its capacity for depriving man of enjoyment, and making him colder, more statuesque, and more Stoical. But it might also turn out to be the *great pain-bringer!*—And then, perhaps,

---

[7]This poem is a parody of the "Chorus Mysticus" which concludes the second part of Goethe's "Faust." Bayard Taylor's translation of the passage in "Faust" runs as follows:—

[8]Translated by Miss M. D. Petre. Inserted by permission of the editor of the *Nation,* in which it appeared on April 17, 1909.

its counteracting force would be discovered simultaneously, its immense capacity for making new sidereal worlds of enjoyment beam forth!

13.

The Theory of the Sense of Power.—We exercise our power over others by doing them good or by doing them ill—that is all we care for! *Doing ill* to those on whom we have to make our power felt; for pain is a far more sensitive means for that purpose than pleasure:—pain always asks concerning the cause, while pleasure is inclined to keep within itself and not look backward. *Doing good* and being kind to those who are in any way already dependent on us (that is, who are accustomed to think of us as their *raison d'être);* we want to increase their power, because we thus increase our own; or we want to show them the advantage there is in being in our power,—they thus become more contented with their position, and more hostile to the enemies of *our* power and readier to contend with to If we make sacrifices in doing good or in doing ill, it does not alter the ultimate value of our actions; even if we stake our life in the cause, as martyrs for the sake of our church, it is a sacrifice to *our* longing for power, or for the purpose of conserving our sense of power. He who under these circumstances feels that he "is in possession of truth" how many possessions does he not let go, in order to preserve this feeling! What does he not throw overboard, in order to keep himself "up,"—that is to say, *above* the others who lack the truth. Certainly the condition we are in when we do ill is seldom so pleasant, so purely pleasant as that in which we practise kindness,—it is an indication that we still lack power, or it betrays ill-humour at this defect in us; it brings with it new dangers and uncertainties as to the power we already possess, and clouds our horizon by the prospect of revenge, scorn, punishment and failure. Perhaps only tee most susceptible to the sense of power and eager for it, will prefer to impress the seal of power on the resisting individual.—those to whom the sight of the already subjugated person as the object of benevolence is a burden and a tedium. It is a question how a person is accustomed to *season* his life; it is a matter of taste whether a person would rather have the slow or the sudden to safe or the dangerous and daring increase of power,—he seeks this or that seasoning always according to his temperament. An easy booty is something contemptible to proud natures; they have an agreeable sensation only at the sight of men of unbroken spirit who could be enemies to them, and similarly, also, at the sight of all not easily accessible possession; they are often hard toward the sufferer, for he is not worthy of their effort or their pride,—but they show themselves so much the more courteous towards their *equals,* with whom strife and struggle would in any case be full of honour, *if* at any time an occasion for it should present itself. It is under the agreeable feelings of *this* perspective that the members of the knightly caste have habituated themselves to exquisite courtesy toward one another.—Pity is the most pleasant feeling in those who have not much pride, and have no prospect of great conquests: the easy booty—and that is what every sufferer is—is for them an enchanting thing. Pity is said to be the virtue of the gay lady.

14.

What is called Love.—The lust of property, and love: what different associations each of these ideas evoke!—and yet it might be the same impulse twice named: on the one occasion disparaged from the standpoint of those already possessing (in whom the impulse has attained something of repose,—who are now apprehensive for the safety of their "possession"); on the other occasion viewed from the standpoint of the unsatisfied and thirsty, and therefore glorified as "good." Our love of our neighbour,—is it not a striving after new *property*? And similarly our love of knowledge, of truth; and in general all the striving after novelties? We gradually become satiated with the old and securely possessed, and again stretch out our hands; even the finest landscape in which we live for three months is no longer certain of our love, and any kind of more distant coast excites our covetousness: the possession for the most part becomes smaller through possessing. Our pleasure in ourselves seeks to maintain itself by always transforming something new *into ourselves,*—that is just possessing. To become satiated with a possession, that is to become satiated with ourselves. (One can also suffer from excess,—even the desire to cast away, to share out, may assume the honourable name of "love.") When we see any one suffering, we willingly utilise the opportunity then afforded to take possession of him; the beneficent and sympathetic man, for example, does this; he also calls the desire for new possession awakened in him, by the name of "love," and has enjoyment in it, as in a new acquisition suggesting itself to him. The love of the sexes, however, betrays itself most plainly as the striving after possession: the lover wants the unconditioned, sole possession of the person longed for by him; he wants just as absolute power over her soul as over her body; he wants to be loved solely, and to dwell and rule in the other soul as what is highest and most to be desired. When one considers that this means precisely to *exclude* all the world from a precious possession, a happiness, and an enjoyment; when one considers that the lover has in view the impoverishment and privation of all other rivals, and would like to become the dragon of his golden hoard, as the most inconsiderate and selfish of all "conquerors" and exploiters; when one considers finally that to the lover himself, the whole world besides appears indifferent, colourless, and worthless, and that he is ready to make every sacrifice, disturb every arrangement, and put every other interest behind his own,—one is verily surprised that this ferocious lust of property and injustice of sexual love should have been glorified and deified to such an extent at all times; yea, that out of this love the conception of love as the antithesis of egoism should have been derived, when it is perhaps precisely the most unqualified expression of egoism. Here, evidently, the non-possessors and desirers have determined the usage of language,—there were, of course, always too many of them. Those who have been favoured with much possession and satiety, have, to be sure, dropped a word now and then about the "raging demon," as, for instance, the most lovable and most beloved of all the Athenians—Sophocles; but Eros always laughed at such revilers,—they were always his greatest favourites.—There is, of course, here and there on this terrestrial sphere a kind of sequel to love, in which that covetous longing of two persons for one another has yielded to a new desire and covetousness, to a *common*, higher thirst for a superior ideal standing above them: but who knows this love? Who has experienced it? Its right name is *friendship*.

15.

Out of the Distance.—This mountain makes the whole district which it dominates charming in every way, and full of significance. After we have said this to ourselves for the hundredth time, we are so irrationally and so gratefully disposed towards it, as the giver of this charm, that we fancy it must itself be the most charming thing in the district—and so we climb it, and are undeceived. All of a sudden, both it and the landscape around us and under us, are as it were disenchanted; we had forgotten that many a greatness, like many a goodness, wants only to be seen at a certain distance, and entirely from below, not from above,—it is thus only that *it operates.* Perhaps you know men in your neighbourhood who can only look at themselves from a certain distance to find themselves at all endurable, or attractive and enlivening; they are to be dissuaded from self-knowledge.

16.

Across the Plank.—One must be able to dissimulate in intercourse with persons who are ashamed of their feelings; they take a sudden aversion to anyone who surprises them in a state of tenderness, or of enthusiastic and high-running feeling, as if he had seen their secrets. If one wants to be kind to them in such moments one should make them laugh, or say some kind of cold, playful wickedness:—their feeling thereby congeals, and they are again self-possessed. But I give the moral before the story.—We were once on a time so near one another in the course of our lives, that nothing more seemed to hinder our friendship and fraternity, and there was merely a small plank between us. While you were just about to step on it, I asked you: "Do you want to come across the plank to me?" But then you did not want to come any longer; and when I again entreated, you were silent. Since then mountains and torrents, and whatever separates and alienates, have interposed between us, and even if we wanted to come to one another, we could no longer do so! When, however, you now remember that small plank, you have no longer words,—but merely sobs and amazement.

17.

Motivation of Poverty.—We cannot, to be sure, by any artifice make a rich and richly-flowing virtue out of a poor one, but we can gracefully enough reinterpret its poverty into necessity, so that its aspect no longer gives pain to us, and we cease making reproachful faces at fate on account of it. It is thus that the wise gardener does who puts the tiny streamlet of his garden into the arms of a fountain-nymph, and thus motivates the poverty:—and who would not like him need the nymphs!

18.

Ancient Pride.—The ancient savour of nobility is lacking in us, because the ancient slave is lacking in our sentiment. A Greek of noble descent found such immense intermediate stages, and such a distance betwixt his elevation and that ultimate baseness, that he could hardly even see the slave plainly: even Plato no longer saw him entirely. It is otherwise with us, accustomed as we are to the *doctrine* of the equality of men, although not to the equality itself. A being who has not the free disposal of himself and has not got leisure,—that is not regarded by us as anything contemptible; there is perhaps too much of this kind of slavishness in each of us, in accordance with the conditions of our social order and activity, which are fundamentally different from those of the ancients.—The Greek philosopher went through life with the secret feeling that there were many more slaves than people supposed—that is to say, that every one was a slave who was not a philosopher. His pride was puffed up when he considered that even the mightiest of the earth were thus to be looked upon as slaves. This pride is also unfamiliar to us, and impossible; the word "slave" has not its full force for us even in simile.

19.

Evil.—Test the life of the best and most productive men and nations, and ask yourselves whether a tree which is to grow proudly heavenward can dispense with bad weather and tempests: whether disfavour and opposition from without, whether every kind of hatred, jealousy, stubbornness, distrust, severity, greed, and violence do not belong to the *favouring* circumstances without which a great growth even in virtue is hardly possible? The poison by which the weaker nature is destroyed is strengthening to the strong individual—and he does not call it poison.

20.

Dignity of Folly.—Several millenniums further on in the path of the last century!—and in everything that man does the highest prudence will be exhibited: but just thereby prudence will have lost all its dignity. It will then, sure enough, be necessary to be prudent, but it will also be so usual and common, that a more fastidious taste will feel this necessity as *vulgarity.* And just as a tyranny of truth and science would be in a position to raise the value of falsehood, a tyranny of prudence could force into prominence a new species of nobleness. To be noble—that might then mean, perhaps, to be capable of follies.

21.

To the Teachers of Unselfishness.—The virtues of a man are called *good,* not in respect to the results they have for himself, but in respect to the results which we expect therefrom for ourselves and for society:—we have all along had very little unselfishness, very little "non-egoism" in our praise of the virtues! For otherwise it could not but have been seen that the virtues (such as diligence, obedience, chastity, piety, justice) are mostly *injurious* to their possessors, as impulses which rule in them too vehemently and ardently, and do not want to be kept in co-ordination with the other impulses by the reason. If you have a virtue, an actual, perfect virtue (and not merely a kind of impulse towards virtue!)—you are its *victim!* But your neighbour praises your virtue precisely on that account! One praises the diligent man though he injures his sight, or the originality and freshness of his spirit, by his diligence; the youth is honoured and regretted who has "worn himself out by work," because one passes the judgment that "for society as a whole the loss of the best individual is only a small sacrifice! A pity that this sacrifice should be necessary! A much greater pity it is true, if the individual should think differently and regard his preservation and development as more important than his work in the service of society!" And so one regrets this youth, not on his own account, but because a devoted *instrument,* regardless of self—a so-called "good man," has been lost to society by his death. Perhaps one further considers the question, whether it would not have been more advantageous for the interests of society if he had laboured with less disregard of himself, and had preserved himself longer-indeed one readily admits an advantage therefrom but one esteems the other advantage, namely, that a *sacrifice* has been made, and that the disposition of the sacrificial animal has once more been *obviously* endorsed—as higher and more enduring. It is accordingly, on the one part, the instrumental character in the virtues which is praised when the virtues are praised, and on the other part the blind, ruling impulse in every virtue which refuse to let itself be kept within bounds by the general advantage to the individual; in short, what is praised is the unreason in the virtues, in consequence of which the individual allows himself to be transformed into a function of the whole. The praise of the virtues is the praise of something which is privately injurious to the individual; it is praise of impulses which deprive man of his noblest self-love, and the power to take the best care of himself. To be sure, for the teaching and embodying of virtuous habits a series of effects of virtue are displayed, which make it appear that virtue and private advantage are closely related,—and there is in fact such a relationship! Blindly furious diligence, for example, the typical virtue of an instrument, is represented as the way to riches and honour, and as the most benefi-cial antidote to tedium and passion: but people are silent concerning its danger, its greatest dangerousness. Education proceeds in this manner throughout: it endeav-ours, by a series of enticements and advantages, to determine the individual to a certain mode of thinking and acting, which, when it has become habit, impulse and passion, rules in him and over him, *in opposition to his ultimate advantage*, but "for the general good." How often do I see that blindly furious diligence does indeed create riches and honours, but at the same time deprives the organs of the refinement by virtue of which alone an enjoyment of riches and honours is possible; so that really the main expedient for combating tedium and passion, simultaneously blunts the senses and makes the spirit refractory towards new stimuli! (The busiest of all ages—our age—does not know how to make anything out of its great diligence and wealth, except always more and more wealth, and more and more diligence; there is even more genius needed for laying out wealth than for acquiring it!—Well, we shall have our "grandchildren"!) If the education succeeds, every virtue of the individual is a public utility, and a private disadvantage in respect to the highest pri-vate end,—probably some psycho-æsthetic stunting, or even premature dissolution. One should consider successively from the same standpoint the virtues of obedience, chastity, piety, and justice. The praise of the unselfish, self-sacrificing, virtuous person—he, consequently, who does not expend his whole energy and reason for *his own* conservation, development, elevation, furtherance and augmentation of power, but lives as regards himself unassumingly and thoughtlessly, perhaps even indifferently or ironically—this praise has in any case not originated out of the spirit of unselfishness! The "neighbour" praises unselfishness because *he profits by it!* If the neighbour were "unselfishly" disposed himself, he would reject that destruction of power, that injury for *his* advantage, he would thwart such inclinations in their origin, and above all he would manifest his unselfishness just by *not giving it a good name!* The fundamental contradiction in that morality which at present stands in high honour is here indicated: the *motives* to such a morality are in antithesis to its *principle!* That with which this morality wishes to prove itself, refutes it out of its criterion of what is moral! The maxim, "Thou shalt renounce thyself and offer thyself as a sacrifice," in order not to be inconsistent with its own morality, could only be decreed by a being who himself renounced his own advantage thereby, and who perhaps in the required self-sacrifice of individuals brought about his own dissolution. As soon; however, as the neighbour (or society) recommended altruism *on account of its utility,* the precisely antithetical proposition, "Thou shalt seek thy advantage even at the expense of everybody else," was brought into use: accordingly, "thou shalt," and "thou shalt not," are preached in one breath!

22.

L'Ordre du jour pour le Roi.—The day commences: let us begin to arrange for this day the business and fêtes of our most gracious lord, who at present is still pleased to repose. His Majesty has bad weather to-day: we shall be careful not to call it bad; we shall not speak of the weather,—but we shall go through to-day's business somewhat more ceremoniously and make the fêtes somewhat more festive than would otherwise be necessary. His Majesty may perhaps even be sick: we shall give the last good news of the evening at breakfast, the arrival of M. Montaigne, who knows how to joke so pleasantly about his sickness,—he suffers from stone. We shall receive several persons (persons!—what would that old inflated frog, who will be among them, say, if he heard this word! "I am no person," he would say, "but always the thing itself")—and the reception will last longer than is pleasant to anybody; a sufficient reason for telling about the poet who wrote over his door, "He who enters here will do me an honour; he who does not—a favour."—That is, forsooth, saying a discourteous thing in a courteous manner! And perhaps this poet is quite justified on his part in being discourteous; they say that his rhymes are better than the rhymester. Well, let him still make many of them, and withdraw himself as much as possible from the world: and that is doubtless the significance of his well-bred rudeness! A prince, on the other hand, is always of more value than his "verse," even when—but what are we about? We gossip,' and the whole court believes that we have already been at work and racked our brains: there is no light to be seen earlier than that which burns in our window.—Hark! Was that not the bell? The devil! The day and the dance commence, and we do not know our rounds! We must then improvise,—all the world improvises its day. To-day, let us for once do like all the world!—And therewith vanished my wonderful morning dream, probably owing to the violent strokes of the tower-clock, which just then announced the fifth hour with all the importance which is peculiar to it. It seems to me that on this occasion the God of dreams wanted to make merry over my habits,—it is my habit to commence the day by arranging it properly, to make it endurable *for myself* and it is possible that I may often have done this too formally, and too much like a prince.

23.

The Characteristics of Corruption.—Let us observe the following characteristics in that condition of society from time to time necessary, which is designated by the word "corruption." Immediately upon the appearance of corruption anywhere, a motley *superstition* gets the upper hand, and the hitherto universal belief of a people becomes colourless and impotent in comparison with it; for superstition is free-thinking of the second rank,—he who gives himself over to it selects certain forms and formulæ which appeal, to him, and permits himself a right of choice. The superstitious man is always much more of a "person," in comparison with the religious man, and a superstitious society will be one in which there are many individuals, and a delight in individuality. Seen from this standpoint superstition always appears as a *progress* in comparison with belief, and as a sign that the intellect becomes more independent and claims to have its rights. Those who reverence the old religion and the religious disposition then complain of corruption,—they have hitherto also determined the usage of language, and have given a bad repute to superstition, even among the freest spirits. Let us learn that it is a symptom of *enlightenment.*—Secondly, a society in which corruption takes a hold is blamed for *effeminacy*: for the appreciation of war, and the delight in war, perceptibly diminish in such a society, and the conveniences of life are now just as eagerly sought after as were military and gymnastic honours formerly. But one is accustomed to overlook the fact that the old national energy and national passion, which acquired a magnificent splendour in war and in the tourney, has now transferred itself into innumerable private passions, and has merely become less visible; indeed in periods of "corruption" the quantity and quality of the expended energy of a people is probably greater than ever, and the individual spends it lavishly, to such an extent as could not be done formerly—he was not then rich enough to do so! And thus it is precisely in times of "effeminacy" that tragedy runs at large in and out of doors, it is then that ardent love and ardent hatred are born, and the flame of knowledge flashes heavenward in full blaze.—Thirdly, as if in amends for the reproach of superstition and effeminacy, it is customary to say of such periods of corruption that they are milder, and that cruelty has then greatly diminished in comparison with the older, more credulous, and stronger period. But to this praise I am just as little able to assent as to that reproach: I only grant so much—namely, that cruelty now becomes more refined, and its older forms are henceforth counter to the taste; but the wounding and torturing by word and look reaches its highest development in times of corruption,—it is now only that *wickedness* is created, and the delight in wickedness. The men of the period of corruption are witty and calumnious; they know that there are yet other ways of murdering than by the dagger and the ambush—they know also that all that is *well said* is believed in.—Fourthly, it is when "morals decay" that those beings whom one calls tyrants first make their appearance; they are the forerunners of the *individual*, and as it were early matured *firstlings*. Yet a little while, and this fruit of fruits hangs ripe and yellow on the tree of a people,—and only for the sake of such fruit did this tree exist! When the decay has reached its worst, and likewise the conflict of all sorts of tyrants, there always arises the Cæsar, the final tyrant, who puts an end to the exhausted struggle for sovereignty, by making the exhaustedness work for him. In his time the individual is usually most mature, and consequently the "culture" is highest and most fruitful, but not on his account nor through him: although the men of highest culture love to flatter their Cæsar by pretending that they are *his* creation. The truth, however, is that they need quietness externally, because they have disquietude and labour internally. In these times bribery and treason are at their height: for the love of the *ego*, then first discovered, is much more powerful than the love of the old, used-up, hackneyed "father-land"; and the need to be secure in one way or other against the frightful fluctuations of fortune, opens even the nobler hands, as soon as a richer and more powerful person shows himself ready to put gold into them. There is then so little certainty with regard to the future; people live only for the day: a psychical condition which enables every deceiver to play an easy game,—people of course only let themselves be misled and bribed "for the present," and reserve for themselves futurity and virtue. The individuals, as is well known, the men who only live for themselves, provide for the moment more than do their opposites, the gregarious men, because they consider themselves just as incalculable as the future; and similarly they attach themselves willingly—to despots, because they believe themselves capable of activities and expedients, which can neither reckon on being understood by the multitude, nor on finding favour with them—but the tyrant or the Cæsar understands the rights of the individual even in his excesses, and has an interest in speaking on behalf of a bolder private morality, and even in giving his hand to it For he thinks of himself, and wishes people to think of him what Napoleon once uttered in his classical style—"I have the right to answer by an eternal 'thus I am' to everything about which complaint is brought against me. I am apart from all the world, I accept conditions from nobody. I wish people also to submit to my fancies, and to take it quite as a simple matter, if I should indulge in this or that diversion." Thus spoke Napoleon once to his wife, when she had reasons for calling in question the fidelity of her husband. The times of corruption are the seasons when the apples fall from the tree: I mean the individuals, the seed-bearers of the future, the pioneers of spiritual colonisation, and of a new construction of national and social unions. Corruption is only an abusive term for the *harvest time* of a people.

24.

Different Dissatisfactions.—The feeble and as it were feminine dissatisfied people, have ingenuity for beautifying and deepening life; the strong dissatisfied people—the masculine persons among them to continue the metaphor—have ingenuity for improving and safeguarding life. The former show their weakness and feminine character by willingly letting themselves be temporarily deceived, and perhaps even by putting up with a little ecstasy and enthusiasm on a time, but on the whole they are never to be satisfied, and suffer from the incurability of their dissatisfaction; moreover they are the patrons of all those who manage to concoct opiate and narcotic comforts, and on that account are averse to those who value the physician higher than the priest,—they thereby encourage the *continuance* of actual distress! If there had not been a surplus of dissatisfied persons of this kind in Europe since the time of the Middle Ages, the remarkable capacity of Europeans for constant *transformation* would perhaps not have originated at all; for the claims of the strong dissatisfied persons are too gross, and really too modest to resist being finally quieted down. China is an instance of a country in which dissatisfaction on a grand scale and the capacity for transformation have died out for many centuries; and the Socialists and state-idolaters of Europe could easily bring things to Chinese conditions and to a Chinese "happiness," with their measures for the amelioration and security of life, provided that they could first of all root out the sicklier, tenderer, more feminine dissatisfaction and Romanticism which are still very abundant among us. Europe is an invalid who owes her best thanks to her incurability and the eternal transformations of her sufferings; these constant new situations, these equally constant new dangers, pains, and make-shifts, have at last generated an intellectual sensitiveness which is almost equal to genius, and is in any case the mother of all genius.

25.

Not Pre-ordained to Knowledge.—There is a pur-blind humility not at all rare, and when a person is afflicted with it, he is once for all disqualified for being a disciple of knowledge. It is this in fact: the moment a man of this kind perceives anything striking, he turns as it were on his heel and says to himself: "You have deceived yourself! Where have your wits been! This cannot be the truth!"—and then, instead of looking at it and listening to it with more attention, he runs out of the way of the striking object as if intimidated, and seeks to get it out of his head as quickly as possible. For his fundamental rule runs thus: "I want to see nothing that contradicts the usual opinion concerning things! Am *I* created for the purpose of discovering new truths? There are already too many of the old ones."

26.

What is Living?—Living—that is to continually eliminate from ourselves what is about to die; Living—that is to be cruel and inexorable towards all that becomes weak and old in ourselves and not only in ourselves. Living—that means, there fore to be without piety toward the dying, the wrenched and the old? To be continually a murderer?—And yet old Moses said: "Thou shalt not kill!"

27.

The Self-Renouncer.—What does the self-renouncer do? He strives after a higher world, he wants to fly longer and further and higher than all men of affirmation—he *throws away many things* that would impede his flight, and several things among them that are not valueless, that are not unpleasant to him: he sacrifices them to his desire for elevation. Now this sacrificing, this casting away, is the very thing which becomes visible in him: on that account one calls him a self-renouncer, and as such he stands before us, enveloped in his cowl, and as the soul of a hair-shirt. With this effect, however, which he makes upon us he is well content: he wants to keep concealed from us his desire, his pride, his intention of flying *above* us.—Yes! He is wiser than we thought, and so courteous towards us—this affirmer! For that is what he is, like us, even in his self-renunciation.

28.

Injuring with ones best Qualities.—Out strong points sometimes drive us so far forward that we cannot any longer endure our weaknesses, and we perish by them: we also perhaps see this result beforehand, but nevertheless do not want it to be otherwise. We then become hard towards that which would fain be spared in us, and our pitilessness is also our greatness. Such an experience, which must in the end cost us our lie, is a symbol of the collective effect of great men upon others and upon their epoch:—it is just with their best abilities, with that which only *they* can do, that they destroy much that is weak, uncertain, evolving, and *willing*, and are thereby injurious. Indeed, the case may happen in which, taken on the whole, they only do injury, because their best is accepted and drunk up as it were solely by those who lose their understanding and their egoism by it, as by too strong a beverage; they become so intoxicated that they go breaking their limbs on all the wrong roads where their drunkenness drives them.

29.

Adventitious Liars.—When people began to combat the unity of Aristotle in France, and consequently also to defend it, there was once more to be seen that which has been seen so often, but seen so unwillingly:—*people imposed false reasons on themselves* on account of which those laws ought to exist, merely for the sake of not acknowledging to themselves that they had *accustomed* themselves to the authority of those laws, and did not want any longer to have things otherwise. And people do so in every prevailing morality and religion, and have always done so: the reasons and intentions behind the habit, are only added surreptitiously when people begin to combat the habit, and *ask* for reasons and intentions. It is here that the great dishonesty of the conservatives of all times hides:—they are adventitious liars.

30.

The Comedy of Celebrated Men.—Celebrated men who *need* their fame, as, for instance, all politicians, no longer select their associates and friends without forethought: from the one they want a portion of the splendour and reflection of his virtues; from the other they want the fear-inspiring power of certain dubious qualities in him, of which everybody is aware; from another they steal his reputation for idleness and basking in the sun, because it is advantageous for their own ends to be regarded temporarily as heedless and lazy:—it conceals the fact that they lie in ambush; they now use the visionaries, now the experts, now the brooders, now the pedants in their neighbourhood, as their actual selves for the time; but very soon they do not need them any longer! And thus while their environment and outside die off continually, everything seems to crowd into this environment, and wants to become a "character" of it; they are like great cities in this respect. Their repute is continually in process of mutation, like their character, for their changing methods require this change, and they show and *exhibit* sometimes this and sometimes that actual or fictitious quality on the stage; their friends and associates, as we have said, belong to these stage properties. On the other hand, that which they aim at must remain so much the more steadfast, and burnished and resplendent in the distance,—and this also sometimes needs its comedy and its stage-play.

31.

Commerce and Nobility.—Buying and selling is now regarded as something ordinary, like the art of reading and writing; everyone is now trained to it even when he is not a tradesman exercising himself daily in the art; precisely as formerly in the period of uncivilised humanity, everyone was a hunter and exercised himself day by day in the art of hunting. Hunting was then something common: but just as this finally became a privilege of the powerful and noble, and thereby lost the character of the commonplace and the ordinary—by ceasing to be necessary and by becoming an affair of fancy and luxury,—so it might become the same some day with buying and selling. Conditions of society are imaginable in which there will be no selling and buying, and in which the necessity for this art will become quite lost; perhaps it may then happen that individuals who are less subjected to the law of the prevailing condition of things will indulge in buying and selling as a *luxury of sentiment.* It is then only that commerce would acquire nobility, and the noble would then perhaps occupy themselves just as readily with commerce as they have done hitherto with war and politics: while on the other hand the valuation of politics might then have entirely altered. Already even politics ceases to be the business of a gentleman; and it is possible that one day it may be found to be so vulgar as to be brought, like all party literature and daily literature, under the rubric: "Prostitution of the intellect."

32.

Undesirable Disciples.—What shall I do with these two youths! called out a philosopher dejectedly, who "corrupted" youths, as Socrates had once corrupted them,—they are unwelcome disciples to me. One of them cannot say "Nay," and the other says "Half and half" to everything. Provided they grasped my doctrine, the former would *suffer* too much, for my mode of thinking requires a martial soul, willingness to cause pain, delight in denying, and a hard skin,—he would succumb by open wounds and internal injuries. And the other will choose the mediocre in everything he represents, and thus make a mediocrity of the whole,—I should like my enemy to have such a disciple.

33.

Outside the Lecture-room.—"In order to prove that man after all belongs to the good-natured animals, I would remind you how credulous he has been for so long a time. It is now only, quite late, and after an immense self-conquest, that he has become a *distrustful* animal,—yes! man is now more wicked than ever."—I do not understand this; why should man now be more distrustful and more wicked?—"Because now he has science,—because he needs to have it!"—

34.

Historia abscondita.—Every great man has a power which operates backward; all history is again placed on the scales on his account, and a thousand secrets of the past crawl out of their lurking-places—into *his* sunlight. There is absolutely no knowing what history may be some day. The past is still perhaps undiscovered in its essence! There is yet so much reinterpreting ability needed!

35.

Heresy and Witchcraft.—To think otherwise than is customary—that is by no means so much the activity of a better intellect, as the activity of strong, wicked inclinations,—severing, isolating, refractory, mischief-loving, malicious inclinations. Heresy is the counterpart of witchcraft, and is certainly just as little a merely harmless affair, or a thing worthy of honour in itself. Heretics and sorcerers are two kinds of bad men; they have it in common that they also feel themselves wicked; their unconquerable delight is to attack and injure whatever rules,—whether it be men or opinions. The Reformation, a kind of duplication of the spirit of the Middle Ages at a time when it had no longer a good conscience, produced both of these kinds of people in the greatest profusion.

36.

Last Words.-It will be recollected that the Emperor Augustus, that terrible man, who had himself as much in his own power and could be silent as well as any wise Socrates, became indiscreet about himself in his last words; for the first time he let his mask fall, when he gave to understand that he had carried a mask and played a comedy,—he had played the father of his country and wisdom on the throne well, even to the point of illusion! *Plaudite amid, comœdia finita est!*—The thought of the dying Nero: *qualis artifex pereo!* was also the thought of the dying Augustus: histrionic conceit! histrionic loquacity! And the very counterpart to the dying Socrates!—But Tiberius died silently, that most tortured of all self-torturers,—*he* was *genuine* and not a stage-player! What may have passed through his head in the end! Perhaps this: "Life—that is a long death. I am a fool, who shortened the lives of so many! Was *I* created for the purpose of being a benefactor? I should have given them eternal life: and then I could have *seen them dying* eternally. I had such good eyes *for that*: *qualis spectator pereo!*" When he seemed once more to regain his powers after a long death-struggle, it was considered advisable to smother him with pillows,—he died a double death.

37.

Owing to three Errors.—Science has been furthered during recent centuries, partly because it was hoped that God's goodness and wisdom would be best understood therewith and thereby—the principal motive in the soul of great Englishmen (like Newton); partly because the absolute utility of knowledge was believed in, and especially the most intimate connection of morality, knowledge, and happiness—the principal motive in the soul of great Frenchmen (like Voltaire); and partly because it was thought that in science there was something unselfish, harmless, self-sufficing, lovable, and truly innocent to be had, in which the evil human impulses did not at all participate—the principal motive in the soul of Spinoza, who felt himself divine, as a knowing being:—it is consequently owing to three errors that science has been furthered.

38.

Explosive People.—When one considers how ready are the forces of young men for discharge, one does not wonder at seeing them decide so uncritically and with so little selection for this or that cause: *that* which attracts them is the sight of eagerness for a cause, as it were the sight of the burning match—not the cause itself. The more ingenious seducers on that account operate by holding out the prospect of an explosion to such persons, and do not urge their cause by means of reasons; these powder-barrels are not won over by means of reasons!

39.

Altered Taste.—The alteration of the general taste is more important than the alteration of opinions; opinions, with all their proving, refuting, and intellectual masquerade, are merely symptoms of altered taste, and are certainly *not* what they are still so often claimed to be, the causes of the altered taste. How does the general taste alter? By the fact of individuals, the powerful and influential persons, expressing and tyrannically enforcing without any feeling of shame, *their hoc est ridiculum, hoc est absurdum;* the decisions, therefore, of their taste and their disrelish:—they thereby lay a constraint upon many people, out of which there gradually grows a habituation for still more, and finally a *necessity for all.* The fact, however, that these individuals feel and "taste" differently, has usually its origin in a peculiarity of their mode of life, nourishment, or digestion, perhaps in a surplus or deficiency of the inorganic salts in their blood and brain, in short in their *physis;* they have, however, the courage to avow their physical constitution, and to lend an ear even to the most delicate tones of its requirements: their æsthetic and moral judgments are those "most delicate tones" of their *physis*.

40.

The Lack of a noble Presence.—Soldiers and their leaders have always a much higher mode of comportment toward one another than workmen and their employers. At present at least, all militarily established civilisation still stands high above all so-called industrial civilisation; the latter, in its present form, is in general the meanest mode of existence that has ever been. It is simply the law of necessity that operates here: people want to live, and have to sell themselves; but they despise him who exploits their necessity and *purchases* the workman. It is curious that the subjection to powerful, fear-inspiring, and even dreadful individuals, to tyrants and leaders of armies, is not at all felt so painfully as the subjection to such undistinguished and uninteresting persons as the captains of industry; in the employer the workman usually sees merely a crafty, blood-sucking dog of a man, speculating on every necessity, whose name, form, character, and reputation are altogether indifferent to him. It is probable that the manufacturers and great magnates of commerce have hitherto lacked too much all those forms and attributes of a *superior race*, which alone make persons interesting; if they had had the nobility of the nobly-born in their looks and bearing, there would perhaps have been no socialism in the masses of the people. For these are really ready for *slavery* of every kind, provided that the superior class above them constantly shows itself legitimately superior, and *born* to command—by its noble presence! The commonest man feels that nobility is not to be improvised, and that it is his part to honour it as the fruit of protracted race-culture,—but the absence of superior presence, and the notorious vulgarity of manufacturers with red, fat hands, brings up the thought to him that it is only chance and fortune that has here elevated the one above the other; well then—so he reasons with himself—let *us* in our turn tempt chance and fortune! Let us in our turn throw the dice!—and socialism commences.

41.

Against Remorse.—The thinker sees in his own actions attempts and questionings to obtain information about something or other; success and failure are *answers* to him first and foremost. To vex himself, however, because something does not succeed, or to feel remorse at all—he leaves that to those who act because they are commanded to do so, and expect to get a beating when their gracious master is not satisfied with the result.

42.

Work and Ennui—In respect to seeking work for the sake of the pay, almost all men are alike at present in civilised countries; to all of them work is a means, and not itself the end; on which account they are not very select in the choice of the work, provided it yields an abundant profit. But still there are rarer men who would rather perish than work without *delight* in their labour: the fastidious people, difficult to satisfy, whose object is not served by an abundant profit, unless the work itself be the reward of all rewards. Artists and contemplative men of all kinds belong to this rare species of human beings; and also the idlers who spend their life in hunting and travelling, or in love-affairs and adventures. They all seek toil and trouble in so far as these are associated with pleasure, and they want the severest and hardest labour, if it be necessary. In other respects, however, they have a resolute indolence, even should impoverishment, dishonour, and danger to health and life be associated therewith. They are not so much afraid of ennui as of labour without pleasure; indeed they require much ennui, if *their* work is to succeed with them. For the thinker and for all inventive spirits ennui is the unpleasant "calm" of the soul which precedes the happy voyage and the dancing breezes; he must endure it, he must *await* the effect it has on him:—it is precisely *this* which lesser natures cannot at all experience! It is common to scare away ennui in every way, just as it is common to labour without pleasure. It perhaps distinguishes the Asiatics above the Europeans, that they are capable of a longer and profounder repose; even their narcotics operate slowly and require patience, in contrast to the obnoxious suddenness of the European poison, alcohol.

43.

What the Laws Betray.—One makes a great mistake when one studies the penal laws of a people, as if they were an expression of its character; the laws do not betray what a people is, but what appears to them foreign, strange, monstrous, and outlandish. The laws concern themselves with the exceptions to the morality of custom; and the severest punishments fall on acts which conform to the customs of the neighbouring peoples. Thus among the Wahabites, there are only two mortal sins: having another God than the Wahabite God, and—smoking (it is designated by them as "the disgraceful kind of drinking"). "And how is it with regard to murder and adultery?"-asked the Englishman with astonishment on learning these things. "Well, God is gracious and pitiful!" answered the old chief.—Thus among the ancient Romans there was the idea that a woman could only sin mortally in two ways: by adultery on the one hand, and—by wine-drinking on the other. Old Cato pretended that kissing among relatives had only been made a custom in order to keep women in control on this point; a kiss meant: did her breath smell of wine? Wives had actually been punished by death who were surprised taking wine: and certainly not merely because women under the influence of wine sometimes unlearn altogether the art of saying No; the Romans were afraid above all things of the orgiastic and Dionysian spirit with which the women of Southern Europe at that time (when wine was still new in Europe) were sometimes visited, as by a monstrous foreignness which subverted the basis of Roman sentiments; it seemed to them treason against Rome, as the embodiment of foreignness.

44.

The Believed Motive.—However important it may be to know the motives according to which mankind has really acted hitherto, perhaps the *belief* in this or that motive, and therefore that which mankind has assumed and imagined to be the actual mainspring of its activity hitherto, is something still more essential for the thinker to know. For the internal happiness and misery of men have always come to them through their belief in this or that motive,—*not* however, through that which was actually the motive! All about the latter has an interest of secondary rank.

45.

Epicurus.—Yes, I am proud of perceiving the character of Epicurus differently from anyone else perhaps, and of enjoying the happiness of the afternoon of antiquity in all that I hear and read of him:—I see his eye gazing out on a broad whitish sea, over the shore-rocks on which the sunshine rests, while great and small creatures play in its light, secure and calm like this light and that eye itself. Such happiness could only have been devised by a chronic sufferer, the happiness of an eye before which the sea of existence has become calm, and which can no longer tire of gazing at the surface and at the variegated, tender, tremulous skin of this sea. Never previously was there such a moderation of voluptuousness.

46.

Our Astonishment—There is a profound and fundamental satisfaction in the fact that science ascertains things that *hold their ground*, and again furnish the basis for new researches:—it could certainly be otherwise. Indeed, we are so much convinced of all the uncertainty and caprice of our judgments, and of the everlasting change of all human laws and conceptions, that we are really astonished *how persistently* the results of science hold their ground! In earlier times people knew nothing of this changeability of all human things; the custom of morality maintained the belief that the whole inner life of man was bound to iron necessity by eternal fetters:—perhaps people then felt a similar voluptuousness of astonishment when they listened to tales and fairy stories. The wonderful did so much good to those men, who might well get tired sometimes of the regular and the eternal. To leave the ground for once! To soar! To stray! To be mad!—that belonged to the paradise and the revelry of earlier times; while our felicity is like that of the shipwrecked man who has gone ashore, and places himself with both feet on the old, firm ground—in astonishment that it does not rock.

47.

The Suppression of the Passions.—When one continually prohibits the expression of the passions as something to be left to the "vulgar," to coarser, bourgeois, and peasant natures—that is, when one does not want to suppress the passions themselves, but only their language and demeanour, one nevertheless realises *therewith* just what one does not want: the suppression of the passions themselves, or at least their weakening and alteration,—as the court of Louis XIV. (to cite the most instructive instance), and all that was dependent on it, experienced. The generation *that followed*, trained in suppressing their expression, no longer possessed the passions themselves, but had a pleasant, superficial, playful disposition in their place,—a generation which was so permeated with the incapacity to be ill-mannered, that even an injury was not taken and retaliated, except with courteous words. Perhaps our own time furnishes the most remarkable counterpart to this period: I see everywhere (in life, in the theatre, and not least in all that is written) satisfaction at all the *coarser* outbursts and gestures of passion; a certain convention of passionateness is now desired,—only not the passion itself! Nevertheless *it* will thereby be at last reached, and our posterity will have a *genuine savagery,* and not merely a formal savagery and unmannerliness.

48.

Knowledge of Distress.—Perhaps there is nothing by which men and periods are so much separated from one another, as by the different degrees of knowledge of distress which they possess; distress of the soul as well as of the body. With respect to the latter, owing to lack of sufficient self-experience, we men of the present day (in spite of our deficiencies and infirmities), are perhaps all of us blunderers and visionaries in comparison with the men of the age of fear—the longest of all ages,—when the individual had to protect himself against violence, and for that purpose had to be a man of violence himself. At that time a man went through a long schooling of corporeal tortures and privations, and found even in a certain kind of cruelty toward himself, in a voluntary use of pain, a necessary means for his preservation; at that time a person trained his environment to the endurance of pain; at that time a person willingly inflicted pain, and saw the most frightful things of this kind happen to others without having any other feeling than for his own security. As regards the distress of the soul however, I now look at every man with respect to whether he knows it by experience or by description; whether he still regards it as necessary to simulate this knowledge, perhaps as an indication of more refined culture; or whether, at the bottom of his heart, he does not at all believe in great sorrows of soul, and at the naming of them calls to mind a similar experience as at the naming of great corporeal sufferings, such as tooth-aches, and stomach-aches. It is thus, however, that it seems to be with most people at present. Owing to the universal inexperience of both kinds of pain, and the comparative rarity of the spectacle of a sufferer, an important consequence results: people now hate pain far more than earlier man did, and calumniate it worse than ever; indeed people nowadays can hardly endure the *thought* of pain, and make out of it an affair of conscience and a reproach to collective existence. The appearance of pessimistic philosophies is not at all the sign of great and dreadful miseries; for these interrogative marks regarding the worth of life appear in periods when the refinement and alleviation of existence already deem the unavoidable gnat-stings of the soul and body as altogether too bloody and wicked; and in the poverty of actual experiences of pain, would now like to make *painful general ideas* appear as suffering of the worst kind.—There might indeed be a remedy for pessimistic philosophies and the excessive sensibility which seems to me the real "distress of the present":—but perhaps this remedy already sounds too cruel, and would itself be reckoned among the symptoms owing to which people at present conclude that "existence is something evil." Well! the remedy for "the distress" is *distress*.

49.

Magnanimity and allied Qualities.—Those paradoxical phenomena, such as the sudden coldness in the demeanour of good-natured men, the humour of the melancholy, and above all *magnanimity*, as a sudden renunciation of revenge or of the gratification of envy—appear in men in whom there is a powerful inner impulsiveness, in men of sudden satiety and sudden disgust. Their satisfactions are so rapid and violent that satiety, aversion and flight into the antithetical taste, immediately follow upon them: in this contrast the convulsion of feeling liberates itself, in one person by sudden coldness, in another by laughter, and in a third by tear and self-sacrifice. The magnanimous person appears to me—at least that kind of magnanimous person who has always made most impression—as a man with the strongest thirst for vengeance, to whom a gratification presents itself close at hand, and who *already* drinks it off *in imagination* so copiously, thoroughly, and to the last drop, that an excessive, rapid disgust follows this rapid licentiousness;—he now elevates himself "above himself," as one says, and forgives his enemy, yea, blesses and honours him. With this violence done to himself, however, with this mockery of his impulse to revenge, even still so powerful he merely yields to the new impulse, the disgust which has become powerful, and does this just as impatiently and licentiously, as a short time previously he *forestalled*, and as it were exhausted, the joy of revenge with his fantasy. In magnanimity there is the same amount of egoism as in revenge, but a different quality of egoism.

50.

The Argument of Isolation.—The reproach of conscience, even in the most conscientious, is weak against the feeling: "This and that are contrary to the good morals of *your* society." A cold glance or a wry mouth on the part of those among whom and for whom one has been educated, is still *feared* even by the strongest. What is really feared there? Isolation! as the argument which demolishes even the best arguments for a person or cause!—It is thus that the gregarious instinct speaks in us.

51.

Sense for Truth.—Commend me to all scepticism where I am permitted to answer: "Let us put it to the test!" But I don't wish to hear anything more of things and questions which do not admit of being tested. That is the limit of my "sense for truth": for bravery has there lost its right.

52.

What others Know of us.—That which we know of ourselves and have in our memory is not so decisive for the happiness of our life as is generally believed. One day it flashes upon our mind what *others* know of us (or think they know)—and then we acknowledge that it is the more powerful. We get on with our bad conscience more easily than with our bad reputation.

53.

Where Goodness Begins.—Where bad eyesight can no longer see the evil impulse as such, on account of its refinement,—there man sets up the kingdom of goodness; and the feeling of having now gone over into the kingdom of goodness brings all those impulses (such as the feelings of security, of comfortableness, of benevolence) into simultaneous activity, which were threatened and confined by the evil impulses. Consequently, the duller the eye so much the further does goodness extend! Hence the eternal cheerfulness of the populace and of children! Hence the gloominess and grief (allied to the bad conscience) of great thinkers.

54.

The Consciousness of Appearance.—How wonderfully and novelly, and at the same time how awfully and ironically, do I feel myself situated with respect to collective existence, with my knowledge! I have *discovered* for myself that the old humanity and animality, yea, the collective primeval age, and the past of all sentient being, continues to meditate, love, hate, and reason in me,—I have suddenly awoke in the midst of this dream, but merely to the consciousness that I just dream, and that I *must* dream on in order not to perish; just as the sleep-walker must dream on in order not to tumble down. What is it that is now "appearance" to me! Verily, not the antithesis of any kind of essence,—what knowledge can I assert of any kind of essence whatsoever, except merely the predicates of its appearance! Verily not a dead mask which one could put upon an unknown X, and which to be sure one could also remove! Appearance is for me the operating and living thing itself; which goes so far in its self-mockery as to make me feel that here there is appearance, and Will o' the Wisp, and spirit-dance, and nothing more,—that among all these dreamers, I also, the "thinker," dance my dance, that the thinker is a means of prolonging further the terrestrial dance, and in so far is one of the masters of ceremony of existence, and that the sublime consistency and connectedness of all branches of knowledge is perhaps, and will perhaps, be the best means for *maintaining* the universality of the dreaming, the complete, mutual understandability of all those dreamers, and thereby *the duration of the dream.*

55.

The Ultimate Nobility of Character.—What then makes a person "noble"? Certainly not that he makes sacrifices; even the frantic libertine makes sacrifices. Certainly not that he generally follows his passions; there are contemptible passions. Certainly not that he does something for others, and without selfishness; perhaps the effect of selfishness is precisely at its greatest in the noblest persons.—But that the passion which seizes the noble man is a peculiarity, without his knowing that it is so: the use of a rare and singular measuring-rod, almost a frenzy: the feeling of heat in things which feel cold to all other persons: a divining of values for which scales have not yet been invented: a sacrificing on altars which are consecrated to an unknown God: a bravery without the desire for honour: a self-sufficiency which has superabundance, and imparts to men and things. Hitherto, therefore, it has been the rare in man, and the unconsciousness of this rareness, that has made men noble. Here, however, let us consider that everything ordinary, immediate, and indispensable, in short, what has been most preservative of the species, and generally the *rule* in mankind hitherto, has been judged unreasonable and calumniated in its entirety by this standard, in favour of the exceptions. To become the advocate of the rule—that may perhaps be: the ultimate form and refinement in which nobility of character will reveal itself on earth.

56.

The Desire for Suffering.—When I think of the desire to do something, how it continually tickles and stimulates millions of young Europeans, who cannot endure themselves and all their ennui,—I conceive that there must be a desire in them to suffer something, in order to derive from their suffering a worthy motive for acting, for doing something. Distress is necessary! Hence the cry of the politicians, hence the many false trumped-up, exaggerated "states of distress" of all possible kinds, and the blind readiness to believe in them. This young world desires that there should arrive or appear *from the outside*—*not* happiness—but misfortune; and their imagination is already busy beforehand to form a monster out of it, so that they may afterwards be able to fight with a monster. If these distress-seekers felt the power to benefit themselves, to do something for themselves from internal sources, they would also understand how to create a distress of their own, specially their own, from internal sources. Their inventions might then be more refined, and their gratifications might sound like good music: while at present they fill the world with their cries of distress, and consequently too often with the *feeling of distress* in the first place! They do not know what to make of themselves—and so they paint the misfortune of others on the wall; they always need others! And always again other others!—Pardon me, my friends, I have ventured to paint my *happiness* on the wall.

BOOK SECOND

57.

To the Realists.—Ye sober beings, who feel yourselves armed against passion and fantasy, and would gladly make a pride and an ornament out of your emptiness, ye call yourselves realists, and give to understand that the world is actually constituted as it appears to you; before you alone reality stands unveiled, and ye yourselves would perhaps be the best part of it,—oh, ye dear images of Sais! But are not ye also in your unveiled condition still extremely passionate and dusky beings compared with the fish, and still all too like an enamoured artist?[9]—and what is "reality" to

---

[9]This poem is a parody of the "Chorus Mysticus" which concludes the second part of Goethe's

an enamoured artist! Ye still carry about with you the valuations of things which had their origin in the passions and infatuations of earlier centuries! There is still a secret and ineffaceable drunkenness embodied in your sobriety! Your love of "reality," for example—oh, that is an old, primitive "love"! In every feeling, in every sense-impression, there is a portion of this old love: and similarly also some kind of fantasy, prejudice, irrationality, ignorance, fear, and whatever else has become mingled and woven into it. There is that mountain! There is that cloud! What is "real" in them? Remove the phantasm and the whole human *element* therefrom, ye sober ones! Yes, if ye could do *that!* If ye could forget your origin, your past, your preparatory schooling,—your whole history as man and beast! There is no "reality" for us—nor for you either, ye sober ones,—we are far from being so alien to one another as ye suppose; and perhaps our good-will to get beyond drunkenness is just as respectable as your belief that ye are altogether *incapable* of drunkenness.

58.

Only as Creators!—It has caused me the greatest trouble, and for ever causes me the greatest trouble, to perceive that unspeakably more depends upon *what things are called*, than on what they are. The reputation, the name and appearance, the importance, the usual measure and weight of things—each being in origin most frequently an error and arbitrariness thrown over the things like a garment, and quite alien to their essence and even to their exterior—have gradually, by the belief therein and its continuous growth from generation to generation, grown as it were on-and-into things and become their very body; the appearance at the very beginning becomes almost always the essence in the end, and *operates* as the essence! What a fool he would be who would think it enough to refer here to this origin and this nebulous veil of illusion, in order to *annihilate* that which virtually passes for the world—namely, so-called "reality"! It is only as creators that we can annihilate!—But let us not forget this: it suffices to create new names and valuations and probabilities, in order in the long run to create new "things."

59.

We Artists!—When we love a woman we have readily a hatred against nature, on recollecting all the disagreeable natural functions to which every woman is subject; we prefer not to think of them at all, but if once our soul touches on these things it twitches impatiently, and glances, as we have said, contemptuously at nature:—we are hurt; nature seems to encroach upon our possessions, and with the profanest hands. We then shut our ears against all physiology, and we decree in secret that

---

"Faust." Bayard Taylor's translation of the passage in "Faust" runs as follows:—

"we will hear nothing of the fact that man is something else than *soul and form!*" "The man under the skin" is an abomination and monstrosity, a blasphemy of God and of love to all lovers.—Well, just as the lover still feels with respect to nature and natural functions, so did every worshipper of God and his "holy omnipotence" feel formerly: in all that was said of nature by astronomers, geologists, physiologists, and physicians, he saw an encroachment on his most precious possession, and consequently an attack,—and moreover also an impertinence of the assailant! The "law of nature" sounded to him as blasphemy against God; in truth he would too willingly have seen the whole of mechanics traced back to moral acts of volition and arbitrariness:—but because nobody could render him this service, he *concealed* nature and mechanism from himself as best he could, and lived in a dream. Oh, those men of former times understood how to *dream*, and did not need first to go to sleep!—and we men of the present day also still understand it too well, with all our good-will for wakefulness and daylight! It suffices to love, to hate, to desire, and in general to feel *immediately* the spirit and the power of the dream come over us, and we ascend, with open eyes and indifferent to all danger, the most dangerous paths, to the roofs and towers of fantasy, and without any giddiness, as persons born for climbing—we the night-walkers by day! We artists! We concealers of naturalness! We moon-struck and God-struck ones! We death-silent, untiring wanderers on heights which we do not see as heights, but as our plains, as our places of safety!

60.

Women and their Effect in the Distance.—Have I still ears? Am I only ear, and nothing else besides? Here I stand in the midst of the surging of the breakers, whose white flames fork up to my feet;—from all sides there is howling, threatening, crying, and screaming at me, while in the lowest depths the old earth-shaker sings his aria hollow like a roaring bull; he beats such an earth-shaker's measure thereto, that even the hearts of these weathered rock-monsters tremble at the sound. Then, suddenly, as if born out of nothingness, there appears before the portal of this hellish labyrinth, only a few fathoms distant,—a great sailing-ship gliding silently along like a ghost. Oh, this ghostly beauty! With what enchantment it seizes me! What? Has all the repose and silence in the world embarked here? Does my happiness itself sit in this quiet place, my happier ego, my second immortalised self? Still not dead, but also no longer living? As a ghost-like, calm, gazing, gliding, sweeping, neutral being? Similar to the ship, which, with its white sails, like an immense butterfly, passes over the dark sea! Yes! Passing *over* existence! That is it! That would be it!—It seems that the noise here has made me a visionary? All great noise causes one to place happiness in the calm and the distance. When a man is in the midst of *his* hubbub, in the midst of the breakers of his plots and plans, he there sees perhaps calm, enchanting beings glide past him, for whose happiness and retirement he longs—*they are women.* He almost thinks that there with the women dwells his better self; that in these calm places even the loudest breakers become still as death, and life itself a dream of life. But still! but still! my noble enthusiast, there is also in the most beautiful sailing-ship so much noise and bustling, and alas, so much petty, pitiable bustling! The enchantment and the most powerful effect of women is, to use the language of philosophers, an effect at a distance, an *actio in distans;* there belongs thereto, however, primarily and above all,—*distance!*

61.

In Honour of Friendship.—That the sentiment of friendship was regarded by antiquity as the highest sentiment, higher even than the most vaunted pride of the self-sufficient and wise, yea, as it were its sole and still holier brotherhood, is very well expressed by the story of the Macedonian king who made the present of a talent to a cynical Athenian philosopher from whom he received it back again. "What?" said the king, "has he then no friend?" He therewith meant to say, "I honour this pride of the wise and independent man, but I should have honoured his humanity still higher, if the friend in him had gained the victory over his pride. The philosopher has lowered himself in my estimation, for he showed that he did not know one of the two highest sentiments—and in fact the higher of them!"

62.

Love.—Love pardons even the passion of the beloved.

63.

Woman in Music—How does it happen that warm and rainy winds bring the musical mood and the inventive delight in melody with them? Are they not the same winds that fill the churches and give women amorous thoughts?

64.

Sceptics.—I fear that women who have grown old are more sceptical in the secret recesses of their hearts than any of the men; they believe in the superficiality of existence as in its essence, and all virtue and profundity is to them only the disguising of this "truth," the very desirable disguising of a *pudendum,*—an affair, therefore, of decency and modesty, and nothing more!

65.

Devotedness.—There are noble women with a certain poverty of spirit, who, in order to *express* their profoundest devotedness, have no other alternative but to offer their virtue and modesty: it is the highest thing they have. And this present is often accepted without putting the recipient under such deep obligation as the giver supposed,—a very melancholy story!

66.

The Strength of the Weak.—Women are all skilful in exaggerating their weaknesses, indeed they are inventive in weaknesses, so as to seem quite fragile ornaments to which even a grain of dust does harm; their existence is meant to bring home to man's mind his coarseness, and to appeal to his conscience. They thus defend themselves against the strong and all "rights of might."

67.

Self-dissembling.—She loves him now and has since been looking forth with as quiet confidence as a cow; but alas! It was precisely his delight that she seemed so fitful and absolutely incomprehensible! He had rather too much steady weather in himself already! Would she not do well to feign her old character? to feign indifference? Does not—love itself advise her *to do so? Vivat comœdia!*

68.

Will and Willingness.—Some one brought a youth to a wise man, and said, "See, this is one who is being corrupted by women!" The wise man shook his head and smiled. "It is men," he called out, "who corrupt women; and everything that women lack should be atoned for and improved in men—for man creates for himself the ideal of woman, and woman moulds herself according to this ideal."—"You are too tender-hearted towards women," said one of the bystanders, "you do not know them!" The wise man answered: "Man's attribute is will, woman's attribute is willingness—such is the law of the sexes, verily! a hard law for woman! All human beings are innocent of their existence, women, however, are doubly innocent; who could have enough of salve and gentleness for them!"—"What about salve! What about gentleness!" called out another person in the crowd, "we must educate women better!"—"We must educate men better," said the wise man, and made a sign to the youth to follow him.—The youth, however, did not follow him.

69.

Capacity for Revenge—That a person cannot and consequently will not defend himself, does not yet cast disgrace upon him in our eyes; but we despise the person who has neither the ability nor the good-will for revenge—whether it be a man or a woman. Would a woman be able to captivate us (or, as people say, to "fetter" us) whom we did not credit with knowing how to employ the dagger (any kind of dagger) skilfully *against us* under certain circumstances? Or against herself; which in a certain case might be the severest revenge (the Chinese revenge).

70.

The Mistresses of the Masters—A powerful contralto voice, as we occasionally hear it in the theatre, raises suddenly for us the curtain on possibilities in which we usually do not believe; all at once we are convinced that somewhere in the world there may be women with high, heroic, royal souls, capable and prepared for magnificent remonstrances, resolutions, and self-sacrifices, capable and prepared for domination over men, because in them the best in man, superior to sex, has become a corporeal ideal. To be sure, it is not the intention of the theatre that such voices should give such a conception of women; they are usually intended to represent the ideal male lover, for example, a Romeo; but, to judge by my experience, the theatre regularly miscalculates here, and the musician also, who expects such effects from such a voice. People do not believe in *these* lovers; these voices still contain a tinge of the motherly and housewifely character, and most of all when love is in their tone.

71.

On Female Chastity.—There is something quite astonishing and extraordinary in the education of women of the higher class; indeed, there is perhaps nothing more paradoxical. All the world is agreed to educate them with as much ignorance as possible *in eroticis*, and to inspire their soul with a profound shame of such things, and the extremest impatience and horror at the suggestion of them. It is really here only that all the "honour" of woman is at stake; what would one not forgive them in other respects! But here they are intended to remain ignorant to the very backbone:—they are intended to have neither eyes, ears, words, nor thoughts for this, their "wickedness"; indeed knowledge here is already evil. And then! To be hurled as with an awful thunderbolt into reality and knowledge with marriage—and indeed by him whom they most love and esteem: to have to encounter love and shame in contradiction, yea, to have to feel rapture, abandonment, duty, sympathy, and fright at the unexpected proximity of God and animal, and whatever else besides! all at once!—There, in fact, a psychic entanglement has been effected which is quite unequalled! Even the sympathetic curiosity of the wisest discerner of men does not suffice to divine how this or that woman gets along with the solution of this enigma and the enigma of this solution; what dreadful, far-reaching suspicions must awaken thereby in the poor unhinged soul; and forsooth, how the ultimate philosophy and scepticism of the woman casts anchor at this point!—Afterwards the same profound silence as before and often even a silence to herself, a shutting of her eyes to herself.—Young wives on that account make great efforts to appear superficial and thoughtless the most ingenious of them simulate a kind of impudence.—Wives easily feel their husbands as a question-mark to their honour, and their children as an apology or atonement,—they require children, and wish for them in quite another spirit than a husband wishes for them.—In short, one cannot be gentle enough towards women!

72.

Mothers.—Animals think differently from men with respect to females; with them the female is regarded as the productive being. There is no paternal love among them, but there is such a thing as love of the children of a beloved, and habituation to them. In the young, the females find gratification for their lust of dominion; the young are a property, an occupation, something quite comprehensible to them, with which they can chatter: all this conjointly is maternal love,—it is to be compared to the love of the artist for his work. Pregnancy has made the females gentler, more expectant, more timid, more submissively inclined; and similarly intellectual pregnancy engenders the character of the contemplative, who are allied to women in character:—they are the masculine mothers.—Among animals the masculine sex is regarded as the beautiful sex.

73.

Saintly Cruelty.—A man holding a newly born child in his hands came to a saint. "What should I do with this child," he asked, "it is wretched, deformed, and has not even enough of life to die" "Kill it," cried the saint with a dreadful voice, "kill it, and then hold it in thy arms for three days and three nights to brand it on thy memory:—thus wilt thou never again beget a child when it is not the time for thee to beget."—When the man had heard this he went away disappointed; and many found fault with the saint because he had advised cruelty; for he had advised to kill the child. "But is it not more cruel to let it live?" asked the saint.

74.

The Unsuccessful—Those poor women always fail of success who become agitated and uncertain, and talk too much in presence of him whom they love; for men are most successfully seduced by a certain subtle and phlegmatic tenderness.

75.

The Third Sex.—"A small man is a paradox, but still a man,—but a small woman seems to me to be of another sex in comparison with well-grown ones"—said an old dancing-master. A small woman is never beautiful—said old Aristotle.

76.

The greatest Danger.—Had there not at all times been a larger number of men who regarded the cultivation of their mind—their "rationality"—as their pride, their obligation, their virtue, and were injured or shamed by all play of fancy and extravagance of thinking—as lovers of "sound common sense":—mankind would long ago have perished! Incipient *insanity* has hovered, and hovers continually over mankind as its greatest danger: it is precisely the breaking out of inclination in feeling, seeing, and hearing; the enjoyment of the unruliness of the mind; the delight in human unreason. It is not truth and certainty that is the antithesis of the world of the insane, but the universality and all-obligatoriness of a belief, in short, non-voluntariness in forming opinions. And the greatest labour of human beings hitherto has been to agree with one another regarding a number of things, and to impose upon themselves a *law of agreement*—indifferent whether these things are true or false. This is the discipline of the mind which has preserved mankind;—but the counter-impulses are still so powerful that one can really speak of the future of mankind with little confidence. The ideas of things still continually shift and move, and will perhaps alter more than ever in the future; it is continually the most select spirits themselves who strive against universal obligatoriness—the investigators of *truth* above all! The accepted belief, as the belief of all the world, continually engenders a disgust and a new longing in the more ingenious minds; and already the slow *tempo* which it demands for all intellectual processes (the imitation of the tortoise, which is here recognised as the rule) makes the artists and poets runaways:—it is in these impatient spirits that a downright delight in delirium breaks out, because delirium has such a joyful *tempo!* Virtuous intellects, therefore, are needed—ah! I want to use the least ambiguous word,—*virtuous stupidity* is needed, imperturbable conductors of the *slow* spirits are needed, in order that the faithful of the great collective belief may remain with one another and dance their dance further: it is a necessity of the first importance that here enjoins and demands. *We others are the exceptions and the danger,—*we eternally need protection—Well, there can actually be something said in favour of the exceptions *provided that they never want to become the rule.*

77.

The Animal with good Conscience.—It is not unknown to me that there is vulgarity in everything that pleases Southern Europe—whether it be Italian opera (for example, Rossini's and Bellini's), or the Spanish adventure-romance (most readily accessible to us in the French garb of Gil Blas)—but it does not offend me, any more than the vulgarity which one encounters in a walk through Pompeii, or even in the reading of every ancient book: what is the reason of this? Is it because shame is lacking here, and because the vulgar always comes forward just as sure and certain of itself as anything noble, lovely, and passionate in the same kind of music or romance? "The animal has its rights like man, so let it run about freely; and you, my dear fellow-man, are still this animal, in spite of all!"—that seems to me the moral of the case, and the peculiarity of southern humanity. Bad taste has its rights like good taste, and even a prerogative over the latter when it is the great requisite, the sure satisfaction, and as it were a universal language, an immediately intelligible mask and attitude; the excellent, select taste on the other hand has always something of a seeking, tentative character, not fully certain that it understands,—it is never, and has never been popular! The *masque* is and remains popular! So let all this masquerade run along in the melodies and cadences, in the leaps and merriment of the rhythm of these operas! Quite the ancient life! What does one understand of it, if one does not understand the delight in the masque, the good conscience of all masquerade! Here is the bath and the refreshment of the ancient spirit:—and perhaps this bath was still more necessary for the rare and sublime natures of the ancient world than for the vulgar.—On the other hand, a vulgar turn in northern works, for example in German music, offends me unutterably. There is *shame* in it, the artist has lowered himself in his own sight, and could not even avoid blushing: we are ashamed with him, and are so hurt because we surmise that he believed he had to lower himself on our account.

78.

What we should be Grateful for.—It is only the artists, and especially the theatrical artists, who have furnished men with eyes and ears to hear and see with some pleasure what everyone is in himself, what he experiences and aims at: it is only *they* who have taught us how to estimate the hero that is concealed in each of these common-place men, and the art of looking at ourselves from a distance as heroes, and as it were simplified and transfigured—the art of "putting ourselves on the stage" before ourselves. It is thus only that we get beyond some of the paltry details in ourselves! Without that art we should be nothing but foreground, and would live absolutely under the spell of the perspective which makes the closest and the commonest seem immensely large and like reality in itself.—Perhaps there is merit of a similar kind in the religion which commanded us to look at the sinfulness of every individual man with a magnifying-glass, and made a great, immortal criminal of the sinner; in that it put eternal perspectives around man, it taught him to see himself from a distance, and as something past, something entire.

79.

The Charm of Imperfection.—I see here a poet, who, like so many men, exercises a higher charm by his imperfections than by all that is rounded off and takes perfect shape under his hands,—indeed, he derives his advantage and reputation far more from his actual limitations than from his abundant powers. His work never expresses altogether what he would really like to express, what he *would like to have seen*: he appears to have had the foretaste of a vision and never the vision itself:—but an extraordinary longing for this vision has remained in his soul; and from this he derives his equally extraordinary eloquence of longing and craving. With this he raises those who listen to him above his work and above all "works," and gives them wings to rise higher than hearers have ever risen before, thus making them poets and seers themselves; they then show an admiration for the originator of their happiness, as if he had led them immediately to the vision of his holiest and ultimate verities, as if he had reached his goal, and had actually *seen* and communicated his vision. It is to the advantage of his reputation that he has not really arrived at his goal.

80.

Art and Nature.—The Greeks (or at least the Athenians) liked to hear good talking: indeed they had an eager inclination for it, which distinguished them more than anything else from non-Greeks. And so they required good talking even from passion on the stage, and submitted to the unnaturalness of dramatic verse with delight:—in nature, forsooth, passion is so sparing of words! so dumb and confused! Or if it finds words, so embarrassed and irrational and a shame to itself! We have now, all of us, thanks to the Greeks, accustomed ourselves to this unnaturalness on the stage, as we endure that other unnaturalness, the *singing* passion, and willingly endure it, thanks to the Italians.—It has become a necessity to us, which we cannot satisfy out of the resources of actuality, to hear men talk well and in full detail in the most trying situations: it enraptures us at present when the tragic hero still finds words, reasons, eloquent gestures, and on the whole a bright spirituality, where life approaches the abysses, and where the actual man mostly loses his head, and certainly his fine language. This kind of *deviation from nature* is perhaps the most agreeable repast for man's pride: he loves art generally on account of it, as the expression of high, heroic unnaturalness and convention. One rightly objects to the dramatic poet when he does not transform everything into reason and speech, but always retains a remnant of *silence*:—just as one is dissatisfied with an operatic musician who cannot find a melody for the highest emotion, but only an emotional, "natural" stammering and crying. Here nature *has to* be contradicted!

Here the common charm of illusion *has to* give place to a higher charm! The Greeks go far, far in this direction—frightfully far! As they constructed the stage as narrow as possible and dispensed with all the effect of deep backgrounds, as they made pantomime and easy motion impossible to the actor, and transformed him into a solemn, stiff, masked bogey, so they have also deprived passion itself of its deep background, and have dictated to it a law of fine talk; indeed, they have really done everything to counteract the elementary effect of representations that inspire pity and terror: *they did not want pity and terror,*—with due deference, with the highest deference to Aristotle! but he certainly did not hit the nail, to say nothing of the head of the nail, when he spoke about the final aim of Greek tragedy! Let us but look at the Grecian tragic poets with respect to *what* most excited their diligence, their inventiveness, and their emulation,—certainly it was not the intention of subjugating the spectators by emotion! The Athenian went to the theatre *to hear fine talking!* And fine talking was arrived at by Sophocles!—pardon me this heresy!—It is very different with *serious opera:* all its masters make it their business to prevent their personages being understood. "An occasional word picked up may come to the assistance of the inattentive listener; but on the whole the situation must be self-explanatory,—the *talking* is of no account!"—so they all think, and so they have all made fun of the words. Perhaps they have only lacked courage to express fully their extreme contempt for words: a little additional insolence in Rossini, and he would have allowed la-la-la-la to be sung throughout—and it might have been the rational course! The personages of the opera are *not* meant to be believed "in their words," but in their tones! That is the difference, that is the fine *unnaturalness* on account of which people go to the opera! Even the *recitativo secco* is not really intended to be heard as words and text: this kind of half-music is meant rather in the first place to give the musical ear a little repose (the repose from *melody,* as from the sublimest, and on that account the most straining enjoyment of this art),—but very soon something different results, namely, an increasing impatience, an increasing resistance, a new longing for *entire* music, for melody.—How is it with the art of Richard Wagner as seen from this standpoint? Is it perhaps the same? Perhaps otherwise? It would often seem to me as if one needed to have learned by heart both the words *and* the music of his creations before the performances; for without that—so it seemed to me—me *may hear* neither the words, nor even the music.

81.

Grecian Taste—"What is beautiful in it?"—asked a certain geometrician, after a performance of the *Iphigenia*—"there is nothing proved in it!" Could the Greeks have been so far from this taste? In Sophocles at least "everything is proved."

82.

Esprit Un-Grecian.—The Greeks were exceedingly logical and plain in all their thinking; they did not get tired of it, at least during their long flourishing period, as is so often the case with the French; who too willingly made a little excursion into the opposite, and in fact endure the spirit of logic only when it betrays its *sociable* courtesy, its sociable self-renunciation, by a multitude of such little excursions into its opposite. Logic appears to them as necessary as bread and water, but also like these as a kind of prison-fare, as soon as it is to be taken pure and by itself. In good society one must never want to be in the right absolutely and solely, as all pure logic requires; hence the little dose of irrationality in all French *esprit.*—The social sense of the Greeks was far less developed than that of the French in the present and the past; hence, so little *esprit* in their cleverest men, hence, so little wit, even in their wags, hence—alas! But people will not readily believe these tenets of mine, and how much of the kind I have still on my soul!—*Est res magna tacere*—says Martial, like all garrulous people.

83.

Translations.—One can estimate the amount of the historical sense which an age possesses by the way in which it makes *translations* and seeks to embody in itself past periods and literatures. The French of Corneille, and even the French of the Revolution, appropriated Roman antiquity in a manner for which we would no longer have the courage—owing to our superior historical sense. And Roman antiquity itself: how violently, and at the same time how naïvely, did it lay its hand on everything excellent and elevated belonging to the older Grecian antiquity! How they translated these writings into the Roman present! How they wiped away intentionally and unconcernedly the wing-dust of the butterfly moment! It is thus that Horace now and then translated Alcæus or Archilochus, it is thus that Propertius translated Callimachus and Philetas (poets of equal rank with Theocritus, if we *be allowed* to judge): of what consequence was it to them that the actual creator experienced this and that, and had inscribed the indication thereof in his poem!—as poets they were averse to the antiquarian, inquisitive spirit which precedes the historical sense; as poets they did not respect those essentially personal traits and names, nor anything peculiar to city, coast, or century, such as its costume and mask, but at once put the present and the Roman in its place. They seem to us to ask: "Should we not make the old new for ourselves, and adjust *ourselves* to it? Should we not be allowed to inspire this dead body with our soul? for it is dead indeed: how loathsome is everything dead!"—They did not know the pleasure of the historical sense; the past and the alien was painful to them, and as Romans it was an incitement to a Roman conquest. In fact, they conquered when they translated,—not only in that they omitted the historical: they added also allusions to the present; above all, they struck out the name of the poet and put their own in its place—not with the feeling of theft, but with the very best conscience of the *Imperium Romanum*.

84.

The Origin of Poetry.—The lovers of the fantastic in man, who at the same time represent the doctrine of instinctive morality, draw this conclusion: "Granted that utility has been honoured at all times as the highest divinity, where then in all the world has poetry come from?—this rhythmising of speech which thwarts rather than furthers plainness of communication, and which, nevertheless, has sprung up everywhere on the earth, and still springs up, as a mockery of all useful purpose! The wildly beautiful irrationality of poetry refutes you, ye utilitarians! The wish *to get rid of* utility in some way—that is precisely what has elevated man, that is what has inspired him to morality and art!" Well, I must here speak for once to please the utilitarians,—they are so seldom in the right that it is pitiful! In the old times which called poetry into being, people had still utility in view with respect to it, and a very important utility—at the time when rhythm was introduced into speech, that force which arranges all the particles of the sentence anew, commands the choosing of the words, recolours the thought, and makes it more obscure, more foreign, and more distant: to be sure a *superstitious utility!* It was intended that a human entreaty should be more profoundly impressed upon the Gods by virtue of rhythm, after it had been observed that men could remember a verse better than an unmetrical speech. It was likewise thought that people could make themselves audible at greater distances by the rhythmical beat; the rhythmical prayer seemed to come nearer to the ear of the Gods. Above all, however, people wanted to have the advantage of the elementary conquest which man experiences in himself when he hears music: rhythm is a constraint; it produces an unconquerable desire to yield, to join in; not only the step of the foot, but also the soul itself follows the measure,—probably the soul of the Gods also, as people thought! They attempted, therefore, to *constrain* the Gods by rhythm, and to exercise a power over them; they threw poetry around the Gods like a magic noose. There was a still more wonderful idea, and it has perhaps operated most powerfully of all in the originating of poetry. Among the Pythagoreans it made its appearance as a philosophical doctrine and as an artifice of teaching: but long before there were philosophers music was acknowledged to possess the power of unburdening the emotions, of purifying the soul, of soothing the *ferocia animi*—and this was owing to the rhythmical element in music. When the proper tension and harmony of the soul were lost a person had to *dance* to the measure of the singer,—that was the recipe of this medical art. By means of it Terpander quieted a tumult, Empedocles calmed a maniac, Damon purged a love-sick youth; by means of it even the maddened, revengeful Gods were treated for the purpose of a cure. This was effected by driving the frenzy and wantonness of their emotions to the highest pitch, by making the furious mad, and the revengeful intoxicated with vengeance all the orgiastic cults seek to discharge the *ferocia* of a deity all at once, and thus make an orgy, so that the deity may feel freer and quieter afterwards, and leave man in peace. *Melos*, according to its root, signifies a soothing agency, not because the song is gentle itself, but because its after-effect is gentle.—And not only in the religious song, but also in the secular song of the most ancient times, the prerequisite is that the rhythm should exercise a magical influence; for example, in drawing water, or in rowing: the song is for the enchanting of the spirits supposed to be active thereby; it makes them obliging, involuntary and the instruments of man. And as often as a person acts he has occasion to sing, *every* action is dependent on the assistance of spirits: magic song and incantation appear to be the original form of poetry. When verse also came to be used in oracles—the Greeks said that the hexameter was invented at Delphi,—the rhythm was here also intended to exercise a compulsory influence. To make a prophecy—that means originally (according to what seems to me the probable derivation of the Greek word) to determine something; people thought they could determine the future by winning Apollo over to their side: he who, according to the most ancient idea, is far more than a foreseeing deity. According as the formula is pronounced with literal and rhythmical correctness, it determines the future: the formula, however, is the invention of Apollo, who as the God of rhythm, can also determine the goddesses of fate—Looked at and investigated as a whole, was there ever anything *more serviceable* to the ancient superstitious species of human being than rhythm? People could do everything with it: they could make labour go on magically; they could compel a God to appear, to be near at hand, and listen to them; they could arrange the future for themselves according to their will; they could unburden their own souls of any kind of excess (of anxiety, of mania, of sympathy, of revenge), and not only their own souls, but the souls of the most evil spirits,—without verse a person was nothing, by means of verse a person became almost a God. Such a fundamental feeling no longer allows itself to be fully eradicated,—and even now, after millenniums of long labour in combating such superstition, the very wisest of us occasionally becomes the fool of rhythm, be it only that one *perceives* a thought to be *truer* when it has a metrical form and approaches with a divine hopping. Is it not a very funny thing that the most serious philosophers, however anxious they are in other respects for strict certainty, still appeal to *poetical sayings* in order to give their thoughts force and credibility? and yet it is more dangerous to a truth when the poet assents to it than when he contradicts it! For, as Homer says, "Minstrels speak much falsehood!"—

85.

The Good and the Beautiful.—Artists, glorify continually—they do nothing else,—and indeed they glorify all those conditions and things that have a repu-tation, so that man may feel himself good or great, or intoxicated, or merry, or pleased and wise by it. Those *select* things and conditions whose value for human *happiness* is regarded as secure and determined, are the objects of artists: they are ever lying in wait to discover such things, to transfer them into the domain of art. I mean to say that they are not themselves the valuers of happiness and of the happy ones, but they always press close to these valuers with the greatest curiosity and longing, in order immediately to use their valuations advantageously. As besides their impatience, they have also the big lungs of heralds and the feet of runners, they are generally always among the first to glorify the *new* excellency, and often *seem* to be the first who have called it good and valued it as good. This, however, as we have said, is an error; they are only faster and louder than the actual valuers:—And who then are these?—They are the rich and the leisurely.

86.

The Theatre.—This day has given me once more strong and elevated sentiments, and if I could have music and art in the evening, I know well what music and art I should *not* like to have; namely, none of that which would fain intoxicate its hearers and *excite* them to a crisis of strong and high feeling,—those men with commonplace souls, who in the evening are not like victors on triumphal cars, but like tired mules to whom life has rather too often applied the whip. What would those men at all know of "higher moods," unless there were expedients for causing ecstasy and idealistic strokes of the whip!—and thus they have their inspirers as they have their wines. But what is their drink and their drunkenness to *me*! Does the inspired one need wine? He rather looks with a kind of disgust at the agency and the agent which are here intended to produce an effect without sufficient reason,—an imitation of the high tide of the soul! What? One gives the mole wings and proud fancies—before going to sleep, before he creeps into his hole? One sends him into the theatre and puts great magnifying-glasses to his blind and tired eyes? Men, whose life is not "action" but business, sit in front of the stage and look at strange beings to whom life is more than business? "This is proper," you say, "this is entertaining, this is what culture wants!"—Well then! culture is too often lacking in me, for this sight is too often disgusting to me. He who has enough of tragedy and comedy in himself surely prefers to remain away from the theatre; or as an exception, the whole procedure—theatre and public and poet included—becomes for him a truly tragic and comic play, so that the performed piece counts for little in comparison. He who is something like Faust and Manfred, what does it matter to him about the Fausts and Manfreds of the theatre!—while it certainly gives him something to think about *that* such figures are brought into the theatre at all. The *strongest* thoughts and passions before those who are not capable of thought and passion—but of *intoxication* only! And *those* as a means to this end! And theatre and music the hashish-smoking and betel-chewing of Europeans! Oh, who will narrate to us the whole history of narcotics!—It is almost the history of "culture," the so-called higher culture!

87.

The Conceit of Artists. I think artists often do not know what they can do best, because they are too conceited, and have set their minds on something loftier than those little plants appear to be, which can grow up to perfection on their soil, fresh, rare, and beautiful. The final value of their own garden and vineyard is superciliously underestimated by them, and their love and their insight are not of the same quality. Here is a musician, who, more than any one else, has the genius for discovering the tones peculiar to suffering, oppressed, tortured souls, and who can endow even dumb animals with speech. No one equals him in the colours of the late autumn, in the indescribably touching happiness of a last, a final, and all too short enjoyment; he knows a chord for those secret and weird midnights of the soul when cause and effect seem out of joint, and when every instant something may originate "out of nothing." He draws his resources best of all out of the lower depths of human happiness, and so to speak, out of its drained goblet, where the bitterest and most nauseous drops have ultimately, for good or for ill, commingled with the sweetest. He knows the weary shuffling along of the soul which can no longer leap or fly, yea, not even walk; he has the shy glance of concealed pain, of understanding without comfort, of leave-taking without avowal; yea, as the Orpheus of all secret misery, he is greater than anyone; and in fact much has been added to art by him which was hitherto inexpressible and not even thought worthy of art, and which was only to be scared away, by words, and not grasped many small and quite microscopic features of the soul: yes, he is the master of miniature. But he does not *wish* to be so! His *character* is more in love with large walls and daring frescoes! He fails to see that his *spirit* has a different taste and inclination, and prefers to sit quietly in the corners of ruined houses:—concealed in this way, concealed even from himself, he there paints his proper masterpieces, all of which are very short, often only one bar in length,—there only does he become quite good, great, and perfect, perhaps there only.—But he does not know it! He is too conceited to know it.

88.

Earnestness for the Truth.—Earnest for the truth! What different things men understand by these words! Just the same opinions, and modes of demonstration and testing which a thinker regards as a frivolity in himself, to which he has succumbed with shame at one time or other,—just the same opinions may give to an artist, who comes in contact with them and accepts them temporarily, the consciousness that the profoundest earnestness for the truth has now taken hold of him, and that it is worthy of admiration that, although an artist, he at the same time exhibits the most ardent desire for the antithesis of the apparent. It is thus possible that a person may, just by his pathos of earnestness, betray how superficially and sparingly his intellect has hitherto operated in the domain of knowledge.—And is not everything that we consider *important* our betrayer? It shows where our motives lie, and where our motives are altogether lacking.

89.

Now and Formerly.—Of what consequence is all our art in artistic products, if that higher art, the art of the festival, be lost by us? Formerly all artistic products were exhibited on the great festive-path of humanity, as tokens of remembrance, and monuments of high and happy moments. One now seeks to allure the exhausted and sickly from the great suffering-path of humanity for a wanton moment by means of works of art; one furnishes them with a little ecstasy and insanity.

90.

Lights and Shades.—Books and writings are different with different thinkers. One writer has collected together in his book all the rays of light which he could quickly plunder and carry home from an illuminating experience; while another gives only the shadows, and the grey and black replicas of that which on the previous day had towered up in his soul.

91.

Precaution.—Alfieri, as is well known, told a great many falsehoods when he narrated the history of his life to his astonished contemporaries. He told falsehoods owing to the despotism toward himself which he exhibited, for example, in the way in which he created his own language, and tyrannised himself into a poet:—he finally found a rigid form of sublimity into which he *forced* his life and his memory; he must have suffered much in the process.—I would also give no credit to a history of Plato's life written by himself, as little as to Rousseau's, or to the *Vita nuova* of Dante.

92.

Prose and Poetry.—Let it be observed that the great masters of prose have almost always been poets as well, whether openly, or only in secret and for the "closet"; and in truth one only writes good prose *in view of poetry!* For prose is an uninterrupted, polite warfare with poetry; all its charm consists in the fact that poetry is constantly avoided and contradicted; every abstraction wants to have a gibe at poetry, and wishes to be uttered with a mocking voice; all dryness and coolness is meant to bring the amiable goddess into an amiable despair; there are often approximations and reconciliations for the moment, and then a sudden recoil and a burst of laughter; the curtain is often drawn up and dazzling light let in just while the goddess is enjoying her twilights and dull colours; the word is often taken out of her mouth and chanted to a melody while she holds her fine hands before her delicate little ears:—and so there are a thousand enjoyments of the warfare, the defeats included, of which the unpoetic, the so-called prose—men know nothing at all:—they consequently write and speak only bad prose! *Warfare is the father of all good things*, it is also the father of good prose!—There have been four very singular and truly poetical men in this century who have arrived at mastership in prose, for which otherwise this century is not suited, owing to lack of poetry, as we have indicated. Not to take Goethe into account, for he is reasonably claimed by the century that produced him, I look only on Giacomo Leopardi, Prosper Mérimée, Ralph Waldo Emerson, and Walter Savage Landor the author of *Imaginary Conversations*, as worthy to be called masters of prose.

93.

But why, then, do you Write?—A: I do not belong to those who *think* with the wet pen in hand; and still less to those who yield themselves entirely to their passions before the open ink-bottle, sitting on their chair and staring at the paper. I am always vexed and abashed by writing; writing is a necessity for me,—even to speak of it in a simile is disagreeable. B: But why, then, do you write? A: Well, my dear Sir, to tell you in confidence, I have hitherto found no other means of *getting rid of* my thoughts. B: And why do you wish to get rid of them? A: Why I wish? Do I really wish! I must—B: Enough! Enough!

94.

Growth after Death.—Those few daring words about moral matters which Fontenelle threw into his immortal *Dialogues of the Dead,* were regarded by his age as paradoxes and amusements of a not unscrupulous wit; even the highest judges of taste and intellect saw nothing more in them,—indeed, Fontenelle himself perhaps saw nothing more. Then something incredible takes place: these thoughts become truths! Science proves them! The game becomes serious! And we read those dialogues with a feeling different from that with which Voltaire and Helvetius read them, and we involuntarily raise their originator into another and *much higher* class of intellects than they did.—Rightly?' Wrongly?

95.

Chamfort.—That such a judge of men and of the multitude as Chamfort should side with the multitude, instead of standing apart in philosophical resignation and defence—I am at a loss to explain this, except as follows:—There was an instinct in him stronger than his wisdom, and it had never been gratified: the hatred against all *noblesse* of blood; perhaps his mother's old and only too explicable hatred, which was consecrated in him by love of her,—an instinct of revenge from his boyhood, which waited for the hour to avenge his mother. But then the course of his life, his genius, and alas! most of all, perhaps, the paternal blood in his veins, had seduced him to rank and consider himself equal to the *noblesse*—for many, many years! In the end, however, he could not endure the sight of himself, the "old man" under the old *régime,* any longer; he got into a violent, penitential passion, and *in this state* he put on the raiment of the populace as *his* special kind of hair-shirt! His bad conscience was the neglect of revenge.—If Chamfort had then been a little more of the philosopher, the Revolution would not have had its tragic wit and its sharpest sting; it would have been regarded as a much more stupid affair, and would have had no such seductive influence on men's minds. But Chamfort's hatred and revenge educated an entire generation; and the most illustrious men passed through his school. Let us but consider that Mirabeau looked up to Chamfort as to his higher and older self, from whom he expected (and endured) impulses, warnings, and condemnations,—Mirabeau, who as a man belongs to an entirely different order of greatness, as the very foremost among the statesman-geniuses of yesterday and to-day.—Strange, that in spite of such a friend and advocate—we possess Mirabeau's letters to Chamfort—this wittiest of all moralists has remained unfamiliar to the

French, quite the same as Stendhal, who has perhaps had the most penetrating eyes and ears of any. Frenchman of *this* century. Is it because the latter had really too much of the German and the Englishman in his nature for the Parisians to endure him?—while Chamfort, a man with ample knowledge of the profundities and secret motives of the soul, gloomy, suffering, ardent—a thinker who found laughter necessary as the remedy of life, and who almost gave himself up as lost every day that he had not laughed,—seems much more like an Italian, and related by blood to Dante and Leopardi, than like a Frenchman. One knows Chamfort's last words: "*Ah! mon ami*," he said to Sieyès, "*je m'en vais enfin de ce monde, où il faut que le cœur se brise ou se bronze—*." These were certainly not the words of a dying Frenchman.

96.

Two Orators.—Of these two orators the one arrives at a full understanding of his case only when he yields himself to emotion; it is only this that pumps sufficient blood and heat into his brain to compel his high intellectuality to reveal itself The other attempts, indeed, now and then to do the same: to state his case sonorously, vehemently, and spiritedly with the aid of emotion,—but usually with bad success. He then very soon speaks obscurely and confusedly; he exaggerates, makes omissions, and excites suspicion of the justice of his case: indeed, he himself feels this suspicion, and the sudden changes into the coldest and most repulsive tones (which raise a doubt in the hearer as to his passionateness being genuine) are thereby explicable. With him emotion always drowns the spirit; perhaps because it is stronger than in the former. But he is at the height of his power when he resists the impetuous storm of his feeling, and as it were scorns it; it is then only that his spirit emerges fully from its concealment, a spirit logical, mocking and playful, but nevertheless awe-inspiring.

97.

The Loquacity of Authors.—There is a loquacity of anger—frequent in Luther, also in Schopenhauer. A loquacity which comes from too great a store of conceptual formulæ, as in Kant. A loquacity which comes from delight in ever new modifications of the same idea: one finds it in Montaigne. A loquacity of malicious natures: whoever reads writings of our period will recollect two authors in this connection. A loquacity which comes from delight in fine words and forms of speech: by no means rare in Goethe's prose. A loquacity which comes from pure satisfaction in noise and confusion of feelings: for example in Carlyle.

98.

In Honour of Shakespeare.—The best thing I could say in honour of Shakespeare, *the man,* is that he believed in Brutus, and cast not a shadow of suspicion on the kind of virtue which Brutus represents! It is to him that Shakespeare consecrated his best tragedy—it is at present still called by a wrong name,—to him, and to the most terrible essence of lofty morality. Independence of soul!—that is the question at issue! No sacrifice can be too great there: one must be able to sacrifice to it even one's dearest friend, although he be the grandest of men, the ornament of the world, the genius without peer,—if one really loves freedom as the freedom of great souls, and if *this* freedom be threatened by him:—it is thus that Shakespeare must have felt! The elevation in which he places Cæsar is the most exquisite honour he could confer upon Brutus; it is thus only that he lifts into vastness the inner problem of his hero, and similarly the strength of soul which could cut *this knot!*—And was it actually political freedom that impelled the poet to sympathy with Brutus,—and made him the accomplice of Brutus? Or was political freedom merely a symbol for something inexpressible? Do we perhaps stand before some sombre event or adventure of the poet's own soul, which has remained unknown, and of which he only cared to speak symbolically? What is all Hamlet-melancholy in comparison with the melancholy of Brutus!—and perhaps Shakespeare also knew this, as he knew the other, by experience! Perhaps he also had his dark hour and his bad angel, just as Brutus had them!—But whatever similarities and secret relationships of that kind there may have been, Shakespeare cast himself on the ground and felt unworthy and alien in presence of the aspect and virtue of Brutus:—he has inscribed the testimony thereof in the tragedy itself. He has twice brought in a poet in it, and twice heaped upon him such an impatient and extreme contempt, that it sounds like a cry,—like the cry of self-contempt. Brutus, even Brutus loses patience when the poet appears, self-important, pathetic and obtrusive, as poets usually are,—persons who seem to abound in the possibilities of greatness, even moral greatness, and nevertheless rarely attain even to ordinary uprightness in the philosophy of practice and of life "He may know the times, *but I know his temper,*—away with the jigging fool!"—shouts Brutus. We may translate this back into the soul of the poet that composed it.

99.

The Followers of Schopenhauer.—What one sees at the contact of civilized peoples with barbarians,—namely, that the lower civilization regularly accepts in the first place the vices, weaknesses and excesses of the higher; then, from that point onward, feels the influence of a charm; and finally, by means of the appropriated vices and weaknesses also allows something of the valuable influence of the higher culture to leaven it:-one can also see this close at hand and without journeys to barbarian peoples, to be sure, somewhat refined and spiritualised, and not so readily palpable. What are the German followers of *Schopenhauer* still accustomed to receive first of all from their master?—those who, when placed beside his superior culture, must deem themselves sufficiently barbarous to be first of all barbarously fascinated and seduced by him. Is it his hard matter-of-fact sense, his inclination to clearness and rationality, which often makes him appear so English, and so unlike Germans? Or the strength of his intellectual conscience, which *endured* a life-long contradiction of "being" and "willing," and compelled him to contradict himself constantly even in his writings on almost every point? Or his purity in matters relating to the Church and the Christian God?—for here he was pure as no German philosopher had been hitherto, so that he lived and died "as a Voltairian." Or his immortal doctrines of the intellectuality of intuition, the apriority of the law of causality, the instrumental nature of the intellect, and the non-freedom of the will? No, nothing of this en-chants, nor is felt as enchanting; but Schopenhauer's mystical embarrassments and shufflings in those passages where the matter-of-fact thinker allowed himself to be seduced and corrupted by the vain impulse to be the unraveller of the world's riddle: his undemonstrable doctrine of *one will* ("all causes are merely occasional causes of the phenomenon of the will at such a time and at such a place," "the will to live, whole and undivided, is present in every being, even in the smallest, as perfectly as in the sum of all that was, is, and will be"); his *denial of the individual* ("all lions are really only one lion," "plurality of individuals is an appearance," as also *development* is only an ap-pearance: he calls the opinion of Lamarck "an ingenious, absurd error"); his fantasy about *genius* ("in æsthetic contemplation the individual is no longer an individual, but a pure, will-less, painless, timeless subject of knowledge," "the subject, in that it entirely merges in the contemplated object, has become this object itself"); his nonsense about *sympathy,* and about the outburst of the *principium individuationis* thus rendered possible, as the source of all morality; including also such assertions as, "dying is really the design of existence," "the possibility should not be absolutely denied that a magical effect could proceed from a person already dead":—these, and similar *extravagances* and vices of the philosopher, are always first accepted and made articles of faith; for vices and extravagances are always easiest to imitate, and do not require a long preliminary practice. But let us speak of the most celebrated of the living Schopenhauerians, Richard Wagner.—It has happened to him as it has already happened to many an artist: he made a mistake in the interpretation of the characters he created, and misunderstood the unexpressed philosophy of the art peculiarly his own. Richard Wagner allowed himself to be misled by Hegel's influence till the middle of his life; and he did the same again when later on he read Schopenhauer's doctrine between the lines of his characters, and began to express himself with such terms as "will," "genius," and "sympathy." Nevertheless it will remain true that nothing is more counter to Schopenhauer's spirit than the essentially Wagnerian element in Wagner's heroes: I mean the innocence of the supremest selfishness, the belief in strong passion as the good in itself, in a word, the Siegfried trait in the countenances of his heroes. "All that still smacks more of Spinoza than of me,"—Schopenhauer would probably have said. Whatever good reasons, therefore, Wagner might have had to be on the outlook for other philosophers than Schopenhauer, the enchantment to which he succumbed in respect to this thinker, not only made him blind towards all other philosophers, but even towards science itself; his entire art is more and more inclined to become the counterpart and complement of the Schopenhauerian philosophy, and it always renounces more emphatically the higher ambition to become the counterpart and complement of human knowledge and science. And not only is he allured thereto by the whole mystic pomp of this philosophy (which would also have allured a Cagliostro), the peculiar airs and emotions of the philosopher have all along been seducing him as well! For example, Wagner's indignation about the corruption of the German language is Schopenhauerian; and if one should commend his imitation in this respect, it is nevertheless not to be denied that Wagner's style itself suffers in no small degree from all the tumours and turgidities, the sight of which made Schopenhauer so furious; and that, in respect to the German-writing Wagnerians, Wagneromania is beginning to be as dangerous as only some kinds of Hegelomania have been. From Schopenhauer comes Wagner's hatred of the Jews, to whom he cannot do justice even in their greatest exploit: are not the Jews the inventors of Christianity! The attempt of Wagner to construe Christianity as a seed blown away from Buddhism, and his endeavour to initiate a Buddhistic era in Europe, under a temporary approximation to Catholic-Christian formulas and sentiments, are both Schopenhauerian. Wagner's preaching in favour of pity in dealing with animals is Schopenhauerian; Schopenhauer's predecessor here, as is well known, was Voltaire, who already perhaps, like his successors, knew how to disguise his hatred of certain men and things as pity towards animals. At least Wagner's hatred of science, which manifests itself in his preaching, has certainly not been inspired by the spirit of charitableness and kindness—nor by the *spirit* at all, as is sufficiently obvious.—Finally, it is of little importance what the philosophy of an artist is, provided it is only a supplementary philosophy, and does not do any injury to his art itself. We cannot be sufficiently on our guard against taking a dislike to an artist on account of an occasional, perhaps very unfortunate and presumptuous masquerade; let us not forget that the dear artists are all of them something of actors—and must be so; it would be difficult for them to hold out in the long run without stage-playing. Let us be loyal to Wagner in that which is *true* and original in him,—and especially in this point, that we, his disciples, remain loyal to ourselves in that which is true and original in us. Let us allow him his intellectual humours and spasms, let us in fairness rather consider what strange nutriments and necessaries an art like his *is entitled to,* in order to be able to live and grow! It is of no account that he is often wrong as a thinker; justice and patience are not *his* affair. It is sufficient that his life is right in his own eyes, and maintains its right,—the life which calls to each of us: "Be a man, and do not follow me—but thyself! thyself!" *Our* life, also ought to maintain its right in our own eyes! We also are to grow and blossom out of ourselves, free and fearless, in innocent selfishness! And so, on the contemplation of such a man, these thoughts still ring in my ears to-day, as formerly: "That passion is better than stoicism or hypocrisy; that straight-forwardness, even in evil, is better than losing oneself in trying to observe traditional morality; that the free man is just as able to be good as evil, but that the unemancipated man is a disgrace to nature, and has no share in heavenly or earthly bliss; finally, that *all who wish to be free must become so through themselves,* and that freedom falls to nobody's lot as a gift from Heaven." (*Richard Wagner in Bayreuth,* Vol. I. of this Translation, pp. 199-200).

100.

Learning to do Homage.—One must learn the art of homage, as well as the art of contempt. Whoever goes in new paths and has led many persons therein, discovers with astonishment how awkward and incompetent all of them are in the expression of their gratitude, and indeed how rarely gratitude *is able* even to express itself. It is always as if something comes into people's throats when their gratitude wants to speak so that it only hems and haws, and becomes silent again. The way in which a thinker succeeds in tracing the effect of his thoughts, and their transforming and convulsing power, is almost a comedy: it sometimes seems as if those who have been operated upon felt profoundly injured thereby, and could only assert their independence, which they suspect to be threatened, by all kinds of improprieties. It needs whole generations in order merely to devise a courteous convention of gratefulness; it is only very late that the period arrives when something of spirit and genius enters into gratitude Then there is usually some one who is the great receiver of thanks, not only for the good he himself has done, but mostly for that which has been gradually accumulated by his predecessors, as a treasure of what is highest and best.

101.

Voltaire—Wherever there has been a court, it has furnished the standard of good-speaking and with this also the standard of style for writers The court language, however, is the language of the courtier who *has no profession,* and who even in conversations on scientific subjects avoids all convenient, technical expressions, because they smack of the profession; on that account the technical expression, and everything that betrays the specialist, is a *blemish of style* in countries which have a court culture. At present, when all courts have become caricatures of past and present times, one is astonished to find even Voltaire unspeakably reserved and scrupulous on this point (for example, in his judgments concerning such stylists as Fontenelle and Montesquieu),—we are now, all of us, emancipated from court taste, while Voltaire was its *perfecter!*

102.

A Word for Philologists.—It is thought that there are books so valuable and royal that whole generations of scholars are well employed when through their efforts these books are kept genuine and intelligible,—to confirm this belief again and again is the purpose of philology. It presupposes that the rare men are not lacking (though they may not be visible), who actually know how to use such valuable books:—those men perhaps who write such books themselves, or could write them. I mean to say that philology presupposes a noble belief,—that for the benefit of some few who are always "to come," and are not there, a very great amount of painful, and even dirty labour has to be done beforehand: it is all labour *in usum Delphinorum.*

103.

German Music.—German music, more than any other, has now become European music; because the changes which Europe experienced through the Revolution have therein alone found expression: it is only German music that knows how to express the agitation of popular masses, the tremendous artificial uproar, which does not even need to be very noisy,—while Italian opera, for example, knows only the choruses of domestics or soldiers, but not "the people." There is the additional fact that in all German music a profound *bourgeois* jealousy of the *noblesse* can be traced, especially a jealousy of *esprit* and *élégance,* as the expressions of a courtly, chivalrous, ancient, and self-confident society. It is not music like that of Goethe's musician at the gate, which was pleasing also "in the hall," and to the king as well; it is not here said: "The knights looked on with martial air; with bashful eyes the ladies." Even the Graces are not allowed in German music without a touch of remorse; it is only with Pleasantness, the country sister of the Graces that the German begins to feel morally at ease—and from this point up to his enthusiastic, learned, and often gruff "sublimity" (the Beethoven-like sublimity), he feels more and more so. If we want to imagine the man of *this* music,—well, let us just imagine Beethoven as he appeared beside Goethe, say, at their meeting at Teplitz: as semi-barbarism beside culture, as the masses beside the nobility, as the good-natured man beside the good and more than "good" man, as the visionary beside the artist, as the man needing comfort beside the comforted, as the man given to exaggeration and distrust beside the man of reason, as the crank and self-tormenter, as the foolishly enraptured, blessedly unfortunate, sincerely immoderate man! as the pretentious and awkward man,—and altogether as the "untamed man": it was thus that Goethe conceived and characterised him, Goethe, the exceptional German, for whom a music of equal rank has not yet been found!—Finally, let us consider whether the present continually extending contempt of melody and the stunting of the sense for melody among Germans should not be understood as a democratic impropriety and an after-effect of the Revolution? For melody has such an obvious delight in conformity to law, and such an aversion to everything evolving, unformed and arbitrary, that it sounds like a note out of the *ancient* European regime, and as a seduction and guidance back to it.

104.

The Tone of the German Language.—We know whence the German originated which for several centuries has been the universal literary language of Germany. The Germans, with their reverence for everything that came from the *court,* intentionally took the chancery style as their pattern in all that they had to *write,* especially in their letters, records, wills, &c. To write in the chancery style, that was to write in court and government style,—that was regarded as something select, compared with the language of the city in which a person lived. People gradually drew this inference, and spoke also as they wrote,—they thus became still more select in the forms of their words, in the choice of their terms and modes of expression, and finally also in their tones: they affected a court tone when they spoke, and the affectation at last became natural. Perhaps nothing quite similar has ever happened elsewhere:—the predominance of the literary style over the talk, and the formality and affectation of an entire people becoming the basis of a common and no longer dialectical language. I believe that the sound of the German language in the Middle

Ages, and especially after the Middle Ages, was extremely rustic and vulgar; it has ennobled itself somewhat during the last centuries, principally because it was found necessary to imitate so many French, Italian, and Spanish sounds, and particularly on the part of the German (and Austrian) nobility, who could not at all content themselves with their mother-tongue. But notwithstanding this practice, German must have sounded intolerably vulgar to Montaigne, and even to Racine: even at present, in the mouths of travellers among the Italian populace, it still sounds very coarse, sylvan, and hoarse, as if it had originated in smoky rooms and outlandish districts.—Now I notice that at present a similar striving after selectness of tone is spreading among the former admirers of the chancery style, and that the Germans are beginning to accommodate themselves to a peculiar "witchery of sound," which might in the long run become an actual danger to the German language,—for one may seek in vain for more execrable sounds in Europe. Something mocking, cold, indifferent and careless in the voice: that is what at present sounds "noble" to the Germans—and I hear the approval of this nobleness in the voices of young officials, teachers, women, and trades-people; indeed, even the little girls already imitate this German of the officers. For the officer, and in fact the Prussian officer is the inventor of these tones: this same officer, who as soldier and professional man possesses that admirable tact for modesty which the Germans as a whole might well imitate (German professors and musicians included!). But as soon as he speaks and moves he is the most inmodest and inelegant figure in old Europe—no doubt unconsciously to himself! And unconsciously also to the good Germans, who gaze at him as the man of the foremost and most select society, and willingly let him "give them his tone." And indeed he gives it to them!—in the first place it is the sergeant-majors and non-commissioned officers that imitate his tone and coarsen it. One should note the roars of command, with which the German cities are absolutely surrounded at present, when there is drilling at all the gates: what presumption, furious imperiousness, and mocking coldness speaks in this uproar! Could the Germans actually be a musical people?—It is certain that the Germans martialise themselves at present in the tone of their language: it is probable that, being exercised to speak martially, they will finally write martially also. For habituation to definite tones extends deeply into the character:—people soon have the words and modes of expression, and finally also the thoughts which just suit these tones! Perhaps they already write in the officers' style; perhaps I only read too little of what is at present written in Germany to know this. But one thing I know all the surer: the German public decorations which also reach places abroad, are not inspired by

German music, but just by that new tone of tasteless arrogance. Almost in every speech of the foremost German statesman, and even when he makes himself heard through his imperial mouth-piece, there is an accent which the ear of a foreigner repudiates with aversion: but the Germans endure it,—they endure themselves.

105.

The Germans as Artists.—When once a German actually experiences passion (and not only, as is usual, the mere inclination to it), he then behaves just as he must do in passion, and does not think further of his behaviour. The truth is, however, that he then behaves very awkwardly and uglily, and as if destitute of rhythm and melody; so that onlookers are pained or moved thereby, but nothing more—*unless* he elevate himself to the sublimity and enrapturedness of which certain passions are capable. Then even the German becomes *beautiful*. The consciousness of the *height at which* beauty begins to shed its charm even over Germans, forces German artists to the height and the super-height, and to the extravagances of passion: they have an actual, profound longing, therefore, to get beyond, or at least to look beyond the ugliness and awkwardness—into a better, easier, more southern, more sunny world. And thus their convulsions are often merely indications that they would like to *dance*: these poor bears in whom hidden nymphs and satyrs, and sometimes still higher divinities, carry on their game!

106.

Music as Advocate.—"I have a longing for a master of the musical art," said an innovator to his disciple, "that he may learn from me my ideas and speak them more widely in his language: I shall thus be better able to reach men's ears and hearts. For by means of tones one can seduce men to every error and every truth: who could *refute* a tone?"—"You would, therefore, like to be regarded as irrefutable?" said his disciple. The innovator answered: "I should like the germ to become a tree. In order that a doctrine may become a tree, it must be believed in for a considerable period; in order that it may be believed in it must be regarded as irrefutable. Storms and doubts and worms and wickedness are necessary to the tree, that it may manifest its species and the strength of its germ; let it perish if it is not strong enough! But a germ is always merely annihilated,—not refuted!"—When he had said this, his disciple called out impetuously: "But I believe in your cause, and regard it as so strong that I will say everything against it, everything that I still have in my heart."—The innovator laughed to himself and threatened the disciple with his finger. "This kind of discipleship," said he then, "is the best, but it is dangerous, and not every kind of doctrine can stand it."

107.

Our Ultimate Gratitude to Art.—If we had not approved of the Arts and invented this sort of cult of the untrue, the insight into the general untruth and falsity of things now given us by science—an insight into delusion and error as conditions of intelligent and sentient existence—would be quite unendurable. *Honesty* would have disgust and suicide in its train. Now, however, our honesty has a counterpoise which helps us to escape such consequences;—namely, Art, as the *good-will* to illusion. We do not always restrain our eyes from rounding off and perfecting in imagination: and then it is no longer the eternal imperfection that we carry over the river of Becoming—for we think we carry a *goddess*, and are proud and artless in rendering this service. As an æsthetic phenomenon existence is still *endurable* to us; and by Art, eye and hand and above all the good conscience are given to us, *to be able* to make such a phenomenon out of ourselves. We must rest from ourselves occasionally by contemplating and looking down upon ourselves, and by laughing or weeping *over* ourselves from an artistic remoteness: we must discover the *hero*, and likewise the *fool*, that is hidden in our passion for knowledge; we must now and then be joyful in our folly, that we may continue to be joyful in our wisdom! And just because we are heavy and serious men in our ultimate depth, and are rather weights than men, there is nothing that does us so much good as the *fool's cap and bells:* we need them in presence of ourselves—we need all arrogant, soaring, dancing, mocking, childish and blessed Art, in order not to lose the *free dominion over things* which our ideal demands of us. It would be *backsliding* for us, with our susceptible integrity, to lapse entirely into morality, and actually become virtuous monsters and scarecrows, on account of the over-strict requirements which we here lay down for ourselves. We ought also to *be able* to stand *above* morality, and not only stand with the painful stiffness of one who every moment fears to slip and fall, but we should also be able to soar and play above it! How could we dispense with Art for that purpose, how could we dispense with the fool?—And as long as you are still *ashamed* of yourselves in any way, you still do not belong to us!

BOOK THIRD

108.

New Struggles.—After Buddha was dead people showed his shadow for centuries afterwards in a cave,—an immense frightful shadow. God is dead:—but as the human race is constituted, there will perhaps be caves for millenniums yet, in which people will show his shadow.—And we—we have still to overcome his shadow!

109.

Let us be on our Guard.—Let us be on our guard against thinking that the world is a living being. Where could it extend itself? What could it nourish itself with? How could it grow and increase? We know tolerably well what the organic is; and we are to reinterpret the emphatically derivative, tardy, rare and accidental, which we only perceive on the crust of the earth, into the essential, universal and eternal, as those do who call the universe an organism? That disgusts me. Let us now be on our guard against believing that the universe is a machine; it is assuredly not constructed with a view to *one* end; we invest it with far too high an honour with the word "machine." Let us be on our guard against supposing that anything so methodical as the cyclic motions of our neighbouring stars obtains generally and throughout the universe; indeed a glance at the Milky Way induces doubt as to whether there are not many cruder and more contradictory motions there, and even stars with continuous, rectilinearly gravitating orbits, and the like. The astral arrangement in which we live is an exception; this arrangement, and the relatively long durability which is determined by it, has again made possible the exception of exceptions, the formation of organic life. The general character of the world, on the other hand, is to all eternity chaos; not by the absence of necessity, but in the sense of the absence of order, structure, form, beauty, wisdom, and whatever else our æsthetic humanities are called. Judged by our reason, the unlucky casts are far oftenest the rule, the exceptions are not the secret purpose; and the whole musical box repeats eternally its air, which can never be called a melody,—and finally the very expression, "unlucky cast" is already an anthropomorphising which involves blame. But how could we presume to blame or praise the universe! Let us be on our guard against ascribing to it heartlessness and unreason, or their opposites; it is neither perfect, nor beautiful, nor noble; nor does it seek to be anything of the kind, it does not at all attempt to imitate man! It is altogether unaffected by our æsthetic and moral judgments! Neither has it any self-preservative instinct, nor instinct at all; it also knows no law. Let us be on our guard against saying that there are laws in nature. There are only necessities: there is no one who commands, no one who obeys, no one who transgresses. When you know that there is no design, you know also that there is no chance: for it is only where there is a world of design that the word "chance" has a meaning. Let us be on our guard against saying that death is contrary to life. The living being is only a species of dead being, and a very rare species.—Let us be on our guard against thinking that the world eternally creates the new. There are no eternally enduring substances; matter is just another such error as the God of the Eleatics. But when shall we be at an end with our foresight and precaution! When will all these shadows of God cease to obscure us? When shall we have nature entirely undeified! When shall we be permitted to *naturalise* ourselves by means of the pure, newly discovered, newly redeemed nature?

110.

Origin of Knowledge.—Throughout immense stretches of time the intellect produced nothing but errors; some of them proved to be useful and preservative of the species: he who fell in with them, or inherited them, waged the battle for himself and his offspring with better success. Those erroneous articles of faith which were successively transmitted by inheritance, and have finally become almost the property and stock of the human species, are, for example, the following:—that there are enduring things, that there are equal things, that there are things, substances, and bodies, that a thing is what it appears, that our will is free, that what is good for me is also good absolutely. It was only very late that the deniers and doubters of such propositions came forward,—it was only very late that truth made its appearance as the most impotent form of knowledge. It seemed as if it were impossible to get along with truth, our organism was adapted for the very opposite; all its higher functions, the perceptions of the senses, and in general every kind of sensation, co-operated with those primevally embodied, fundamental errors. Moreover, those propositions became the very standards of knowledge according to which the "true" and the "false" were determined—throughout the whole domain of pure logic. The *strength* of conceptions does not, therefore, depend on their degree of truth, but on their antiquity, their embodiment, their character as conditions of life. Where life and knowledge seemed to conflict, there has never been serious contention; denial and doubt have there been regarded as madness. The exceptional thinkers like the Eleatics, who, in spite of this, advanced and maintained the antitheses of the natural errors, believed that it was possible also *to live* these counterparts: it was they who devised the sage as the man of immutability, impersonality and universality of intuition, as one and all at the same time, with a special faculty for that reverse kind of knowledge; they were of the belief that their knowledge was at the same time the principle of *life*. To be able to affirm all this, however, they had to *deceive* themselves concerning their own condition: they had to attribute to themselves impersonality and unchanging permanence, they had to mistake the nature of the philosophic individual, deny the force of the impulses in cognition, and conceive of reason generally as an entirely free and self-originating activity; they kept their eyes shut to the fact that they also had reached their doctrines in contradiction to valid methods, or through their longing for repose or for exclusive possession or for domination. The subtler development of sincerity and of scepticism finally made these men impossible; their life also, and their judgments, turned out to be dependent on the primeval impulses and fundamental errors of all sentient being.—The subtler sincerity and scepticism arose wherever two antithetical maxims appeared to be *applicable* to life, because both of them were compatible with the fundamental errors; where, therefore, there could be contention concerning a higher or lower degree of *utility* for life; and likewise where new maxims proved to be, not necessarily useful, but at least not injurious, as expressions of an intellectual impulse to play a game that was like all games innocent and happy. The human brain was gradually filled with such judgments and convictions; and in this tangled skein there arose ferment, strife and lust for power. Not only utility and delight, but every kind of impulse took part in the struggle for "truths": the intellectual struggle became a business, an attraction, a calling, a duty, an honour—: cognizing and striving for the true finally arranged themselves as needs among other needs. From that moment, not only belief and conviction, but also examination, denial, distrust and contradiction became *forces*; all "evil" instincts were subordinated to knowledge, were placed in its service, and acquired the prestige of the permitted, the honoured, the useful, and finally the appearance and innocence of the *good*. Knowledge, thus became a portion of life itself, and as life it became a continually growing power: until finally the cognitions and those primeval, fundamental errors clashed with each other, both as life, both as power, both in the same man. The thinker is now the being in whom the impulse to truth and those life-preserving errors wage their first conflict, now that the impulse to truth has also *proved* itself to be a life-preserving power. In comparison with the importance of this conflict everything else is indifferent; the final question concerning the conditions of life is here raised, and the first attempt is here made to answer it by experiment. How far is truth susceptible of embodiment?—that is the question, that is the experiment.

111.

Origin of the Logical.—Where has logic originated in men's heads? Undoubtedly out of the illogical, the domain of which must originally *have* been immense. But numberless beings who reasoned otherwise than we do at present, perished; albeit that they may have come nearer to truth than we! Whoever, for example, could not discern the "like" often enough with regard to food, and with regard to animals dangerous to him, whoever, therefore, deduced too slowly, or was too circumspect in his deductions, had smaller probability of survival than he who in all similar cases immediately divined the equality. The preponderating inclination, however, to deal with the similar as the equal—an illogical inclination, for there is nothing equal in itself—first created the whole basis of logic. It was just so (in order that the conception of substance should originate, this being indispensable to logic, although in the strictest sense nothing actual corresponds to it) that for a long period the changing process in things had to be overlooked, and remain unperceived; the beings not seeing correctly had an advantage over those who saw everything "in flux." In itself every high degree of circumspection in conclusions, every sceptical inclination, is a great danger to life. No living being might have been preserved unless the contrary inclination—to affirm rather than suspend judgment, to mistake and fabricate rather than wait, to assent rather than deny, to decide rather than be in the right—had been cultivated with extraordinary assiduity.—The course of logical thought and reasoning in our modern brain corresponds to a process and struggle of impulses, which singly and in themselves are all very illogical and unjust; we experience usually only the result of the struggle, so rapidly and secretly does this primitive mechanism now operate in us.

112.

Cause and Effect.—We say it is "explanation"; but it is only in "description" that we are in advance of the older stages of knowledge and science. We describe better,—we explain just as little as our predecessors. We have discovered a manifold succession where the naïve man and investigator of older cultures saw only two things, "cause" and "effect," as it was said; we have perfected the conception of becoming, but have not got a knowledge of what is above and behind the conception. The series of "causes" stands before us much more complete in every case; we conclude that this and that must first precede in order that that other may follow—but we have not *grasped* anything thereby. The peculiarity, for example, in every chemical process seems a "miracle," the same as before, just like all locomotion; nobody has "explained" impulse. How could we ever explain! We operate only with things which do not exist, with lines, surfaces, bodies, atoms, divisible times, divisible spaces—how can explanation ever be possible when we first make everything a *conception*, our conception! It is sufficient to regard science as the exactest humanising of things that is possible; we always learn to describe ourselves more accurately by describing things and their successions. Cause and effect: there is probably never any such duality; in fact there is a *continuum* before us, from which we isolate a few portions;—just as we always observe a motion as isolated points, and therefore do not properly see it, but infer it. The abruptness with which many effects take place leads us into error; it is however only an abruptness for us. There is an infinite multitude of processes in that abrupt moment which escape us. An intellect which could see cause and effect as a *continuum*, which could see the flux of events not according to our mode of perception, as things arbitrarily separated and broken—would throw aside the conception of cause and effect, and would deny all conditionality.

113.

The Theory of Poisons.—So many things have to be united in order that scientific thinking may arise, and all the necessary powers must have been devised, exercised, and fostered singly! In their isolation, however, they have very often had quite a different effect than at present, when they are confined within the limits of scientific thinking and kept mutually in check:—they have operated as poisons; for example, the doubting impulse, the denying impulse, the waiting impulse, the collecting impulse, the disintegrating impulse. Many hecatombs of men were sacrificed ere these impulses learned to understand their juxtaposition and regard themselves as functions of one organising force in one man! And how far are we still from the point at which the artistic powers and the practical wisdom of life shall co-operate with scientific thinking, so that a higher organic system may be formed, in relation to which the scholar, the physician, the artist, and the lawgiver, as we know them at present, will seem sorry antiquities!

114.

The Extent of the Moral.—We construct a new picture, which we see immediately with the aid of all the old experiences which we have had, *always according to the degree* of our honesty and justice. The only experiences are moral experiences, even in the domain of sense-perception.

115.

The Four Errors.—Man has been reared by his errors: firstly, he saw himself always imperfect; secondly,-he attributed to himself—imaginary qualities; thirdly, he felt himself in a false position in relation to the animals and nature; fourthly, he always devised new tables of values, and accepted them for a time as eternal and unconditioned, so that at one time this, and at another time that human impulse or state stood first, and was ennobled in consequence. When one has deducted the effect of these four errors, one has also deducted humanity, humaneness, and "human dignity."

116.

Herd-Instinct.—Wherever we meet with a morality we find a valuation and order of rank of the human impulses and activities. These valuations and orders of rank are always the expression of the needs of a community or herd: that which is in the first place to *its* advantage—and in the second place and third place—is also the authoritative standard for the worth of every individual. By morality the individual is taught to become a function of the herd, and to ascribe to himself value only as a function. As the conditions for the maintenance of one community have been very different from those of another community, there have been very different moralities; and in respect to the future essential transformations of herds and communities, states and societies, one can prophesy that there will still be very divergent moralities. Morality is the herd-instinct in the individual.

117.

The Herd's Sting of Conscience.—In the longest and remotest ages of the human race there was quite a different sting of conscience from that of the present day. At present one only feels responsible for what one intends and for what one does, and we have our pride in ourselves. All our professors of jurisprudence start with this sentiment of individual independence and pleasure, as if the source of right had taken its rise here from the beginning. But throughout the longest period in the life of mankind there was nothing more terrible to a person than to feel himself independent. To be alone, to feel independent, neither to obey nor to rule, to represent an individual—that was no pleasure to a person then, but a punishment; he was condemned "to be an individual." Freedom of thought was regarded as discomfort personified. While we feel law and regulation as constraint and loss, people formerly regarded egoism as a painful thing, and a veritable evil. For a person to be himself, to value himself according to his own measure and weight—that was then quite distasteful. The inclination to such a thing would have been regarded as madness; for all miseries and terrors were associated with being alone. At that time the "free will" had bad conscience in close proximity to it; and the less independently a person acted, the more the herd-instinct, and not his personal character, expressed itself in his conduct, so much the more moral did he esteem himself. All that did injury to the herd, whether the individual had intended it or not, then caused him a sting of conscience—and his neighbour likewise, indeed the whole herd!—It is in this respect that we have most changed our mode of thinking.

118.

Benevolence—Is it virtuous when a cell transforms itself into the function of a stronger cell? It must do so. And is it wicked when the stronger one assimilates the other? It must do so likewise: it is necessary, for it has to have abundant indemnity and seeks to regenerate itself. One has therefore to distinguish the instinct of appropriation and the instinct of submission in benevolence, according as the stronger or the weaker feels benevolent. Gladness and covetousness are united in the stronger person, who wants to transform something to his function: gladness and desire-to-be-coveted in the weaker person, who would like to become a function.—The former case is essentially pity, a pleasant excitation of the instinct of appropriation at the sight of the weak: it is to be remembered, however, that "strong" and "weak" are relative conceptions.

119.

No Altruism!/—I see in many men an excessive impulse and delight in wanting to be a function; they strive after it, and have the keenest scent for all those positions in which precisely *they* themselves can be functions. Among such persons are those women who transform themselves into just that function of a man that is but weakly-developed in him, and then become his purse, or his politics, or his social intercourse. Such beings maintain themselves best when they insert themselves in an alien organism; if they do not succeed they become vexed, irritated, and eat themselves up.

120.

Health of the Soul.—The favourite medico-moral formula (whose originator was Ariston of Chios), "Virtue is the health of the soul," would, for all practical purposes, have to be altered to this: "Thy virtue is the health of thy soul." For there is no such thing as health in itself, and all attempts to define a thing in that way have lamentably failed. It is necessary to know thy aim, thy horizon, thy powers, thy impulses, thy errors, and especially the ideals and fantasies of thy soul, in order to determine *what health* implies even for thy *body*. There are consequently innumerable kinds of physical health; and the more one again permits the unique and unparalleled to raise its head, the more one unlearns the dogma of the "Equality of men," so much the more also must the conception of a normal health, together with a normal diet and a normal course of disease, be abrogated by our physicians. And then only would it be time to turn our thoughts to the health and disease of the *soul*, and make the special virtue of everyone consist in its health; but, to be sure, what appeared as health in one person might appear as the contrary of health in another. In the end the great question might still remain open:—Whether we could *do without* sickness for the development of our virtue, and whether our thirst for knowledge and self-knowledge would not especially need the sickly soul as well as the sound one; in short, whether the mere will to health is not a prejudice, a cowardice, and perhaps an instance of the subtlest barbarism and unprogressiveness?

121.

Life no Argument.—We have arranged for ourselves a world in which we can live—by the postulating of bodies, lines, surfaces, causes and effects, motion and rest, form and content: without these articles of faith no one could manage to live at present! But for all that they are still unproved. Life is no argument; error might be among the conditions of life.

122.

The Element of Moral Scepticism in Christianity.—Christianity also has made a great contribution to enlightenment, and has taught moral scepticism —in a very impressive and effective manner, accusing and embittering, but with untiring patience and subtlety; it annihilated in every individual the belief in his virtues: it made the great virtuous ones, of whom antiquity had no lack, vanish for ever from the earth, those popular men, who, in the belief in their perfection, walked about with the dignity of a hero of the bull-fight. When, trained in this Christian school of scepticism, we now read the moral books of the ancients, for example those of Seneca and Epictetus, we feel a pleasurable superiority, and are full of secret insight and penetration,—it seems to us as if a child talked before an old man, or a pretty, gushing girl before La Rochefoucauld:—we know better what virtue is! After all, however, we have applied the same scepticism to all *religious* states and processes, such as sin, repentance, grace, sanctification, &c., and have allowed the worm to burrow so well, that we have now the same feeling of subtle superiority and insight even in reading all Christian books:—we know also the religious feelings better! And it is time to know them well and describe them well, for the pious ones of the old belief die out also; let us save their likeness and type, at least for the sake of knowledge.

123.

Knowledge more than a Means.—Also *without* this passion—I refer to the passion for knowledge—science would be furthered: science has hitherto increased and grown up without it. The good faith in science, the prejudice in its favour, by which States are at present dominated (it was even the Church formerly), rests fundamentally on the fact that the absolute inclination and impulse has so rarely revealed itself in it, and that science is regarded *not* as a passion, but as a condition and an "ethos." Indeed, *amour-plaisir* of knowledge (curiosity) often enough suffices, *amour-vanité* suffices, and habituation to it, with the afterthought of obtaining honour and bread; it even suffices for many that they do not know what to do with a surplus of leisure, except to continue reading, collecting, arranging, observing and narrating; their "scientific impulse" is their ennui. Pope Leo X once (in the brief to Beroaldus) sang the praise of science; he designated it as the finest ornament and the greatest pride of our life, a noble employment in happiness and in misfortune; "without it," he says finally, "all human undertakings would be without a firm basis,—even with it they are still sufficiently mutable and insecure!" But this rather sceptical Pope, like all other ecclesiastical panegyrists of science, suppressed his ultimate judgment concerning it. If one may deduce from his words what is remarkable enough for such a lover of art, that he places science above art it is alter all, however, only from politeness that he omits to speak of that which he places high above all science: the "revealed truth," and the "eternal salvation o the soul,"—what are ornament, pride, entertainment and security of life to him, in comparison thereto? "Science is something of secondary rank, nothing ultimate or unconditioned, no object of passion"—this judgment was kept back in Leos soul: the truly Christian judgment concerning science! In antiquity its dignity and appreciation were lessened by the fact that, even among its most eager disciples, the striving after *virtue* stood foremost and that people thought they had given the highest praise to knowledge when they celebrated it as the best means to virtue. It is something new in history that knowledge claims to be more than a means.

124.

In the Horizon of the Infinite.—We have left the land and have gone aboard ship! We have broken down the bridge behind us,—nay, more, the land behind us! Well, little ship! look out! Beside thee is the ocean; it is true it does not always roar, and sometimes it spreads out like silk and gold and a gentle reverie. But times will come when thou wilt feel that it is infinite, and that there is nothing more frightful than infinity. Oh, the poor bird that felt itself free, and now strikes against the walls of this cage! Alas, if home-sickness for the land should attack thee, as if there had been more *freedom* there,—and there is no "land" any longer!

125.

The Madman.—Have you ever heard of the madman who on a bright morning lighted a lantern and ran to the market-place calling out unceasingly: "I seek God! I seek God!"—As there were many people standing about who did not believe in God, he caused a great deal of amusement. Why! is he lost? said one. Has he strayed away like a child? said another. Or does he keep himself hidden? Is he afraid of us?

Has he taken a sea-voyage? Has he emigrated?—the people cried out laughingly, all in a hubbub. The insane man jumped into their midst and transfixed them with his glances. "Where is God gone?" he called out. "I mean to tell you! *We have killed him,*—you and I! We are all his murderers! But how have we done it? How were we able to drink up the sea? Who gave us the sponge to wipe away the whole horizon? What did we do when we loosened this earth from its sun? Whither does it now move? Whither do we move? Away from all suns? Do we not dash on unceasingly? Back-wards, sideways, forewards, in all directions? Is there still an above and below? Do we not stray, as through infinite nothingness? Does not empty space breathe upon us? Has it not become colder? Does not night come on continually, darker and darker? Shall we not have to light lanterns in the morning? Do we not hear the noise of the grave-diggers who are burying God? Do we not smell the divine putrefaction?—for even Gods putrefy! God is dead! God remains dead! And we have killed him! How shall we console ourselves, the most murderous of all murderers? The holiest and the mightiest that the world has hitherto possessed, has bled to death under our knife,—who will wipe the blood from us? With what water could we cleanse ourselves? What lustrums, what sacred games shall we have to devise? Is not the magnitude of this deed too great for us? Shall we not ourselves have to become Gods, merely to seem worthy of it? There never was a greater event,—and on account of it, all who are born after us belong to a higher history than any history hitherto!"—Here the madman was silent and looked again at his hearers; they also were silent and looked at him in surprise. At last he threw his lantern on the ground, so that it broke in pieces and was extinguished. "I come too early," he then said, "I am not yet at the right time. This prodigious event is still on its way, and is travelling,—it has not yet reached men's ears. Lightning and thunder need time, the light of the stars needs time, deeds need time, even after they are done, to be seen and heard. This deed is as yet further from them than the furthest star,—*and yet they have done it!*"—It is further stated that the madman made his way into different churches on the same day, and there intoned his *Requiem æternam deo.* When led out and called to account, he always gave the reply: "What are these churches now, if they are not the tombs and monuments of God?"—

126.

Mystical Explanations.—Mystical explanations are regarded as profound; the truth is that they do not even go the length of being superficial.

127.

After-Effect of the most Ancient Religiousness.—The thoughtless man thinks that the

Will is the only thing that operates, that willing is something simple, manifestly given, underived, and comprehensible in itself. He is convinced that when he does anything, for example, when he delivers a blow, it is *he* who strikes, and he has struck because he *willed* to strike. He does not notice anything of a problem therein, but the feeling of *willing* suffices to him, not only for the acceptance of cause and effect, but also for the belief that he *understands* their relationship. Of the mechanism of the occurrence, and of the manifold subtle operations that must be performed in order that the blow may result, and likewise of the incapacity of the Will in itself to effect even the smallest part of those operations—he knows nothing. The Will is to him a magically operating force; the belief in the Will as the cause of effects is the belief in magically operating forces. In fact, whenever he saw anything happen, man originally believed in a Will as cause, and in personally *willing* beings operating in the background,—the conception of mechanism was very remote from him. Because, however, man for immense periods of time believed only in persons (and not in matter, forces, things, &c.), the belief in cause and effect has become a fundamental belief with him, which he applies everywhere when anything happens,—and even still uses instinctively as a piece of atavism of remotest origin. The propositions, "No effect without a cause," and "Every effect again implies a cause," appear as generalisations of several less general propositions:—"Where there is operation there has been *willing*." "Operating is only possible on *willing* beings." "There is never a pure, resultless experience of activity, but every experience involves stimulation of the Will" (to activity, defence, revenge or retaliation). But in the primitive period of the human race, the latter and the former propositions were identical, the first were not generalisations of the second, but the second were explanations of the first.—Schopenhauer, with his assumption that all that exists is something *volitional*, has set a primitive mythology on the throne; he seems never to have attempted an analysis of the Will, because he *believed* like everybody in the simplicity and immediateness of all volition:—while volition is in fact such a cleverly practised mechanical process that it almost escapes the observing eye. I set the following propositions against those of Schopenhauer:—Firstly, in order that Will may arise, an idea of pleasure and pain is necessary. Secondly, that a vigorous excitation may be felt as pleasure or pain, is the affair of the *interpreting* intellect, which, to be sure, operates thereby for the most part unconsciously to us, and one and the same excitation *may* be interpreted as pleasure or pain. Thirdly, it is only in an intellectual being that there is pleasure, displeasure and Will; the immense majority of organisms have nothing of the kind.

128.

The Value of Prayer.—Prayer has been devised for such men as have never any thoughts of their own, and to whom an elevation of the soul is unknown, or passes unnoticed; what shall these people do in holy places and in all important situations in life which require repose and some kind of dignity? In order at least that they may not *disturb,* the wisdom of all the founders of religions, the small as well as the great, has commended to them the formula of prayer, as a long mechanical labour of the lips, united with an effort of the memory, and with a uniform, prescribed attitude of hands and feet—*and* eyes! They may then, like the Tibetans, chew the cud of their *"om mane padme hum,"* innumerable times, or, as in Benares, count the name of the God Ram-Ram-Ram (etc., with or without grace) on their fingers; or honour Vishnu with his thousand names of invocation, Allah with his ninety-nine; or they may make use of the prayer-wheels and the rosary: the main thing is that they are settled down for a time at this work, and present a tolerable appearance; their mode of prayer is devised for the advantage of the pious who have thought and elevation of their own. But even these have their weary hours when a series of venerable words and sounds, and a mechanical, pious ritual does them good. But supposing that these rare men—in every religion the religious man is an exception—know how to help themselves, the poor in spirit do not know, and to forbid them the prayer-babbling would mean to take their religion from them, a fact which Protestantism brings more and more to light. All that religion wants with such persons is that they should *keep still* with their eyes, hands, legs, and all their organs: they thereby become temporarily beautified and—more human-looking!

129.

The Conditions for God.—"God himself cannot subsist without wise men," said Luther, and with good reason; but "God can still less subsist without unwise men,"—good Luther did not say that!

130.

A Dangerous Resolution.—The Christian resolution to find the world ugly and bad, has made the world ugly and bad.

131.

Christianity and Suicide.—Christianity made use of the excessive longing for suicide at the time of its origin as a lever for its power: it left only two forms of suicide, invested them with the highest dignity and the highest hopes, and forbade all others with dreadful threatenings. But martyrdom and the slow self-annihilation of the ascetic were permitted.

132.

Against Christianity.—It is now no longer our reason, but our taste that decides against Christianity.

133.

Axioms.—An unavoidable hypothesis on which mankind must always fall back again, is in the long run *more powerful* than the most firmly believed belief in something untrue (like the Christian belief). In the long run: that means a hundred thousand years hence.

134.

Pessimists as Victims.—When a profound dislike of existence gets the upper hand, the after-effect of a great error in diet of which a people has been long guilty comes to light. The spread of Buddhism (*not* its origin) is thus to a considerable extent dependent on the excessive and almost exclusive rice-fare of the Indians, and on the universal enervation that results therefrom. Perhaps the modern, European discontentedness is to be looked upon as caused by the fact that the world of our forefathers, the whole Middle Ages, was given to drink, owing to the influence of German tastes in Europe: the Middle Ages, that means the alcoholic poisoning of Europe.—The German dislike of life (including the influence of the cellar-air and stove-poison in German dwellings), is essentially a cold-weather complaint.

135.

Origin of Sin—Sin, as it is at present felt wherever Christianity prevails or has prevailed is a Jewish feeling and a Jewish invention; and in respect to this background of all Christian morality Christianity has in fact aimed at "Judaising" the whole world. To what an extent this has succeeded in Europe is traced most accurately in our remarkable alienness to Greek antiquity—a world without the feeling of sin—in our sentiments even at present; in spite of all the good will to approximation and assimilation, which whole generations and many distinguished individuals have not failed to display. "Only when thou *repentest* is God gracious to thee"—that would arouse the laughter or the wrath of a Greek: he would say, "Slaves may have such sentiments." Here a mighty being, an almighty being, and yet a revengeful being, is presupposed; his power is so great that no injury whatever can be done to him except in the point of honour. Every sin is an infringement of respect, a *crimen læsæ majestatis divinæ*—and nothing more! Contrition, degradation, rolling-in-the-dust,—these are the first and last conditions on which his favour depends: the restoration, therefore, of his divine honour! If injury be caused otherwise by sin, if a profound, spreading evil be propagated by it, an evil which, like a disease, attacks and strangles one man after another—that does not trouble this honour-craving Oriental in heaven; sin is an offence against him, not against mankind!—to him on whom he has bestowed his favour he bestows also this indifference to the natural consequences of sin. God and mankind are here thought of as separated as so antithetical that sin against the latter cannot be at all possible,—all deeds are to be looked upon *solely with respect to their supernatural consequences,* and not with respect to their natural results: it is thus that the Jewish feeling, to which all that is natural seems unworthy in itself, would have things. The *Greeks,* on the other hand, were more familiar with the thought that transgression also may have dignity,—even theft, as in the case of Prometheus, even the slaughtering of cattle as the expression of frantic jealousy, as in the case of Ajax; in their need to attribute dignity to transgression and embody it therein, they invented *tragedy,*—an art and a delight, which in its profoundest essence has remained alien to the Jew, in spite of all his poetic endowment and taste for the sublime.

136.

The Chosen People.—The Jews, who regard themselves as the chosen people among the nations, and that too because they are the moral genius among the nations (in virtue of their capacity for *despising* the human in themselves *more* than any other people)—the Jews have a pleasure in their divine monarch and saint similar to that which the French nobility had in Louis XIV. This nobility had allowed its power and autocracy to be taken from it, and had become contemptible: in order not to feel this, in order to be able to forget it, an *unequalled* royal magnificence, royal authority and plenitude of power was needed, to which there was access only for the nobility. As in accordance with this privilege they raised themselves to the elevation of the court, and from that elevation saw everything under them,—saw everything contemptible,—they got beyond all uneasiness of conscience. They thus elevated intentionally the tower of the royal power more and more into the clouds, and set the final coping-stone of their own power thereon.

137.

Spoken in Parable.—A Jesus Christ was only possible in a Jewish landscape—I mean in one over which the gloomy and sublime thunder-cloud of the angry Jehovah hung continually. Here only was the rare, sudden flashing of a single sunbeam through the dreadful, universal and continuous nocturnal-day regarded as a miracle of "love," as a beam of the most unmerited "grace." Here only could Christ dream of his rainbow and celestial ladder on which God descended to man; everywhere else the clear weather and the sun were considered the rule and the commonplace.

138.

The Error of Christ.—The founder of Christianity thought there was nothing from which men suffered so much as from their sins:—it was his error, the error of him who felt himself without sin, to whom experience was lacking in this respect! It was thus that his soul filled with that marvellous, fantastic pity which had reference to a trouble that even among his own people, the inventors of sin, was rarely a great trouble! But Christians understood subsequently how to do justice to their master, and how to sanctify his error into a "truth."

139.

Colour of the Passions.—Natures such as the apostle Paul, have an evil eye for the passions; they learn to know only the filthy, the distorting, and the heart-breaking in them,—their ideal aim, therefore, is the annihilation of the passions; in the divine they see complete purification from passion. The Greeks, quite otherwise than Paul and the Jews, directed their ideal aim precisely to the passions, and loved, elevated, embellished and deified them: in passion they evidently not only felt themselves happier, but also purer and diviner than otherwise.—And now the Christians? Have they wished to become Jews in this respect? Have they perhaps become Jews?

140.

Too Jewish.—If God had wanted to become an object of love, he would first of all have had to forgo judging and justice:-a judge, and even a gracious judge, is no object of love. The founder of Christianity showed too little of the finer feelings in this respect—being a Jew.

141.

Too Oriental.—What? A God who loves men provided that they believe in him, and who hurls frightful glances and threatenings at him who does not believe in this love! What? A conditioned love as the feeling of an almighty God! A love which has not even become master of the sentiment of honour and of the irritable desire for vengeance! How Oriental is all that! "If I love thee, what does it concern thee?"[10] is already a sufficient criticism of the whole of Christianity.

142.

Frankincense.—*Buddha* says: "Do not flatter thy benefactor!" Let one repeat this saying in a Christian church:—it immediately purifies the air.

143.

The Greatest Utility of Polytheism.—For the individual to set up his *own* ideal and

---

[10]This poem is a parody of the "Chorus Mysticus" which concludes the second part of Goethe's "Faust." Bayard Taylor's translation of the passage in "Faust" runs as follows:—

derive from it his laws, his pleasures and his rights—*that* has perhaps been hitherto regarded as the most monstrous of all human aberrations, and as idolatry in itself; in fact, the few who have ventured to do this have always needed to apologise to themselves, usually in this wise: "Not I! not I! but *a God*, through my instrumentality!" It was in the marvellous art and capacity for creating Gods—in polytheism—that this impulse was permitted to discharge itself, it was here that it became purified, perfected, and ennobled; for it was originally a commonplace and unimportant impulse, akin to stubbornness, disobedience and envy. To be *hostile* to this impulse towards the individual ideal,—that was formerly the law of every morality. There was then only one norm, "the man"—and every people believed that it *had* this one and ultimate norm. But above himself, and outside of himself, in a distant over-world, a person could see a *multitude of norms*: the one God was not the denial or blasphemy of the other Gods! It was here that individuals were first permitted, it was here that the right of individuals was first respected. The inventing of Gods, heroes, and supermen of all kinds, as well as co-ordinate men and undermen—dwarfs, fairies, centaurs, satyrs, demons, devils—was the inestimable preliminary to the justification of the selfishness and sovereignty of the individual: the freedom which was granted to one God in respect to other Gods, was at last given to the individual himself in respect to laws, customs and neighbours. Monotheism, on the contrary, the rigid consequence of the doctrine of one normal human being—consequently the belief in a normal God, beside whom there are only false, spurious Gods—has perhaps been the greatest danger of mankind in the past: man was then threatened by that premature state of inertia, which, so far as we can see, most of the other species of animals reached long ago, as creatures who all believed in one normal animal and ideal in their species, and definitely translated their morality of custom into flesh and blood. In polytheism man's free-thinking and many-sided thinking had a prototype set up: the power to create for himself new and individual eyes, always newer and more individualised: so that these are no *eternal* horizons and perspectives.

144.

Religious Wars.—The greatest advance of the masses hitherto has been religious war, for it proves that the masses have begun to deal reverently with conceptions of things. Religious wars only result when human reason generally has been refined by the subtle disputes of sects; so that even the populace becomes punctilious and regards trifles as important, actually thinking it possible that the "eternal salvation of the soul" may depend upon minute distinctions of concepts.

145.

Danger of Vegetarians.—The immense prevalence of rice-eating impels to the use of opium and narcotics, in like manner as the immense prevalence of potato-eating impels to the use of brandy:—it also impels, however, in its more subtle after-effects to modes of thought and feeling which operate narcotically. This is in accord with the fact that those who promote narcotic modes of thought and feeling, like those Indian teachers, praise a purely vegetable diet, and would like to make it a law for the masses: they want thereby to call forth and augment the need which *they* are in a position to satisfy.

146.

German Hopes.—Do not let us forget that the names of peoples are generally names of reproach. The Tartars, for example, according to their name, are "the dogs"; they were so christened by the Chinese. *"Deutschen"* (Germans) means originally "heathen": it is thus that the Goths after their conversion named the great mass of their unbaptized fellow-tribes, according to the indication in their translation of the Septuagint, in which the heathen are designated by the word which in Greek signifies "the nations." (See Ulfilas.)—It might still be possible for the Germans to make an honourable name ultimately out of their old name of reproach, by becoming the first *non-Christian* nation of Europe; for which purpose Schopenhauer, to their honour, regarded them as highly qualified. The work of *Luther* would thus be consummated,—he who taught them to be anti-Roman, and to say: "Here *I* stand! *I* cannot do otherwise!"—

147.

Question and Answer.—What do savage tribes at present accept first of all from Europeans? Brandy and Christianity, the European narcotics.—And by what means are they fastest ruined?—By the European narcotics.

148.

Where Reformations Originate.—At the time of the great corruption of the church it was least of all corrupt in Germany: it was on that account that the Reformation originated *here*, as a sign that even the beginnings of corruption were felt to be unendurable. For, comparatively speaking, no people was ever more Christian than the Germans at the time of Luther; their Christian culture was just about to burst into bloom with a hundred-fold splendour,—one night only was still lacking; but that night brought the storm which put an end to all.

149.

The Failure of Reformations.—It testifies to the higher culture of the Greeks, even in rather early ages, that attempts to establish new Grecian religions frequently failed; it testifies that quite early there must have been a multitude of dissimilar individuals in Greece, whose dissimilar troubles were not cured by a single recipe of faith and hope. Pythagoras and Plato, perhaps also Empedocles, and already much earlier the Orphic enthusiasts, aimed at founding new religions; and the two first-named were so endowed with the qualifications for founding religions, that one cannot be sufficiently astonished at their failure: they just reached the point of founding sects. Every time that the Reformation of an entire people fails and only sects raise their heads, one may conclude that the people already contains many types, and has begun to free itself from the gross herding instincts and the morality of, custom,—a momentous state of suspense, which one is accustomed to disparage as decay of morals and corruption, while it announces the maturing of the egg and the early rupture of the shell. That Luther's Reformation succeeded in the north, is a sign that the north had remained backward in comparison with the south of Europe, and still had requirements tolerably uniform in colour and kind; and there would have been no Christianising of Europe at all, if the culture of the old world of the south had not been gradually barbarized by an excessive admixture of the blood of German barbarians, and thus lost its ascendency. The more universally and unconditionally an individual, or the thought of an individual, can operate, so much more homogeneous and so much lower must be the mass that is there operated upon; while counter-strivings betray internal counter-requirements, which also want to gratify and realise themselves. Reversely, one may always conclude with regard to an actual elevation of culture, when powerful and ambitious natures only produce a limited and sectarian effect: this is true also for the separate arts, and for the provinces of knowledge. Where there is ruling there are masses: where there are masses there is need of slavery. Where there is slavery the individuals are but few, and have the instincts and conscience of the herd opposed to them.

150.

Criticism of Saints.—Must one then, in order to have a virtue, be desirous of having it precisely in its most brutal form?—as the Christian saints desired and needed;—those who only *endured* life with the thought that at the sight of their virtue self-contempt might seize every man. A virtue with such an effect I call brutal.

151.

The Origin of Religion.—The metaphysical requirement is not the origin of religions, as Schopenhauer claims, but only a *later sprout* from them. Under the dominance of religious thoughts we have accustomed ourselves to the idea of "another (back, under, or upper) world," and feel an uncomfortable void and privation through the annihilation of the religious illusion;—and then "another world" grows out of this feeling once more, but now it is only a metaphysical world, and no longer a religious one. That however which in general led to the assumption of "another world" in primitive times, was *not* an impulse or requirement, but an *error* in the interpretation of certain natural phenomena, a difficulty of the intellect.

152.

The greatest Change.—The lustre and the hues of all things have changed! We no longer quite understand how earlier men conceived of the most familiar and frequent things,—for example, of the day, and the awakening in the morning: owing to their belief in dreams the waking state seemed to them differently illuminated. And similarly of the whole of life, with its reflection of death and its significance: our "death" is an entirely different death. All events were of a different lustre, for a God shone forth in them; and similarly of all resolutions and peeps into the distant future: for people had oracles, and secret hints, and believed in prognostication. "Truth" was conceived in quite a different manner, for the insane could formerly be regarded as its mouthpiece—a thing which makes *us* shudder, or laugh. Injustice made a different impression on the feelings: for people were afraid of divine retribution, and not only of legal punishment and disgrace. What joy was there in an age when men believed in the devil and tempter! What passion was there when people saw demons lurking close at hand! What philosophy was there when doubt was regarded as sinfulness of the most dangerous kind, and in fact as an outrage on eternal love, as distrust of everything good, high, pure, and compassionate!—We have coloured things anew, we paint them over continually,—but what have we been able to do hitherto in comparison with the *splendid colouring* of that old master!—I mean ancient humanity.

153.

Homo poeta.—"I myself who have made this tragedy of tragedies altogether independently, in so far as it is completed; I who have first entwined the perplexities of morality about existence, and have tightened them so that only a God could unravel them—so Horace demands!—I have already in the fourth act killed all the Gods—for the sake of morality! What is now to be done about the fifth act? Where shall I get the tragic *dénouement!* Must I now think about a comic *dénouement?*"

154.

Differences in the Dangerousness of Life.—You don't know at all what you experience; you run through life as if intoxicated, and now and then fall down a stair. Thanks however to your intoxication you still do not break your limbs: your muscles are too languid and your head too confused to find the stones of the staircase as hard as we others do! For, us life is a greater danger: we are made of glass—alas, if we should *strike against* anything! And all is lost if we should *fall!*

155.

What we Lack.—We love the *grandeur* of Nature, and have discovered it; that is because human grandeur is lacking in our minds. It was the reverse with the Greeks: their feeling towards Nature was quite different from ours.

156.

The most Influential Person.—The fact that a person resists the whole spirit of his age, stops it at the door and calls it to account, *must* exert an influence! It is indifferent whether he wishes to exert an influence; the point is that he *can.*

157.

Mentiri.—Take care!—he reflects: he will have a lie ready immediately. This is a stage in the civilisation of whole nations. Consider only what the Romans expressed by *mentiri!*

158.

An Inconvenient Peculiarity.—To find everything deep is an inconvenient peculiarity: it makes one constantly strain one's eyes, so that in the end one always finds more than one wishes.

159.

Every Virtue has its Time.—The honesty of him who is at present inflexible often causes him remorse; for inflexibility is the virtue of a time different from that in which honesty prevails.

160.

In Intercourse with Virtues.—One can also be undignified and flattering towards a virtue.

161.

To the Admirers of the Age.—The runaway priest and the liberated criminal are continually making grimaces; what they want is a look without a past. But have you ever seen men who know that their looks reflect the future, and who are so courteous to you, the admirers of the "age," that they assume a look without a future?—

162.

Egoism.—Egoism is the *perspective* law of our sentiment, according to which the near appears large and momentous, while in the distance the magnitude and importance of all things diminish.

163.

After a Great Victory.—The best thing in a great victory is that it deprives the conqueror of the fear of defeat. "Why should I not be worsted for once?" he says to himself, "I am now rich enough to stand it."

164.

Those who Seek Repose.—I recognise the minds that seek repose by the many *dark* objects with which they surround themselves: those who want to sleep darken their chambers, or creep into caverns. A hint to those who do not know what they really seek most, and would like to know!

165.

The Happiness of Renunciation.—He who has absolutely dispensed with something for a long time will almost imagine, when he accidentally meets with it again, that he has discovered it,—and what happiness every discoverer has! Let us be wiser than the serpents that lie too long in the same sunshine.

166.

Always in our own Society.—All that is akin to me in nature and history speaks to me, praises me, urges me forward and comforts me—: other things are unheard by me, or immediately forgotten. We are only in our own society always.

167.

Misanthropy and Philanthropy.—We only speak about being sick of men when we can no longer digest them, and yet have the stomach full of them. Misanthropy is the result of a far too eager philanthropy and "cannibalism,"—but who ever bade you swallow men like oysters, my Prince Hamlet?

168.

Concerning an Invalid.—"Things go badly with him!"—What is wrong?—" He suffers from the longing to be praised, and finds no sustenance for it."—Inconceivable! All the world does honour to him, and he is reverenced not only in deed but in word!—"Certainly, but he is dull of hearing for the praise. When a friend praises him it sounds to him as if the friend praised himself; when an enemy praises him, it sounds to him as if the enemy wanted to be praised for it; when, finally, some one else praises him—there are by no means so many of these, he is so famous!—he is offended because they neither want him for a friend nor for an enemy; he is accustomed to say: 'What do I care for those who can still pose as the all-righteous towards me!'"

169.

Avowed Enemies.—Bravery in presence of an enemy is a thing by itself: a person may possess it and still be a coward and an irresolute num-skull. That was Napoleon's opinion concerning the "bravest man" he knew, Murat:—whence it follows that avowed enemies are indispensable to some men, if they are to attain to *their* virtue, to their manliness, to their cheerfulness.

170.

With, the Multitude.—He has hitherto gone with the multitude and is its pane-gyrist; but one day he will be its opponent! For he follows it in the belief that his laziness will find its advantage thereby: he has not yet learned that the multitude is not lazy enough for him! that it always presses forward! that it does not allow any one to stand still!—And he likes so well to stand still!

171.

Fame.—When the gratitude of many to one casts aside all shame, then fame originates.

172.

The Perverter of Taste.—A: "You are a perverter of taste—they say so everywhere!" B: "Certainly! I pervert every one's taste for his party:—no party forgives me for that."

173.

To be Profound and to Appear Profound.—He who knows that he is profound strives for clearness; he who would like to appear profound to the multitude strives for obscurity. The multitude thinks everything profound of which it cannot see the bottom; it is so timid and goes so unwillingly into the water.

174.

Apart.—Parliamentarism, that is to say, the public permission to choose be-tween five main political opinions, insinuates itself into the favour of the numerous class who would fain *appear* independent and individual, and like to fight for their opinions. After all, however, it is a matter of indifference whether one opinion is imposed upon the herd, or five opinions are permitted to it.—He who diverges from the five public opinions and goes apart, has always the whole herd against him.

175.

Concerning Eloquence.—What has hitherto had the most convincing eloquence? The rolling of the drum: and as long as kings have this at their command, they will always be the best orators and popular leaders.

176.

Compassion.—The poor, ruling princes! All their rights now change unexpectedly into claims, and all these claims immediately sound like pretensions! And if they but say "we," or "my people," wicked old Europe begins laughing. Verily, a chief-master-of-ceremonies of the modern world would make little ceremony with them; perhaps he would decree that "*les souverains rangent aux parvenus.*"

177.

On "Educational Matters."—In Germany an important educational means is lacking for higher men; namely, the laughter of higher men; these men do not laugh in Germany.

178.

For Moral Enlightenment.—The Germans must be talked out of their Mephistopheles—and out of their Faust also. These are two moral prejudices against the value of knowledge.

179.

Thoughts.—Thoughts are the shadows of our sentiments—always however obscurer, emptier and simpler.

180.

The Good Time for Free Spirits.—Free Spirits take liberties even with regard to Science—and meanwhile they are allowed to do so,—while the Church still remains!—In so far they have now their good time.

181.

Following and Leading.—A: "Of the two, the one will always follow, the other will always lead, whatever be the course of their destiny. *And yet* the former is superior to the other in virtue and intellect." B: "And yet? And yet? That is spoken for the others; not for me, not for us!—*Fit secundum regulam.*"

182.

In Solitude.—When one lives alone one does not speak too loudly, and one does not write too loudly either, for one fears the hollow reverberation—the criticism of the nymph Echo.—And all voices sound differently in solitude!

183.

The Music of the Best Future.—The first musician for me would be he who knew only the sorrow of the profoundest happiness, and no other sorrow: there has not hitherto been such a musician.

184.

Justice.—Better allow oneself to be robbed than have scarecrows around one—that is my taste. And under all circumstances it is just a matter of taste—and nothing more!

185.

Poor.—He is now poor, but not because everything has been taken from him, but because he has thrown everything away:—what does he care? He is accustomed to find new things.—It is the poor who misunderstand his voluntary poverty.

186.

Bad Conscience.—All that he now does is excellent and proper—and yet he has a bad conscience with it all. For the exceptional is his task.

187.

Offensiveness in Expression.—This artist offends me by the way in which he expresses his ideas, his very excellent ideas: so diffusely and forcibly, and with such gross rhetorical artifices, as if he were speaking to the mob. We feel always as if "in bad company" when devoting some time to his art.

188.

Work.—How closely work and the workers now stand even to the most leisurely of us! The royal courtesy in the words: "We are all workers," would have been a cynicism and an indecency even under Louis XIV.

189.

The Thinker.—He is a thinker: that is to say, he knows how to take things more simply than they are.

190.

Against Eulogisers.—A: "One is only praised by one's equals!" B: "Yes! And he who praises you says: 'You are my equal!'"

191.

Against many a Vindication.—The most perfidious manner of injuring a cause is to vindicate it intentionally with fallacious arguments.

192.

The Good-natured.—What is it that distinguishes the good-natured, whose countenances beam kindness, from other people? They feel quite at ease in presence of a new person, and are quickly enamoured of him; they therefore wish him well; their first opinion is: "He pleases me." With them there follow in succession the wish to appropriate (they make little scruple about the person's worth), rapid appropriation, joy in the possession, and actions in favour of the person possessed.

193.

Kant's Joke.—Kant tried to prove, in a way that dismayed "everybody," that "everybody" was in the right:—that was his secret joke. He wrote against the learned, in favour of popular prejudice; he wrote, however, for the learned and not for the people.

194.

The "Open-hearted" Man.—That man acts probably always from concealed motives; for he has always communicable motives on his tongue, and almost in his open hand.

195.

Laughable!—See! See! He runs *away* from men—: they follow him, however, because he runs *before* them,—they are such a gregarious lot!

196.

The Limits of our Sense of Hearing.—We hear only the questions to which we are capable of finding an answer.

197.

Caution therefore!—There is nothing we are fonder of communicating to others than the seal of secrecy—together with what is under it.

198.

Vexation of the Proud Man.—The proud man is vexed even with those who help him forward: he looks angrily at his carriage-horses.

199.

Liberality.—Liberality is often only a form of timidity in the rich.

200.

Laughing.—To laugh means to love mischief, but with a good conscience.

201.

In Applause.—In applause there is always some kind of noise: even in self-applause.

202.

A Spendthrift.—He has not yet the poverty of the rich man who has counted all his treasure,—he squanders his spirit with the irrationalness of the spendthrift Nature.

203.

Hic niger est.—Usually he has no thoughts,—but in exceptional cases bad thoughts come to him.

204.

Beggars and Courtesy.—"One is not discourteous when one knocks at a door with a stone when the bell-pull is awanting"—so think all beggars and necessitous persons, but no one thinks they are in the right.

205.

Need.—Need is supposed to be the cause of things; but in truth it is often only the result of things.

206.

During the Rain.—It rains, and I think of the poor people who now crowd together with their many cares, which they are unaccustomed to conceal; all of them, therefore, ready and anxious to give pain to one another, and thus provide themselves with a pitiable kind of comfort, even in bad weather. This, this only, is the poverty of the poor!

207.

The Envious Man.—That is an envious man—it is not desirable that he should have children; he would be envious of them, because he can no longer be a child.

208.

A Great Man!—Because a person is "a great man," we are not authorised to infer that he is a man. Perhaps he is only a boy, or a chameleon of all ages, or a bewitched girl.

209.

A Mode of Asking for Reasons.—There is a mode of asking for our reasons which not only makes us forget our best reasons, but also arouses in us a spite and repugnance against reason generally:-a very stupefying mode of questioning, and really an artifice of tyrannical men!

210.

Moderation in Diligence.—One must not be anxious to surpass the diligence of one's father—that would make one ill.

211.

Secret Enemies.—To be able to keep a secret enemy—that is a luxury which the morality even of the highest-minded persons can rarely afford.

212.

Not Letting oneself be Deluded.—His spirit has bad manners, it is hasty and always stutters with impatience; so that one would hardly suspect the deep breathing and the large chest of the soul in which it resides.

213.

The Way to Happiness.—A sage asked of a fool the way to happiness. The fool answered without delay, like one who had been asked the way to the next town: "Admire yourself, and live on the street!" "Hold," cried the sage, "you require too much; it suffices to admire oneself!" The fool replied: "But how can one constantly admire without constantly despising?"

214.

Faith Saves.—Virtue gives happiness and a state of blessedness only to those who have a strong faith in their virtue:—not, however, to the more refined souls whose virtue consists of a profound distrust of themselves and of all virtue. After all, therefore, it is "faith that saves" here also!—and be it well observed, *not* virtue!

215.

The Ideal and the Material.—You have a noble ideal before your eyes: but are you also such a noble stone that such a divine image could be formed out of you? And without that—is not all your labour barbaric sculpturing? A blasphemy of your ideal?

216.

Danger in the Voice.—With a very loud voice a person is almost incapable of reflecting on subtle matters.

217.

Cause and Effect.—Before the effect one believes in other causes than after the effect.

218.

My Antipathy.—I do not like those people who, in order to produce an effect, have to burst like bombs, and in whose neighbourhood one is always in danger of suddenly losing one's hearing—or even something more.

219.

The Object of Punishment.—The object of punishment is to improve him *who punishes,*—that is the ultimate appeal of those who justify punishment.

220.

Sacrifice.—The victims think otherwise than the spectators about sacrifice and sacrificing: but they have never been allowed to express their opinion.

221.

Consideration.—Fathers and sons are much more considerate of one another than mothers and daughters.

222.

Poet and Liar.—The poet sees in the liar his foster-brother whose milk he has drunk up; the latter has thus remained wretched, and has not even attained to a good conscience.

223.

Vicariousness of the Senses.—"We have also eyes in order to hear with them,"—said an old confessor who had grown deaf; "and among the blind he that has the longest ears is king."

224.

Animal Criticism.—I fear the animals regard man as a being like themselves, seriously endangered by the loss of sound animal understanding;—they regard him perhaps as the absurd animal, the laughing animal, the crying animal, the unfortunate animal.

225.

The Natural.—"Evil has always had the great effect! And Nature is evil! Let us therefore be natural!"—so reason secretly the great aspirants after effect, who are too often counted among great men.

226.

The Distrustful and their Style.—We say the strongest things simply, provided people are about us who believe in our strength:—such an environment educates to "simplicity of style." The distrustful, on the other hand, speak emphatically; they make things emphatic.

227.

Fallacy, Fallacy.—He cannot rule himself; therefore that woman concludes that it will be easy to rule him, and throws out her lines to catch him;—the poor creature, who in a short time will be his slave.

228.

Against Mediators.—He who attempts to mediate between two decided thinkers is rightly called mediocre: he has not an eye for seeing the unique; similarising and equalising are signs of weak eyes.

229.

Obstinacy and Loyalty.—Out of obstinacy he holds fast to a cause of which the questionableness has become obvious,—he calls that, however, his "loyalty."

230.

Lack of Reserve.—His whole nature fails to *convince*—that results from the fact that he has never been reticent about a good action he has performed.

231.

The "Plodders."—Persons slow of apprehension think that slowness forms part of knowledge.

232.

Dreaming.—Either one does not dream at all, or one dreams in an interesting manner. One must learn to be awake in the same fashion:—either not at all, or in an interesting manner.

233.

The most Dangerous Point of View.—What I now do, or neglect to do, is as important *for all that is to come*, as the greatest event of the past: in this immense perspective of effects all actions are equally great and small.

234.

Consolatory Words of a Musician.—"Your life does not sound into people's ears: for them you live a dumb life, and all refinements of melody, all fond resolutions in following or leading the way, are concealed from them. To be sure you do not parade the thoroughfares with regimental music,—but these good people have no right to say on that account that your life is lacking in music. He that hath ears let him hear."

235.

Spirit and Character.—Many a one attains his full height of character, but his spirit is not adapted to the elevation,—and many a one reversely.

236.

To Move the Multitude.—Is it not necessary for him who wants to move the multitude to give a stage representation of himself? Has he not first to translate himself into the grotesquely obvious, and then *set forth* his whole personality and cause in that vulgarised and simplified fashion?

237.

The Polite Man.—"He is so polite!"—Yes, he has always a sop for Cerberus with him, and is so timid that he takes everybody for Cerberus, even you and me,—that is his "politeness."

238.

Without Envy.—He is wholly without envy, but there is no merit therein: for he wants to conquer a land which no one has yet possessed and hardly any one has even seen.

239.

The Joyless Person.—A single joyless person is enough to make constant displeasure and a clouded heaven in a household; and it is only by a miracle that such a person is lacking!—Happiness is not nearly such a contagious disease;—how is that?

240.

On the Sea-Shore.—I would not build myself a house (it is an element of my happiness not to be a house-owner!). If I had to do so, however, I should build it, like many of the Romans, right into the sea,—I should like to have some secrets in common with that beautiful monster.

241.

Work and Artist.—This artist is ambitious and nothing more; ultimately, however, his work is only a magnifying-glass, which he offers to every one who looks in his direction.

242.

Suum cuique.—However great be my greed of knowledge, I cannot appropriate aught of things but what already belongs to me,—the property of others still remains in the things. How is it possible for a man to be a thief or a robber?

243.

Origin of "Good" and "Bad."—He only will devise an improvement who can feel that "this is not good."

244.

Thoughts and Words.—Even our thoughts we are unable to render completely in words.

245.

Praise in Choice.—The artist chooses his subjects; that is his mode of praising.

246.

Mathematics.—We want to carry the refinement and rigour of mathematics into all the sciences, as far as it is in any way possible, not in the belief that we shall apprehend things in this way, but in order thereby to *assert* our human relation to things. Mathematics is only a means to general and ultimate human knowledge.

247.

Habits.—All habits make our hand wittier and our wit unhandier.

248.

Books.—Of what account is a book that never carries us away beyond all books?

249.

The Sigh of the Seeker of Knowledge.—"Oh, my covetousness! In this soul there is no disinterestedness—but an all-desiring self, which, by means of many individuals, would fain see as with *its own* eyes, and grasp as with *its own* hands—a self bringing back even the entire past, and wanting to lose nothing that could in anyway belong to it! Oh, this flame of my covetousness! Oh, that I were reincarnated in a hundred individuals!"—He who does not know this sigh by experience, does not know the passion of the seeker of knowledge either.

250.

Guilt.—Although the most intelligent judges of the witches, and even the witches themselves, were convinced of the guilt of witchcraft, the guilt, nevertheless, was not there. So it is with all guilt.

251.

Misunderstood Sufferers.—Great natures suffer otherwise than their worshippers imagine; they suffer most severely from the ignoble, petty emotions of certain evil moments; in short, from doubt of their own greatness;—not however from the sacrifices and martyrdoms which their tasks require of them. As long as Prometheus sympathises with men and sacrifices himself for them, he is happy and proud in himself; but on becoming envious of Zeus and of the homage which mortals pay him—then Prometheus suffers!

252.

Better to be in Debt.—"Better to remain in debt than to pay with money which does not bear our stamp!"—that is what our sovereignty prefers.

253.

Always at Home.—One day we attain our *goal*—and then refer with pride to the long journeys we have made to reach it. In truth, we did not notice that we travelled. We got into the habit of thinking that we were *at home* in every place.

254.

Against Embarrassment.—He who is always thoroughly occupied is rid of all embarrassment.

255.

Imitators.—A: "What? You don't want to have imitators?" B: "I don't want people to do anything *after* me; I want every one to do something *before* himself (as a pattern to himself)—just as *I* do." A: "Consequently—?"

256.

Skinniness.—All profound men have their happiness in imitating the flying-fish at times, and playing on the crests of the waves; they think that what is best of all in things is their surface: their skinniness—*sit venia verbo.*

257.

From Experience.—A person often does not know how rich he is, until he learns from experience what rich men even play the thief on him.

258.

The Deniers of Chance.—No conqueror believes in chance.

259.

From Paradise.—"Good and Evil are God's prejudices"—said the serpent.

260.

One times One.—One only is always in the wrong, but with two truth begins.—One only cannot prove himself right; but two are already beyond refutation.

261.

Originality.—What is originality? To *see* something that does not yet bear a name, that cannot yet be named, although it is before everybody's eyes. As people are usually constituted, it is the name that first makes a thing generally visible to them.—Original persons have also for the most part been the namers of things.

262.

Sub specie æterni.—A: "You withdraw faster and faster from the living; they will soon strike you out of their lists!"—B: "It is the only way to participate in the privilege of the dead." A: "In what privilege?"—B: "No longer having to die."

263.

Without Vanity.—When we love we want our defects to remain concealed,—not out of vanity, but lest the person loved should suffer therefrom. Indeed, the lover would like to appear as a God,—and not out of vanity either.

264.

What we Do.—What we do is never understood, but only praised and blamed.

265.

Ultimate Scepticism.—But what after all are man's truths?—They are his *irrefutable* errors.

266.

Where Cruelty is Necessary.—He who is great is cruel to his second-rate virtues and judgments.

267.

With a high Aim.—With a high aim a person is superior even to justice, and not only to his deeds and his judges.

268.

What makes Heroic?—To face simultaneously one's greatest suffering and one's highest hope.

269.

What dost thou Believe in?—In this: That the weights of all things must be determined anew.

270.

What Saith thy Conscience?—"Thou shalt become what thou art."

271.

Where are thy Greatest Dangers?—In pity.

272.

What dost thou Love in others?—My hopes.

273.

Whom dost thou call Bad?—Him who always wants to put others to shame.

274.

What dost thou think most humane?—To spare a person shame.

275.

What is the Seal of Attained Liberty?—To be no longer ashamed of oneself.

BOOK FOURTH

SANCTUS JANUARIUS

Thou who with cleaving fiery lances
    The stream of my soul from
    its ice dost free,
Till with a rush and a roar it advances
To enter with glorious hoping the sea:
Brighter to see and purer ever,
Free in the bonds of thy sweet constraint,—
So it praises thy wondrous endeavour,
January, thou beauteous saint!

Genoa, January 1882.

276.

For the New Year.—I still live, I still think; I must still live, for I must still think.
Sum, ergo cogito: cogito, ergo sum. To-day everyone takes the liberty of expressing his
wish and his favourite thought: well, I also mean to tell what I have wished for
myself to-day, and what thought first crossed my mind this year,—a thought which
ought to be the basis, the pledge and the sweetening of all my future life! I want
more and more to perceive the necessary characters in things as the beautiful:—I
shall thus be one of those who beautify things. *Amor fati:* let that henceforth be my
love! I do not want to wage war with the ugly. I do not want to accuse, I do not want
even to accuse the accusers. *Looking aside,* let that be my sole negation! And all in all,
to sum up: I wish to be at any time hereafter only a yea-sayer!

277.

Personal Providence.—There is a certain climax in life, at which, notwithstanding
all our freedom, and however much we may have denied all directing reason and
goodness in the beautiful chaos of existence, we are once more in great danger of

intellectual bondage, and have to face our hardest test. For now the thought of a personal Providence first presents itself before us with its most persuasive force, and has the best of advocates, apparentness, in its favour, now when it is obvious that all and everything that happens to us always *turns out for the best.* The life of every day and of every hour seems to be anxious for nothing else but always to prove this proposition anew; let it be what it will, bad or good weather, the loss of a friend, a sickness, a calumny, the non-receipt of a letter, the spraining of one's foot, a glance into a shop-window, a counter-argument, the opening of a book, a dream, a deception:—it shows itself immediately, or very soon afterwards, as something "not permitted to be absent,"—it is full of profound significance and utility precisely *for us!* Is there a more dangerous temptation to rid ourselves of the belief in the Gods of Epicurus, those careless, unknown Gods, and believe in some anxious and mean Divinity, who knows personally every little hair on our heads, and feels no disgust in rendering the most wretched services? Well—I mean in spite of all this! we want to leave the Gods alone (and the serviceable genii likewise), and wish to content ourselves with the assumption that our own practical and theoretical skilfulness in explaining and suitably arranging events has now reached its highest point. We do not want either to think too highly of this dexterity of our wisdom, when the wonderful harmony which results from playing on our instrument sometimes surprises us too much: a harmony which sounds too well for us to dare to ascribe it to ourselves. In fact, now and then there is one who plays *with* us—beloved Chance: he leads our hand occasionally, and even the all-wisest Providence could not devise any finer music than that of which our foolish hand is then capable.

278.

The Thought of Death.—It gives me a melancholy happiness to live in the midst of this confusion of streets, of necessities, of voices: how much enjoyment, impatience and desire, how much thirsty life and drunkenness of life comes to light here every moment! And yet it will soon be so still for all these shouting, lively, life-loving people! How everyone's shadow, his gloomy travelling-companion stands behind him! It is always as in the last moment before the departure of an emigrant-ship: people have more than ever to say to one another, the hour presses, the ocean with its lonely silence waits impatiently behind all the noise—so greedy, so certain of its prey! And all, all, suppose that the past has been nothing, or a small matter, that the near future is everything: hence this haste, this crying, this self-deafening and self-overreaching! Everyone wants to be foremost in this future,—and yet death and the stillness of death are the only things certain and common to all in this future!

How strange that this sole thing that is certain and common to all, exercises almost no influence on men, and that they are the *furthest* from regarding themselves as the brotherhood of death! It makes me happy to see that men do not want to think at all of the idea of death! I would fain do something to make the idea of life even a hundred times *more worthy of their attention.*

279.

Stellar Friendship.—We were friends, and have become strangers to each other. But this is as it ought to be, and we do not want either to conceal or obscure the fact, as if we had to be ashamed of it. We are two ships, each of which has its goal and its course; we may, to be sure, cross one another in our paths, and celebrate a feast together as we did before,—and then the gallant ships lay quietly in one harbour, and in one sunshine, so that it might have been thought they were already at their goal, and that they had had one goal. But then the almighty strength of our tasks forced us apart once more into different seas and into different zones, and perhaps we shall never see one another again,—or perhaps we may see one another, but not know one another again; the different seas and suns have altered us! That we had to become strangers to one another is the law to which we are *subject*: just by that shall we become more sacred to one another! Just by that shall the thought of our former friendship become holier! There is probably some immense, invisible curve and stellar orbit in which our courses and goals, so widely different, may be *comprehended* as small stages of the way,—let us raise ourselves to this thought! But our life is too short, and our power of vision too limited for us to be more than friends in the sense of that sublime possibility.—And so we will *believe* in our stellar friendship, though we should have to be terrestrial enemies to one another.

280.

Architecture for Thinkers.—An insight is needed (and that probably very soon) as to what is specially lacking in our great cities—namely, quiet, spacious, and widely extended places for reflection, places with long, lofty colonnades for bad weather, or for too sunny days, where no noise of wagons or of shouters would penetrate, and where a more refined propriety would prohibit loud praying even to the priest: buildings and situations which as a whole would express the sublimity of self-communion and seclusion from the world. The time is past when the Church possessed the monopoly of reflection, when the *vita contemplativa* had always in the first place to be the *vita religiosa:* and everything that the Church has built expresses this thought. I know not how we could content ourselves with their structures, even if they should be divested of their ecclesiastical purposes: these structures speak a far too pathetic and too biassed speech, as houses of God and places of splendour for supernatural intercourse, for us godless ones to be able to think *our thoughts* in them. We want to have *ourselves* translated into stone and plant, we want to go for a walk in *ourselves* when we wander in these halls and gardens.

281.

Knowing how to Find the End.—Masters of the first rank are recognised by knowing in a perfect manner how to find the end, in the whole as well as in the part; be it the end of a melody or of a thought, be it the fifth act of a tragedy or of a state affair. The masters of the second degree always become restless towards the end, and seldom dip down into the sea with such proud, quiet equilibrium as for example, the mountain-ridge at *Porto fino*—where the Bay of Genoa sings its melody to an end.

282.

The Gait.—There are mannerisms of the intellect by which even great minds betray that they originate from the populace, or from the semi-populace—it is principally the gait and step, of their thoughts which betray them; they cannot *walk*. It was thus that even Napoleon, to his profound chagrin, could not walk "legitimately" and in princely fashion on occasions when it was necessary to do so properly, as in great coronation processions and on similar occasions: even there he was always just the leader of a column—proud and brusque at the same time, and very self-conscious of it all.—It is something laughable to see those writers who make the folding robes of their periods rustle around them: they want to cover their *feet*.

283.

Pioneers.—I greet all the signs indicating that a more manly and warlike age is commencing, which will, above all, bring heroism again into honour! For it has to prepare the way for a yet higher age, and gather the force which the latter will one day require,—the age which will carry heroism into knowledge, and *wage war* for the sake of ideas and their consequences. For that end many brave pioneers are now needed, who, however, cannot originate out of nothing,—and just as little out of the sand and slime of present-day civilisation and the culture of great cities: men silent, solitary and resolute, who know how to be content and persistent in invisible activity: men who with innate disposition seek in all things that which is *to be overcome* in them: men to whom cheerfulness, patience, simplicity, and contempt of the great vanities belong just as much as do magnanimity in victory and indulgence to the trivial vanities of all the vanquished: men with an acute and independent judgment regarding all victors, and concerning the part which chance has played in the winning of victory and fame: men with their own holidays, their own work-days, and their own periods of mourning; accustomed to command with perfect assurance, and equally ready, if need be, to obey, proud in the one case as in the other, equally serving their own interests: men more imperilled, more productive, more happy! For believe me!—the secret of realising the largest productivity and the greatest enjoyment of existence is *to live in danger!* Build your cities on the slope of Vesuvius! Send your ships into unexplored seas! Live in war with your equals and with yourselves! Be robbers and spoilers, ye knowing ones, as long as ye cannot be rulers and possessors! The time will soon pass when you can be satisfied to live like timorous deer concealed in the forests. Knowledge will finally stretch out her hand for that which belongs to her:—she means to *rule* and *possess,* and you with her!

284.

Belief in Oneself—In general, few men have belief in themselves:—and of those few some are endowed with it as a useful blindness or partial obscuration of intellect (what would they perceive if they could see *to the bottom of themselves!*). The others must first acquire the belief for themselves: everything good, clever, or great that they do, is first of all an argument against the sceptic that dwells in them: the question is how to convince or persuade *this sceptic,* and for that purpose genius almost is needed. They are signally dissatisfied with themselves.

285.

Excelsior!—"Thou wilt never more pray, never more worship, never more repose in infinite trust—thou refusest to stand still and dismiss thy thoughts before an ultimate wisdom, an ultimate virtue, an ultimate power,—thou hast no constant guardian and friend in thy seven solitudes—thou livest without the outlook on a mountain that has snow on its head and fire in its heart—there is no longer any requiter for thee, nor any amender with, his finishing touch—there is no longer any reason in that which happens, or any love in that which will happen to thee—there is no longer any resting-place for thy weary heart, where it has only to find and no longer to seek, thou art opposed to any kind of ultimate peace, thou desirest the eternal recurrence of war and peace:—man of renunciation, wilt thou renounce in all these things? Who will give thee the strength to do so? No one has yet had this strength!"—There is a lake which one day refused to flow away, and threw up a dam at the place where it had hitherto discharged: since then this lake has always risen higher and higher. Perhaps the very renunciation will also furnish us with the strength with which the renunciation itself can be borne; perhaps man will ever rise higher and higher from that point onward, when he no longer *flows out* into a God.

286.

A Digression.—Here are hopes; but what will you see and hear of them, if you have not experienced glance and glow and dawn of day in your own souls? I can only suggest—I cannot do more! To move the stones, to make animals men—would you have me do that? Alas, if you are yet stones and animals, you must seek your Orpheus!

287.

Love of Blindness.—"My thoughts," said the wanderer to his shadow, "ought to show me where I stand, but they should not betray to me *whither I go.* I love ignorance of the future, and do not want to come to grief by impatience and anticipatory tasting of promised things."

288.

Lofty Moods.—It seems to me that most men do not believe in lofty moods, unless it be for the moment, or at the most for a quarter of an hour,—except the few who know by experience a longer duration of high feeling. But to be absolutely a man with a single lofty feeling, the incarnation of a single lofty mood—that has hitherto been only a dream and an enchanting possibility: history does not yet give us any trustworthy example of it Nevertheless one might also some day produce such men—when a multitude of favourable conditions have been created and established, which at present even the happiest chance is unable to throw together. Perhaps that very state which has hitherto entered into our soul as an exception, felt with horror now and then, may be the usual condition of those future souls: a continuous movement between high and low, and the feeling of high and low, a constant state of mounting as on steps, and at the same time reposing as on clouds.

289.

Aboard Ship!—When one considers how a full philosophical justification of his mode of living and thinking operates upon every individual—namely, as a warming, blessing, and fructifying sun, specially shining on him; how it makes him independent of praise and blame, self-sufficient, rich and generous in the bestowal of happiness and kindness; how it unceasingly transforms the evil to the good, brings all the energies to bloom and maturity, and altogether hinders the growth of the greater and lesser weeds of chagrin and discontent —one at last cries out importunately: Oh, that many such new suns were created! The evil man, also, the unfortunate man, and the exceptional man, shall each have his philosophy, his rights, and his sunshine! It is not sympathy with them that is necessary!—we must unlearn this arrogant fancy, notwithstanding that humanity has so long learned it and used it exclusively,—we have not to set up any confessor, exorcist, or pardoner for them! It is a new *justice*, however, that is necessary! And a new solution! And new philosophers! The moral earth also is round! The moral earth also has its antipodes! The antipodes also have their right to exist! there is still another world to discover—and more than one! Aboard ship! ye philosophers!

290.

One Thing is Needful—To "give style" to one's character—that is a grand and a rare art! He who surveys all that his nature presents in its strength and in its weakness, and then fashions it into an ingenious plan, until everything appears artistic and rational, and even the weaknesses enchant the eye—exercises that admirable art. Here there has been a great amount of second nature added, there a portion of first nature has been taken away:—in both cases with long exercise and daily labour at the task. Here the ugly, which does not permit of being taken away, has been concealed, there it has been re-interpreted into the sublime. Much of the vague, which refuses to take form, has been reserved and utilised for the perspectives:—it is meant to give a hint of the remote and immeasurable. In the end, when the work has been completed, it is revealed how it was the constraint of the same taste that organised and fashioned it in whole and in part: whether the taste was good or bad is of less importance than one thinks,—it is sufficient that it was *a taste!*—It will be the strong imperious natures which experience their most refined joy in such constraint, in such confinement and perfection under their own law; the passion of their violent volition lessens at the sight of all disciplined nature, all conquered and ministering nature: even when they have palaces to build and gardens to lay out, it is not to their taste to allow nature to be free.—It is the reverse with weak characters who have not power over themselves, and *hate* the restriction of style: they feel that if this repugnant constraint were laid upon them, they would necessarily become *vulgarised* under it: they become slaves as soon as they serve, they hate service. Such intellects—they may be intellects of the first rank—are always concerned with fashioning and interpreting themselves and their surroundings as *free* nature—wild, arbitrary, fantastic, confused and surprising: and it is well for them to do so, because only in this manner can they please themselves! For one thing is needful: namely, that man should *attain to* satisfaction with himself—be it but through this or that fable and artifice: it is only then that man's aspect is at all endurable! He who is dissatisfied with himself is ever ready to avenge himself on that account: we others will be his victims, if only in having always to endure his ugly aspect. For the aspect of the ugly makes one mean and sad.

291.

Genoa.—I have looked upon this city, its villas and pleasure-grounds, and the wide circuit of its inhabited heights and slopes, for a considerable time: in the end I must say that I see *countenances* out of past generations,—this district is strewn with the images of bold and autocratic men. They have *lived* and have wanted to live on—they say so with their houses, built and decorated for centuries, and not for the passing hour: they were well disposed to life, however ill-disposed they may often have been towards themselves. I always see the builder, how he casts his eye on all that is built around him far and near, and likewise on the city, the sea, and the chain of mountains; how he expresses power and conquest with his gaze: all this he wishes to fit into *his* plan, and in the end make it his *property,* by its becoming a portion of the same. The whole district is overgrown with this superb, insatiable egoism of the desire to possess and exploit; and as these men when abroad recognised no frontiers, and in their thirst for the new placed a new world beside the old, so also at home everyone rose up against everyone else, and devised some mode of expressing his superiority, and of placing between himself and his neighbour his personal illimitableness. Everyone won for himself his home once more by over-powering it with his architectural thoughts, and by transforming it into a delightful sight for his race. When we consider the mode of building cities in the north, the law and the general delight in legality and obedience, impose upon us: we thereby divine the propensity to equality and submission which must have ruled in those builders. Here, however, on turning every corner you find a man by himself, who knows the sea, knows adventure, and knows the Orient, a man who is averse to law and to neighbour, as if it bored him to have to do with them, a man who scans all that is already old and established, with envious glances: with a wonderful craftiness of fantasy, he would like, at least in thought, to establish all this anew, to lay his hand upon it, and introduce his meaning into it—if only for the passing hour of a sunny afternoon, when for once his insatiable and melancholy soul feels satiety, and when only what is his own, and nothing strange, may show itself to his eye.

292.

To the Preachers of Morality.—I do not mean to moralise, but to those who do, I would give this advice: if you mean ultimately to deprive the best things and the best conditions of all honour and worth, continue to speak of them in the same way as heretofore! Put them at the head of your morality, and speak from morning till night of the happiness of virtue, of repose of soul, of righteousness, and of reward and punishment in the nature of things: according as you go on in this manner, all these good things will finally acquire a popularity and a street-cry for themselves: but then all the gold on them will also be worn off, and more besides: all the gold *in them* will have changed into lead. Truly, you understand the reverse art of alchemy, the depreciating of the most valuable things! Try, just for once, another recipe, in order not to realise as hitherto the opposite of what you mean to attain: *deny* those good things, withdraw from them the applause of the populace and discourage the spread of them, make them once more the concealed chastities of solitary souls, and say: *morality is something forbidden!* Perhaps you will thus attract to your cause the sort of men who are only of any account, I mean the *heroic*. But then there must be something formidable in it, and not as hitherto something disgusting I Might one not be inclined to say at present with reference to morality what Master Eckardt says: "I pray God to deliver me from God!"

293.

Our Atmosphere.—We know it well: in him who only casts a glance now and then at science, as when taking a walk (in the manner of women, and alas! also like many artists), the strictness in its service, its inexorability in small matters as well as in great, its rapidity in weighing, judging and condemning, produce something of a feeling of giddiness and fright. It is especially terrifying to him that the hardest is here demanded, that the best is done without the reward of praise or distinction; it is rather as among soldiers—almost nothing but blame and sharp reprimand *is heard*; for doing well prevails here as the rule, doing ill as the exception; the rule, however, has, here as everywhere, a silent tongue. It is the same with this "severity of science" as with the manners and politeness of the best society: it frightens the uninitiated. He, however, who is accustomed to it, does not like to live anywhere but in this clear, transparent, powerful, and highly electrified atmosphere, this *manly* atmosphere. Anywhere else it is not pure and airy enough for him: he suspects that *there* his best art would neither be properly advantageous to anyone else, nor a delight to himself, that through misunderstandings half of his life would slip through his fingers, that much foresight, much concealment, and reticence would constantly be necessary,—nothing but great and useless losses of power! In *this* keen and clear element, however, he has his entire power: here he can fly! Why should he again go down into those muddy waters where he has to swim and wade and soil his wings!—No! There it is too hard for us to live! we cannot help it that we are born for the atmosphere, the pure atmosphere, we rivals of the ray of light; and that we should like best to ride like it on the atoms of ether, not away from the

sun, but *towards the sun!* That, however, we cannot do:—so we want to do the only
thing that is in our power: namely, to bring light to the earth, we want to be "the
light of the earth!" And for that purpose we have our wings and our swiftness and
our severity, on that account we are manly, and even terrible like the fire. Let those
fear us, who do not know how to warm and brighten themselves by our influence!

294.

Against the Disparagers of Nature.—They are disagreeable to me, those men in
whom every natural inclination forthwith becomes a disease, something disfiguring,
or even disgraceful. They have seduced us to the opinion that the inclinations and
impulses of men are evil; *they* are the cause of our great injustice to our own nature,
and to all nature! There are enough of men who *may* yield to their impulses gracefully
and carelessly: but they do not do so, for fear of that imaginary "evil thing" in nature!
That is the cause why there is so little nobility to be found among men: the indication
of which will always be to have no fear of oneself, to expect nothing disgraceful from
oneself, to fly without hesitation whithersoever we are impelled—we free-born
birds! Wherever we come, there will always be freedom and sunshine around us.

295.

Short-lived Habits.—I love short-lived habits, and regard them as an invaluable
means for getting a knowledge of *many* things and various conditions, to the very
bottom of their sweetness and bitterness; my nature is altogether arranged for
short-lived habits, even in the needs of its bodily health, and in general, *as far as* I
can see, from the lowest up to the highest matters. I always think that *this* will at last
satisfy me permanently (the short-lived habit has also this characteristic belief of
passion, the belief in everlasting duration; I am to be envied for having found it and
recognised it), and then it nourishes me at noon and at eve, and spreads a profound
satisfaction around me and in me, so that I have no longing for anything else, not
needing to compare, or despise, or hate. But one day the habit has had its time: the
good thing separates from me, not as something which then inspires disgust in
me—but peaceably, and as though satisfied with me, as I am with it; as if we had to
be mutually thankful, and *thus* shook hands for farewell. And already the new habit
waits at the door, and similarly also my belief—indestructible fool and sage that I
am!—that this new habit will be the right one, the ultimate right one. So it is with
me as regards foods, thoughts, men, cities, poems, music, doctrines, arrangements
of the day, and modes of life.—On the other hand, I hate *permanent* habits, and feel
as if a tyrant came into my neighbourhood, and as if my life's breath *condensed*, when
events take such a form that permanent habits seem necessarily to grow out of them:

for example, through an official position, through constant companionship with the same persons, through a settled abode, or through a uniform state of health. Indeed, from the bottom of my soul I am gratefully disposed to all my misery and sickness, and to whatever is imperfect in me, because such things leave me a hundred back-doors through which I can escape from permanent habits. The most unendurable thing, to be sure, the really terrible thing, would be a life without habits, a life which continually required improvisation:—that would be my banishment and my Siberia.

296.

A Fixed Reputation.—A fixed reputation was formerly a matter of the very greatest utility; and wherever society continues to be ruled by the herd-instinct, it is still most suitable for every individual *to give* to his character and business *the appearance* of unalterableness,—even when they are not so in reality. "One can rely on him, he remains the same"—that is the praise which has most significance in all dangerous conditions of society. Society feels with satisfaction that it has a reliable *tool* ready at all times in the virtue of this one, in the ambition of that one, and in the reflection and passion of a third one,—it honours this *tool-like nature*, this self-constancy, this unchangeableness in opinions, efforts, and even in faults, with the highest honours. Such a valuation, which prevails and has prevailed everywhere simultaneously with the morality of custom, educates "characters," and brings all changing, re-learning, and self-transforming into *disrepute.* Be the advantage of this mode of thinking ever so great otherwise, it is in any case the mode of judging which is most injurious *to knowledge:* for precisely the good-will of the knowing one ever to declare himself unhesitatingly as *opposed* to his former opinions, and in general to be distrustful of all that wants to be fixed in him—is here condemned and brought into disrepute. The disposition of the thinker, as incompatible with a "fixed reputation," is regarded as *dishonourable,* while the petrifaction of opinions has all the honour to itself:—we have at present still to live under the interdict of such rules! How difficult it is to live when one feels that the judgment of many millenniums is around one and against one. It is probable that for many millenniums knowledge was afflicted with a bad conscience, and there must have been much self-contempt and secret misery in the history of the greatest intellects.

297.

Ability to Contradict—Everyone knows at present that the ability, to endure contradiction is a good indication of culture. Some people even know that the higher man courts opposition, and provokes it, so as to get a cue to his hitherto unknown partiality. But the *ability* to contradict, the attainment of a *good* conscience in hostility to the accustomed, the traditional and the hallowed,—that is more than both the above-named abilities, and is the really great, new and astonishing thing in our culture, the step of all steps of the emancipated intellect: who knows that?—

298.

A Sigh.—I caught this notion on the way, and rapidly took the readiest, poor words to hold it fast, so that it might not again fly away. But it has died in these dry words, and hangs and flaps about in them—and now I hardly know, when I look upon it, how I could have had such happiness when I caught this bird.

299.

What one should Learn from Artists.—What means have we for making things beautiful, attractive, and desirable, when they are not so?—and I suppose they are never so in themselves! We have here something to learn from physicians, when, for example, they dilute what is bitter, or put wine and sugar into their mixing-bowl; but we have still more to learn from artists, who in fact, are continually concerned in devising such inventions and artifices. To withdraw from things until one no longer sees much of them, until one has even to see things into them, *in order to see them at all*—or to view them from the side, and as in a frame—or to place them so that they partly disguise themselves and only permit of perspective views—or to look at them through coloured glasses, or in the light of the sunset—or to furnish them with a surface or skin which is not fully transparent: we should learn all this from artists, and moreover be wiser than they. For this fine power of theirs usually ceases with them where art ceases and life begins; *we*, however, want to be the poets of our lives, and first of all in the smallest and most commonplace matters.

300.

Prelude to Science.—Do you believe then that the sciences would have arisen and grown up if the sorcerers, alchemists, astrologers and witches had not been their forerunners; those who, with their promisings and foreshadowings, had first to create a thirst, a hunger, and a taste for *hidden and forbidden* powers? Yea, that infinitely more had to be *promised* than could ever be fulfilled, in order that something might be fulfilled in the domain of knowledge? Perhaps the whole of *religion*, also, may appear to some distant age as an exercise and a prelude, in like manner as the prelude and preparation of science here exhibit themselves, though *not* at all practised and regarded as such. Perhaps religion may have been the peculiar means for enabling individual men to enjoy but once the entire self-satisfaction of a God and all his self-redeeming power. Indeed!—one may ask—would man have learned at all to get on the tracks of hunger and thirst for *himself*, and to extract satiety and fullness out of *himself,* without that religious schooling and preliminary history? Had Prometheus first to *fancy* that he had *stolen* the light, and that he did penance for the theft,—in order finally to discover that he had created the light, *in that he had longed for the light,* and that not only man, but also *God,* had been the work of *his* hands and the clay in his hands? All mere creations of the creator?—just as the illusion, the theft, the Caucasus, the vulture, and the whole tragic Prometheia of all thinkers?

301.

Illusion of the Contemplative.—Higher men are distinguished from lower, by seeing and hearing immensely more, and in a thoughtful manner—and it is precisely this that distinguishes man from the animal, and the higher animal from the lower. The world always becomes fuller for him who grows up to the full stature of humanity; there are always more interesting fishing-hooks, thrown out to him; the number of his stimuli is continually on the increase, and similarly the varieties of his pleasure and pain,—the higher man becomes always at the same time happier and unhappier. An *illusion,* however, is his constant accompaniment all along: he thinks he is placed as a *spectator* and *auditor* before the great pantomime and concert of life; he calls his nature a *contemplative nature,* and thereby overlooks the fact that he himself is also a real creator, and continuous poet of life,—that he no doubt differs greatly from the *actor* in this drama, the so-called practical man, but differs still more from a mere onlooker or spectator *before* the stage. There is certainly *vis contemplativa,* and re-examination of his work peculiar to him as poet, but at the same time, and first and foremost, he has the *vis creativa,* which the practical man or doer *lacks,* whatever appearance and current belief may say to the contrary. It is we, who think and feel, that actually and unceasingly *make* something which did not before exist: the whole eternally increasing world of valuations, colours, weights, perspectives, gradations, affirmations and negations. This composition of ours is continually learnt, practised, and translated into flesh and actuality, and even into the commonplace, by the so-called practical men (our actors, as we have said). Whatever has *value* in the present world, has not it in itself, by its nature,—nature is always worthless:—but a value was once given to it, bestowed upon it and it was *we* who gave and bestowed! We only have created the world *which is of any account to man!*—But it is precisely this knowledge that we lack, and when we get hold of it for a moment we have forgotten it the next: we misunderstand our highest power, we contemplative men, and estimate ourselves at too low a rate,—we are neither as *proud nor as happy* as we might be.

302.

The Danger of the Happiest Ones.—To have fine senses and a fine taste; to be accustomed to the select and the intellectually best as our proper and readiest fare; to be blessed with a strong, bold, and daring soul; to go through life with a quiet eye and a firm step, ever ready for the worst as for a festival, and full of longing for undiscovered worlds and seas, men and Gods; to listen to all joyous music, as if there perhaps brave men, soldiers and seafarers, took a brief repose and enjoyment, and in the profoundest pleasure of the moment were overcome with tears and the whole purple melancholy of happiness: who would not like all this to be *his* possession, his condition! It was the *happiness of Homer*! The condition of him who invented the Gods for the Greeks,—nay, who invented *his* Gods for himself! But let us not conceal the fact that with this happiness of Homer in one's soul, one is more liable to suffering than any other creature under the sun! And only at this price do we purchase the most precious pearl that the waves of existence have hitherto washed ashore! As its possessor one always becomes more sensitive to pain, and at last too sensitive: a little displeasure and loathing sufficed in the end to make Homer disgusted with life. He was unable to solve a foolish little riddle which some young fishers proposed to him! Yes, the little riddles are the dangers of the happiest ones!—

303.

Two Happy Ones.—Certainly this man, notwithstanding his youth, understands the *improvisation of life*, and astonishes even the acutest observers. For it seems that he never makes a mistake, although he constantly plays the most hazardous games. One is reminded of the improvising masters of the musical art, to whom even the listeners would fain ascribe a divine *infallibility* of the hand, notwithstanding that they now and then make a mistake, as every mortal is liable to do. But they are skilled and inventive, and always ready in a moment to arrange into the structure of the score the most accidental tone (where the jerk of a finger or a humour brings it about), and to animate the accident with a fine meaning and soul.—Here is quite a different man: everything that he intends and plans fails with him in the long run. That on which he has now and again set his heart has already brought him several times to the abyss, and to the very verge of ruin; and if he has as yet got out of the scrape, it certainly has not been merely with a "black eye." Do you think he is unhappy over it? He resolved long ago not to regard his own wishes and plans as of so much importance. "If this does not succeed with me," he says to himself, "perhaps that will succeed; and on the whole I do not know but that I am under more obligation to thank my failures than any of my successes. Am I made to be headstrong, and to wear the bull's horns? That which constitutes the worth and the sum of life *for me*, lies somewhere else; I know more of life, because I have been so often on the point of losing it; and just on that account I *have* more of life than any of you!"

304.

In Doing we Leave Undone.—In the main all those moral systems are distasteful to me which say: "Do not do this! Renounce! Overcome thyself!" On the other hand I am favourable to those moral systems which stimulate me to do something, and to do it again from morning till evening, to dream of it at night, and think of nothing else but to do it *well*, as well as is possible for *me* alone! From him who so lives there fall off one after the other the things that do not pertain to such a life: without hatred or antipathy, he sees *this* take leave of him to-day, and *that* to-morrow, like the yellow leaves which every livelier breeze strips from the tree: or he does not see at all that they take leave of him, so firmly is his eye fixed upon his goal, and generally forward, not sideways, backward, or downward. "Our doing must determine what we leave undone; in that we do, we leave undone"—so it pleases me, so runs *my placitum*. But I do not mean to strive with open eyes for my impoverishment; I do not like any of the negative virtues whose very essence is negation and self-renunciation.

305.

Self-control—Those moral teachers who first and foremost order man to get himself into his own power, induce thereby a curious infirmity in him—namely, a constant sensitiveness with reference to all natural strivings and inclinations, and as it were, a sort of itching. Whatever may henceforth drive him, draw him, allure or impel him, whether internally or externally—it always seems to this sensitive being as if his self-control were in danger: he is no longer at liberty to trust himself to any instinct, to any free flight, but stands constantly with defensive mien, armed against himself, with sharp distrustful eye, the eternal watcher of his stronghold, to which office he has appointed himself. Yes, he can be *great* in that position! But how unendurable he has now become to others, how difficult even for himself to bear, how impoverished and cut off from the finest accidents of his soul! Yea, even from all further *instruction!* For we must be able to lose ourselves at times, if we want to learn something of what we have not in ourselves.

306.

Stoic and Epicurean.—The Epicurean selects the situations, the persons, and even the events which suits his extremely sensitive, intellectual constitution; he renounces the rest—that is to say, by far the greater part of experience—because it would be too strong and too heavy fare for him. The Stoic, on the contrary, accustoms himself to swallow stones and vermin, glass-splinters and scorpions, without feeling any disgust: his stomach is meant to become indifferent in the end to all that the accidents of existence cast into it:—he reminds one of the Arabic sect of the Assaua, with which the French became acquainted in Algiers; and like those insensible persons, he also likes well to have an invited public at the exhibition of his insensibility, the very thing the Epicurean willingly dispenses with:—he has of course his "garden"! Stoicism may be quite advisable for men with whom fate improvises, for those who live in violent times and are dependent on abrupt and changeable individuals. He, however, who *anticipates* that fate will permit him to spin "a long thread," does well to make his arrangements in Epicurean fashion; all men devoted to intellectual labour have done it hitherto! For it would be a supreme loss to them to forfeit their fine sensibility, and to acquire the hard, stoical hide with hedgehog prickles in exchange.

307.

In Favour of Criticism.—Something now appears to thee as an error which thou formerly lovedst as a truth, or as a probability: thou pushest it from thee and imaginest that thy reason has there gained a victory. But perhaps that error was then, when thou wast still another person—thou art always another person,—just as necessary to thee as all thy present "truths," like a skin, as it were, which concealed and veiled from thee much which thou still mayst not see. Thy new life, and not thy reason, has slain that opinion for thee: *thou dost not require it any longer,* and now it breaks down of its own accord, and the irrationality crawls out of it as a worm into the light. When we make use of criticism it is not something arbitrary and impersonal,—it is, at least very often, a proof that there are lively, active forces in us, which cast a skin. We deny, and must deny, because something in us *wants* to live and affirm itself, something which we perhaps do not as yet know, do not as yet see!—So much in favour of criticism.

308.

The History of each Day.—What is it that constitutes the history of each day for thee? Look at thy habits of which it consists: are they the product of numberless little acts of cowardice and laziness, or of thy bravery and inventive reason? Although the two cases are so different, it is possible that men might bestow the same praise upon thee, and that thou mightst also be equally useful to them in the one case as in the other. But praise and utility and respectability may suffice for him whose only desire is to have a good conscience,—not however for thee, the "trier of the reins," who hast a *consciousness of the conscience!*

309.

Out of the Seventh Solitude.—One day the wanderer shut a door behind him, stood still, and wept. Then he said: "Oh, this inclination and impulse towards the true, the real, the non-apparent, the certain! How I detest it! Why does this gloomy and passionate taskmaster follow just *me?* I should like to rest, but it does not permit me to do so. Are there not a host of things seducing me to tarry! Everywhere there are gardens of Armida for me, and therefore there will ever be fresh separations and fresh bitterness of heart! I must set my foot forward, my weary wounded foot: and because I feel I must do this, I often cast grim glances back at the most beautiful things which could not detain me—*because* they could not detain me!"

310.

Will and Wave.—How eagerly this wave comes hither, as if it were a question of its reaching something! How it creeps with frightful haste into the innermost corners of the rocky cliff! It seems that it wants to forestall some one; it seems that something is concealed there that has value, high value.—And now it retreats somewhat more slowly, still quite white with excitement,—is it disappointed? Has it found what it sought? Does it merely pretend to be disappointed?—But already another wave approaches, still more eager and wild than the first, and its soul also seems to be full of secrets, and of longing for treasure-seeking. Thus live the waves,—thus live we who exercise will!—I do not say more.—But what! Ye distrust me? Ye are angry at me, ye beautiful monsters? Do ye fear that I will quite betray your secret? Well! Just be angry with me, raise your green, dangerous bodies as high as ye can, make a wall between me and the sun—as at present! Verily, there is now nothing more left of the world save green twilight and green lightning-flashes. Do as ye will, ye wanton creatures, roar with delight and wickedness—or dive under again, pour your emeralds down into the depths, and cast your endless white tresses of foam and spray over them—it is all the same to me, for all is so well with you, and I am so pleased with you for it all: how could I betray *you!* For—take this to heart!—I know you and your secret, I know your race! You and I are indeed of one race! You and I have indeed one secret!

311.

Broken Lights.—We are not always brave, and when we are weary, people of our stamp are liable to lament occasionally in this wise:—"It is so hard to cause pain to men—oh, that it should be necessary! What good is it to live concealed, when we do not want to keep to ourselves that which causes vexation? Would it not be more advisable to live in the madding crowd, and compensate individuals for sins that are committed, and must be committed, against mankind in general? Foolish with fools, vain with the vain, enthusiastic with enthusiasts? Would that not be reasonable when there is such an inordinate amount of divergence in the main? When I hear of the malignity of others against me—is not my first feeling that of satisfaction? It is well that it should be so!—I seem to myself to say to them—I am so little in harmony with you, and have so much truth on my side: see henceforth that ye be merry at my expense as often as ye can! Here are my defects and mistakes, here are my illusions, my bad taste, my confusion, my tears, my vanity, my owlish concealment, my contradictions! Here you have something to laugh at! Laugh then, and enjoy yourselves! I am not averse to the law and nature of things, which is that defects and errors should give pleasure!—To be sure, there were once 'more glorious' times, when as soon as any one got an idea, however moderately new it might be, he would think himself so *indispensable* as to go out into the street with it, and call to everybody: 'Behold! the kingdom of heaven is at hand!'—I should not miss myself, if I were a-wanting. We are none of us indispensable!"—As we have said, however, we do not think thus when we are brave; we do not think *about it* at all.

312.

My Dog.—I have given a name to my pain, and call it "a dog,"—it is just as faithful, just as importunate and shameless, just as entertaining, just as wise, as any other dog—and I can domineer over it, and vent my bad humour on it, as others do with their dogs, servants, and wives.

313.

No Picture of a Martyr.—I will take my cue from Raphael, and not paint any more martyr-pictures. There are enough of sublime things without its being necessary to seek sublimity where it is linked with cruelty; moreover my ambition would not be gratified in the least if I aspired to be a sublime executioner.

314.

New Domestic Animals.—I want to have my lion and my eagle about me, that I may always have hints and premonitions concerning the amount of my strength or weakness. Must I look down on them to-day, and be afraid of them? And will the hour come once more when they will look up to me, and tremble?—

315.

The Last Hour.—Storms are my danger. Shall I have my storm in which I perish, as Oliver Cromwell perished in his storm? Or shall I go out as a light does, not first blown out by the wind, but grown tired and weary of itself—a burnt-out light? Or finally, shall I blow myself out, so as *not to burn out?*

316.

Prophetic Men.—Ye cannot divine how sorely prophetic men suffer: ye think only that a fine "gift" has been given to them, and would fain have it yourselves,—but I will express my meaning by a simile. How much may not the animals suffer from the electricity of the atmosphere and the clouds! Some of them, as we see, have a prophetic faculty with regard to the weather, for example, apes (as one can observe very well even in Europe,—and not only in menageries, but at Gibraltar). But it never occurs to us that it is their *sufferings*—that are their prophets! When strong positive electricity, under the influence of an approaching cloud not at all visible, is suddenly converted into negative electricity, and an alteration of the weather is imminent, these animals then behave as if an enemy were approaching them, and prepare for defence, or flight: they generally hide themselves,—they do not think of the bad weather as weather, but as an enemy whose hand they already *feel!*

317.

Retrospect.—We seldom become conscious of the real pathos of any period of life as such, as long as we continue in it, but always think it is the only possible and reasonable thing for us henceforth, and that it is altogether *ethos* and not *pathos*[11]—to speak and distinguish like the Greeks. A few notes of music to-day recalled a winter and a house, and a life of utter solitude to my mind, and at the same time the sentiments in which I then lived: I thought I should be able to live in such a state always. But now I understand that it was entirely pathos and passion, something comparable to this painfully bold and truly comforting music,—it is not one's lot to have these sensations for years, still less for eternities: otherwise one would become too "ethereal" for this planet.

318.

Wisdom in Pain.—In pain there is as much wisdom as in pleasure: like the latter it is one of the best self-preservatives of a species. Were it not so, pain would long ago have been done away with; that it is hurtful is no argument against it, for to be hurtful is its very essence. In pain I hear the commanding call of the ship's captain: "Take in sail!" "Man," the bold seafarer, must have learned to set his sails in a thousand different ways, otherwise he could not have sailed long, for the ocean would soon have swallowed him up. We must also know how to live with reduced energy: as

---

[11]This poem is a parody of the "Chorus Mysticus" which concludes the second part of Goethe's "Faust." Bayard Taylor's translation of the passage in "Faust" runs as follows:—

soon as pain gives its precautionary signal, it is time to reduce the speed—some great danger, some storm, is approaching, and we do well to "catch" as little wind as possible—It is true that there are men who, on the approach of severe pain, hear the very opposite call of command, and never appear more proud, more martial, or more happy than when the storm is brewing; indeed, pain itself provides them with their supreme moments! These are the heroic men, the great *pain-bringers* of mankind: those few and rare ones who need just the same apology as pain generally,—and verily, it should not be denied them! They are forces of the greatest importance for preserving and advancing the species, be it only because they are opposed to smug ease, and do not conceal their disgust at this kind of happiness.

319.

As Interpreters of our Experiences.—One form of honesty has always been lacking among founders of religions and their kin:—they have never made their experiences a matter of the intellectual conscience. "What did I really experience? What then took place in me and around me? Was my understanding clear enough? Was my will directly opposed to all deception of the senses, and courageous in its defence against fantastic notions?"—None of them ever asked these questions, nor to this day do any of the good religious people ask them. They have rather a thirst for things which are *contrary to reason*, and they don't want to have too much difficulty in satisfying this thirst,—so they experience "miracles" and "regenerations," and hear the voices of angels! But we who are different, who are thirsty for reason, want to look as carefully into our experiences as in the case of a scientific experiment, hour by hour, day by day! We ourselves want to be our own experiments, and our own subjects of experiment.

320.

On Meeting Again.—A: Do I quite understand you? You are in search of something? *Where*, in the midst of the present, actual world, is *your* niche and star? Where can *you* lay yourself in the sun, so that you also may have a surplus of well-being, that your existence may justify itself? Let everyone do that for himself—you seem to say, —and let him put talk about generalities, concern for others and society, out of his mind!—B: I want more; I am no seeker. I want to create my own sun for myself.

321.

A New Precaution.—Let us no longer think so much about punishing, blaming, and improving! We shall seldom be able to alter an individual, and if we should succeed in doing so, something else may also succeed, perhaps unawares: *we* may have been altered by him! Let us rather see to it that our own influence on *all that is to come* outweighs and overweighs his influence! Let us not struggle in direct conflict!—all blaming, punishing, and desire to improve comes under this category. But let us elevate ourselves all the higher! Let us ever give to our pattern more shining colours! Let us obscure, the other by our light! No! We do not mean to become *darker* ourselves on his account, like those who punish and are discontented! Let us rather go aside! Let us look away!

322.

A Simile.—Those thinkers in whom all the stars move in cyclic orbits, are not the most profound. He who looks into himself, as into an immense universe, and carries Milky Ways in himself, knows also how irregular all Milky Ways are; they lead into the very chaos and labyrinth of existence.

323.

Happiness in Destiny.—Destiny confers its greatest distinction upon us when it has made us fight for a time on the side of our adversaries. We are thereby *predestined* to a great victory.

324.

In Media Vita.—No! Life has not deceived me! On the contrary, from year to year I find it richer, more desirable and more mysterious—from the day on which the great liberator broke my fetters, the thought that life may be an experiment of the thinker—and not a duty, not a fatality, not a deceit!—And knowledge itself may be for others something different; for example, a bed of ease, or the path to a bed of ease, or an entertainment, or a course of idling,—for me it is a world of dangers and victories, in which even the heroic sentiments have their arena and dancing-floor. *"Life as a means to knowledge"*—with this principle in one's heart, one can not only be brave, but can even *live joyfully and laugh joyfully!* And who could know how to laugh well and live well, who did not first understand the full significance of war and victory?

325.

What Belongs to Greatness.—Who can attain to anything great if he does not feel in himself the force and will *to inflict* great pain? The ability to suffer is a small matter: in that line, weak women and even slaves often attain masterliness. But not to perish from internal distress and doubt when one inflicts great suffering and hears the cry of it—that is great, that belongs to greatness.

326.

Physicians of the Soul and Pain.—All preachers of morality, as also all theologians, have a bad habit in common: all of them try to persuade man that he is very ill, and that a severe, final, radical cure is necessary. And because mankind as a whole has for centuries listened too eagerly to those teachers, something of the superstition that the human race is in a very bad way has actually come over men: so that they are now far too ready to sigh; they find nothing more in life and make melancholy faces at each other, as if life were indeed very hard *to endure*. In truth, they are inordinately assured of their life and in love with it, and full of untold intrigues and subtleties for suppressing everything disagreeable, and for extracting the thorn from pain and misfortune. It seems to me that people always speak *with exaggeration* about pain and misfortune, as if it were a matter of good behaviour to exaggerate here: on the other hand people are intentionally silent in regard to the number of expedients for alleviating pain; as for instance, the deadening of it, feverish flurry of thought, a peaceful position, or good and bad reminiscences, intentions, and hopes,—also many kinds of pride and fellow-feeling, which have almost the effect of anæsthetics: while in the greatest degree of pain fainting takes place of itself. We understand very well how to pour sweetness on our bitterness, especially on the bitterness of our soul; we find a remedy in our bravery and sublimity, as well as in the nobler delirium of submission and resignation. A loss scarcely remains a loss for an hour: in some way or other a gift from heaven has always fallen into our lap at the same moment—a new form of strength, for example: be it but a new opportunity for the exercise of strength! What have the preachers of morality not dreamt concerning the inner "misery" of evil men! What *lies* have they not told us about the misfortunes of impassioned men! Yes, lying is here the right word: they were only too well aware of the overflowing happiness of this kind of man, but they kept silent as death about it; because it was a refutation of their theory, according to which happiness only originates through the annihilation of the passions and the silencing of the will! And finally, as regards the recipe of all those physicians of the soul and their recommendation of a severe radical cure, we may be allowed to ask: Is our life really painful and burdensome enough for us to exchange it with advantage for a Stoical mode of living, and Stoical petrification? We do *not feel sufficiently miserable* to have to feel ill in the Stoical fashion!

327.

Taking Things Seriously.—The intellect is with most people an awkward, obscure and creaking machine, which is difficult to set in motion: they call it "*taking a thing seriously*" when they work with this machine and want to think well—oh, how burdensome must good thinking be to them! That delightful animal, man, seems to lose his good-humour whenever he thinks well; he becomes "serious"! And "where there is laughing and gaiety, thinking cannot be worth anything: "—so speaks the prejudice of this serious animal against all "Joyful Wisdom."—Well, then! Let us show that it is prejudice!

328.

Doing Harm to Stupidity.—It is certain that the belief in the reprehensibility of egoism, preached with such stubbornness and conviction, has on the whole done harm to egoism (*in favour of the herd-instinct,* as I shall repeat a hundred times!), especially by depriving it of a good conscience, and by bidding us seek in it the source of all misfortune. "Thy selfishness is the bane of thy life"—so rang the preaching for millenniums: it did harm, as we have said, to selfishness, and deprived it of much spirit, much cheerfulness, much ingenuity, and much beauty; it stultified and deformed and poisoned selfishness!—Philosophical antiquity, on the other hand, taught that there was another principal source of evil: from Socrates downwards, the thinkers were never weary of preaching that "your thoughtlessness and stupidity, your unthinking way of living according to rule, and your subjection to the opinion of your neighbour, are the reasons why you so seldom attain to happiness,—we thinkers are, as thinkers, the happiest of mortals." Let us not decide here whether this preaching against stupidity was more sound than the preaching against selfishness; it is certain, however, that stupidity was thereby deprived of its good conscience:—those philosophers *did harm to stupidity.*

329.

Leisure and Idleness.—There is an Indian savagery, a savagery peculiar to the Indian blood, in the manner in which the Americans strive after gold: and the breathless hurry of their work—the characteristic vice of the new world—already begins to infect old Europe, and makes it savage also, spreading over it a strange lack of intellectuality. One is now ashamed of repose: even long reflection almost causes remorse of conscience. Thinking is done with a stop-watch, as dining is done with the eyes fixed on the financial newspaper; we live like men who are continually "afraid of letting opportunities slip." "Better do anything whatever, than nothing"—this principle also is a noose with which all culture and all higher taste may be strangled. And just as all form obviously disappears in this hurry of workers, so the sense for form itself, the ear and the eye for the melody of movement, also disappear. The proof of this is the *clumsy perspicuity* which is now everywhere demanded in all positions where a person would like to be sincere with his fellows, in intercourse with friends, women, relatives, children, teachers, pupils, leaders and princes,—one has no longer either time or energy for ceremonies, for roundabout courtesies, for any *esprit* in conversation, or for any *otium* whatever. For life in the hunt for gain continually compels a person to consume his intellect, even to exhaustion, in constant dissimulation, overreaching, or forestalling: the real virtue nowadays is to do something in a shorter time than another person. And so there are only rare hours of sincere intercourse *permitted:* in them, however, people are tired, and would not only like "to let themselves go," but *to stretch their legs* out wide in awkward style. The way people write their *letters* nowadays is quite in keeping with the age; their style and spirit will always be the true "sign of the times." If there be still enjoyment in society and in art, it is enjoyment such as over-worked slaves provide for themselves. Oh, this moderation in "joy" of our cultured and uncultured classes! Oh, this increasing suspiciousness of all enjoyment! *Work* is winning over more and more the good conscience to its side: the desire for enjoyment already calls itself "need of recreation," and even begins to be ashamed of itself. "One owes it to one's health," people say, when they are caught at a picnic. Indeed, it might soon go so far that one could not yield to the desire for the *vita contemplativa* (that is to say, excursions with thoughts and friends), without self-contempt and a bad conscience.—Well! Formerly it was the very reverse: it was "action" that suffered from a bad conscience. A man of good family *concealed* his work when need compelled him to labour. The slave laboured under the weight of the feeling that he did something contemptible:—the "doing" itself was something contemptible. "Only in *otium* and *bellum* is there nobility and honour:" so rang the voice of ancient prejudice!

330.

Applause.—The thinker does not need applause or the clapping of hands, provided he be sure of the clapping of his own hands: the latter, however, he cannot do without. Are there men who could also do without this, and in general without any kind of applause? I doubt it: and even as regards the wisest, Tacitus, who is no calumniator of the wise, says: *quando etiam sapientibus gloriæ cupido novissima exuitur*—that means with him: never.

331.

Better Deaf than Deafened.—Formerly a person wanted to have his *calling*, but that no longer suffices to-day, for the market has become too large,—there has now to be *bawling*. The consequence is that even good throats outcry each other, and the best wares are offered for sale with hoarse voices; without market-place bawling and hoarseness there is now no longer any genius.—It is, sure enough, an evil age for the thinker: he has to learn to find his stillness betwixt two noises, and has to pretend to be deaf until he finally becomes so. As long as he has not learned this, he is in danger of perishing from impatience and headaches.

332.

The Evil Hour.—There has perhaps been an evil hour for every philosopher, in which he thought: What do I matter, if people should not believe my poor arguments!—And then some malicious bird has flown past him and twittered: "What do you matter? What do you matter?"

333.

What does Knowing Mean?—*Non ridere, non lugere, neque detestari, sed intelligere!* says Spinoza, so simply and sublimely, as is his wont. Nevertheless, what else is this *intelligere* ultimately, but just the form in which the three other things become perceptible to us all at once? A result of the diverging and opposite impulses of desiring to deride, lament and execrate? Before knowledge is possible each of these impulses must first have brought forward its one-sided view of the object or event. The struggle of these one-sided views occurs afterwards, and out of it there occasionally arises a compromise, a pacification, a recognition of rights on all three sides, a sort of justice and agreement: for in virtue of the justice and agreement all those impulses can maintain themselves in existence and retain their mutual rights. We, to whose consciousness only the closing reconciliation scenes and final settling of accounts of these long processes manifest themselves, think on that account that *intelligere* is something conciliating, just and good, something essentially antithetical to the impulses; whereas it is only *a certain relation of the impulses to one another.* For a very long time conscious thinking was regarded as the only thinking: it is now only that the truth dawns upon us that the greater part of our intellectual activity goes on unconsciously and unfelt by us; I believe, however, that the impulses which are here in mutual conflict understand rightly how to make themselves felt by *one another,* and how to cause pain:—the violent sudden exhaustion which overtakes all thinkers, may have its origin here (it is the exhaustion of the battle-field). Aye, perhaps in our struggling interior there is much concealed *heroism,* but certainly nothing divine, or eternally-reposing-in-itself, as Spinoza supposed. *Conscious* thinking, and especially that of the philosopher, is the weakest, and on that account also the relatively mildest and quietest mode of thinking: and thus it is precisely the philosopher who is most easily misled concerning the nature of knowledge.

334.

One must Learn to Love.—This is our experience in music: we must first *learn* in general *to hear,* to hear fully, and to distinguish a theme or a melody, we have to isolate and limit it as a life by itself; then we need to exercise effort and good-will in order *to endure* it in spite of its strangeness we need patience towards its aspect and expression and indulgence towards what is odd in it:—in the end there comes a moment when we are *accustomed* to it, when we expect it, when it dawns upon us that we should miss it if it were lacking; and then it goes on to exercise its spell and charm more and more, and does not cease until we have become its humble and enraptured lovers, who want it, and want it again, and ask for nothing better from the world.—It is thus with us, however, not only in music: it is precisely thus that we have *learned to love* everything that we love. We are always finally recompensed for our good-will, our patience reasonableness and gentleness towards what is unfamiliar, by the unfamiliar slowly throwing off its veil and presenting itself to us as a new, ineffable beauty:—that is its *thanks* for our hospitality. He also who loves himself must have learned it in this way: there is no other way. Love also has to be learned.

335.

Cheers for Physics!—How many men are there who know how to observe? And among the few who do know,—how many observe themselves? "Everyone is furthest from himself"—all the "triers of the reins" know that to their discomfort; and the saying, "Know thyself," in the mouth of a God and spoken to man, is almost a mockery. But that the case of self-observation is so desperate, is attested best of all by the manner in which *almost everybody* talks of the nature of a moral action, that prompt, willing, convinced, loquacious manner, with its look, its smile, and its pleasing eagerness! Everyone seems inclined to say to you: "Why, my dear Sir, that is precisely *my* affair! You address yourself with your question to him who *is authorised* to answer, for I happen to be wiser with regard to this matter than in anything else. Therefore, when a man decides that '*this is right*,' when he accordingly concludes that '*it must therefore be done,* and thereupon *does* what he has thus recognised as right and designated as necessary—then the nature of his action is *moral!*" But, my friend, you are talking to me about three actions instead of one: your deciding, for instance, that "this is right," is also an action,—could one not judge either morally or immorally? *Why* do you regard this, and just this, as right?—"Because my conscience tells me so; conscience never speaks immorally, indeed it determines in the first place what shall be moral!"—But why do you *listen* to the voice of your conscience? And in how far are you justified in regarding such a judgment as true and infallible? This *belief*—is there no further conscience for it? Do you know nothing of an intellectual conscience? A conscience behind your "conscience"? Your decision, "this is right," has a previous history in your impulses, your likes and dislikes, your experiences and non-experiences; "*how* has it originated?" you must ask, and afterwards the further question: "*what* really impels me to give ear to it?" You can listen to its command like a brave soldier who hears the command of his officer. Or like a woman who loves him who commands. Or like a flatterer and coward, afraid of the commander. Or like a blockhead who follows because he has nothing to say to the contrary. In short, you can give ear to your conscience in a hundred different ways. But *that* you hear this or that judgment as the voice of conscience, consequently, *that* you feel a thing to be right—may have its cause in the fact that you have never thought about your nature, and have blindly accepted from your childhood what has been designated to you as *right*: or in the fact that hitherto bread and honours have fallen to your share with that which you call your duty,—it is "right" to you, because it seems to be *your* "condition of existence" (that you, however, have a *right* to existence seems to you irrefutable!). The *persistency* of your moral judgment might still be just a proof of personal wretchedness or impersonality; your "moral force" might have its source in your obstinacy—or in your incapacity to perceive new ideals! And to be brief: if you had thought more acutely, observed more accurately, and had learned more, you would no longer under all circumstances call this and that your "duty" and your "conscience": the knowledge *how moral judgments have in general always originated* would make you tired of these pathetic words,—as you have already grown tired of other pathetic words, for instance "sin," "salvation," and "redemption."—And now, my friend, do not talk to me about the categorical imperative! That word tickles my ear, and I must laugh in spite of your presence and your seriousness. In this connection I recollect old Kant, who, as a punishment for having *gained possession surreptitiously* of the "thing in itself"—also a very ludicrous affair!—was imposed upon by the categorical imperative, and with that in his heart *strayed back again* to "God," the "soul," "freedom," and "immortality," like a fox which strays back into its cage: and it had been *his* strength and shrewdness which had *broken open* this cage!—What? You admire the categorical imperative in you? This "persistency" of your so-called moral judgment? This absoluteness of the feeling that "as I think on this matter, so must everyone think"? Admire rather your *selfishness* therein! And the blindness, paltriness, and modesty of your selfishness! For it is selfishness in a person to regard *his* judgment as universal law, and a blind, paltry and modest selfishness besides, because it betrays that you have not yet discovered yourself, that you have not yet created for yourself any personal, quite personal ideal:—for this could never be the ideal of another, to say nothing of all, of every one!—He who still thinks that "each would have to act in this manner in this case," has not yet advanced half a dozen paces in self-knowledge: otherwise he would know that there neither are, nor can be, similar actions,—that every action that has been done, has been done in an entirely unique and inimitable manner, and that it will be the same with regard to all future actions; that all precepts of conduct (and even the most esoteric and subtle precepts of all moralities up to the present), apply only to the coarse exterior,—that by means of them, indeed, a semblance of equality can be attained, *but only a semblance,*—that in outlook and retrospect, *every* action is, and remains, an impenetrable affair, —that our opinions of the "good," "noble" and "great" can never be proved by our actions, because no action is cognisable,—that our opinions, estimates, and tables of values are certainly among the most powerful levers in the mechanism of our actions, that in every single case, nevertheless, the law of their mechanism is untraceable. Let us *confine* ourselves, therefore, to the purification of our opinions and appreciations, and to the *construction of new tables of value of our own:*—we will, however, brood no longer over the "moral worth of our actions"! Yes, my friends! As regards the whole moral twaddle of people about one another, it is time to be disgusted with it! To sit in judgment morally ought to be opposed to our taste! Let us leave this nonsense and this bad taste to those who have nothing else to do, save to drag the past a little distance further through time, and who are never themselves the present,—consequently to the many, to the majority! We, however, *would seek to become what we are,*—the new, the unique, the incomparable, making laws for ourselves and creating ourselves! And for this purpose we must become the best students and discoverers of all the laws and necessities in the world. We must be *physicists* in order to be *creators* in that sense—whereas hitherto all appreciations and ideals have been based on *ignorance* of physics, or in *contradiction* thereto. And therefore, three cheers for physics! And still louder cheers for that which *impels* us thereto—our honesty.

336.

Avarice of Nature—Why has nature been so niggardly towards humanity that she has not let human beings shine, this man more and that man less, according to their inner abundance of light? Why have not great men such a fine visibility in their rising and setting as the sun? How much less equivocal would life among men then be!

337.

Future "Humanity."—When I look at this age with the eye of a distant future, I find nothing so remarkable in the man of the present day as his peculiar virtue and sickness called "the historical sense." It is a tendency to something quite new and foreign in history: if this embryo were given several centuries and more, there might finally evolve out of it a marvellous plant, with a smell equally marvellous, on account of which our old earth might be more pleasant to live in than it has been hitherto. We moderns are just beginning to form the chain of a very powerful, future sentiment, link by link,—we hardly know what we are doing. It almost seems to us as if it were not the question of a new sentiment, but of the decline of all old sentiments:—the historical sense is still something so poor and cold, and many are attacked by it as by a frost, and are made poorer and colder by it. To others it appears as the indication of stealthily approaching age, and our planet is regarded by them as a melancholy invalid, who, in order to forget his present condition, writes the history of his youth. In fact, this is one aspect of the new sentiment. He who knows how to regard the history of man in its entirety as *his own history*, feels in the immense generalisation all the grief of the invalid who thinks of health, of the old man who thinks of the dream of his youth, of the lover who is robbed of his beloved, of the martyr whose ideal is destroyed, of the hero on the evening of the indecisive battle which has brought him wounds and the loss of a friend. But to bear this immense sum of grief of all kinds, to be able to bear it, and yet still be the hero who at the commencement of a second day of battle greets the dawn and his happiness, as one who has an horizon of centuries before and behind him, as the heir of all nobility, of all past intellect, and the obligatory heir (as the noblest) of all the old nobles; while at the same time the first of a new nobility, the equal of which has never been seen nor even dreamt of: to take all this upon his soul, the oldest, the newest, the losses, hopes, conquests, and victories of mankind: to have all this at last in one soul, and to comprise it in one feeling:—this would necessarily furnish a happiness which man has not hitherto known,—a God's happiness, full of power and love, full of tears and laughter, a happiness which, like the sun in the evening, continually gives of its inexhaustible riches and empties into the sea,—and like the sun, too, feels itself richest when even the poorest fisherman rows with golden oars! This divine feeling might then be called—humanity!

338.

The Will to Suffering and the Compassionate.—Is it to your advantage to be above all compassionate? And is it to the advantage of the sufferers when you are so? But let us leave the first question for a moment without an answer.—That from which we suffer most profoundly and personally is almost incomprehensible and inaccessible to every one else: in this matter we are hidden from our neighbour even when he eats at the same table with us. Everywhere, however, where we are *noticed* as sufferers, our suffering is interpreted in a shallow way; it belongs to the nature of the emotion of pity to *divest* unfamiliar suffering of its properly personal character:—our "benefactors" lower our value and volition more than our enemies. In most benefits which are conferred on the unfortunate there is something shocking in the intellectual levity with which the compassionate person plays the rôle of fate: he knows nothing of all the inner consequences and complications which are called misfortune for *me* or for *you!* The entire economy of my soul and its adjustment by "misfortune," the uprising of new sources and needs, the closing up of old wounds, the repudiation of whole periods of the past—none of these things which may be connected with misfortune preoccupy the dear sympathiser. He wishes *to succour,* and does not reflect that there is a personal necessity for misfortune; that terror, want, impoverishment, midnight watches, adventures, hazards and mistakes are as necessary to me and to you as their opposites, yea, that, to speak mystically, the path to one's own heaven always leads through the voluptuousness of one's own hell. No, he knows nothing thereof. The "religion of compassion" (or "the heart") bids him help, and he thinks he has helped best when he has helped most speedily! If you adherents of this religion actually have the same sentiments towards yourselves which you have towards your fellows, if you are unwilling to endure your own suffering even for an hour, and continually forestall all possible misfortune, if you regard suffering and pain generally as evil, as detestable, as deserving of annihilation, and as blots on existence, well, you have then, besides your religion of compassion, yet another religion in your heart (and this is perhaps the mother of the former)—*the religion of smug ease.* Ah, how little you know of the *happiness* of man, you comfortable and good-natured ones!—for happiness and misfortune are brother and sister, and twins, who grow tall together, or, as with you, *remain small together!* But now let us return to the first question.—How is it at all possible for a person to keep to *his* path! Some cry or other is continually calling one aside: our eye then rarely lights on anything without it becoming necessary for us to leave for a moment our own affairs and rush to give assistance. I know there are hundreds of respectable and laudable methods of making me stray *from my course,* and in truth the most "moral" of methods! Indeed, the opinion of the present-day preachers of the morality of compassion goes so far as to imply that just this, and this alone is moral:—to stray from *our* course to that extent and to run to the assistance of our neighbour. I am equally certain that I need only give myself over to the sight of one case of actual distress, and I, too, *am* lost! And if a suffering friend said to me, "See, I shall soon die, only promise to die with me"—I might promise it, just

as—to select for once bad examples for good reasons—the sight of a small, mountain people struggling for freedom,. would bring me to the point of offering them
my hand and my life. Indeed, there is even a secret seduction in all this awakening
of compassion, and calling for help: our "own way" is a thing too hard and insistent,
and too far removed from the love and gratitude of others,—we escape from it and
from our most personal conscience, not at all unwillingly, and, seeking security
in the conscience of others, we take refuge in the lovely temple of the "religion of
pity." As soon now as any war breaks out, there always breaks out at the same time
a certain secret delight precisely in the noblest class of the people: they rush with
rapture to meet the new danger of *death*, because they believe that in the sacrifice
for their country they have finally that long-sought-for permission—the permission
to shirk their aim:—war is for them a detour to suicide, a detour, however, with a
good conscience. And although silent here about some things, I will not, however,
be silent about my morality, which says to me: Live in concealment in order that
thou *mayest* live to thyself. Live *ignorant* of that which seems to thy age to be most
important! Put at least the skin of three centuries betwixt thyself, and the present
day! And the clamour of the present day, the noise of wars and revolutions, ought
to be a murmur to thee! Thou wilt also want to help, but only those whose distress
thou entirely *understandest*, because they have *one* sorrow and *one* hope in common
with thee—thy *friends:* and only in *the* way that thou helpest thyself:—I want to make
them more courageous, more enduring, more simple, more joyful! I want to teach
them that which at present so few understand, and the preachers of fellowship in
sorrow least of all:—namely, *fellowship in joy!*

339.

Vita femina.—To see the ultimate beauties in a work—all knowledge and good-
will is not enough; it requires the rarest, good chance for the veil of clouds to move
for once from the summits, and for the sun to shine on them. We must not only
stand at precisely the right place to see this, our very soul itself must have pulled
away the veil from its heights, and must be in need of an external expression and
simile, so as to have a hold and remain master of itself. All these, however, are so
rarely united at the same time that I am inclined to believe that the highest summit
of all that is good, be it work, deed, man, or nature, has hitherto remained for
most people, and even for the best, as something concealed and shrouded:—that,
however, which unveils itself to us, *unveils itself to us but once.* The Greeks indeed
prayed: "Twice and thrice, everything beautiful!" Ah, they had their good reason
to call on the Gods, for ungodly actuality does not furnish us with the beautiful at

all, or only does so once! I mean to say that the world is overfull of beautiful things, but it is nevertheless poor, very poor, in beautiful moments, and in the unveiling of those beautiful things. But perhaps this is the greatest charm of life: it puts a gold-embroidered veil of lovely potentialities over itself, promising, resisting, modest, mocking, sympathetic, seductive. Yes, life is a woman!

340.

The Dying Socrates.—-I admire the courage and wisdom of Socrates in all that he did, said—and did not say. This mocking and amorous demon and rat-catcher of Athens, who made the most insolent youths tremble and sob, was not only the wisest babbler that has ever lived, but was just as great in his silence. I would that he had also been silent in the last moment of his life,—perhaps he might then have belonged to a still higher order of intellects. Whether it was death, or the poison, or piety, or wickedness—something or other loosened his tongue at that moment, and he said: "O Crito, I owe a cock to Asclepios." For him who has ears, this ludicrous and terrible "last word" implies: "O Crito, *life is a long sickness!*" Is it possible! A man like him, who had lived cheerfully and to all appearance as a soldier,—was a pessimist! He had merely put on a good demeanour towards life, and had all along concealed his ultimate judgment, his profoundest sentiment! Socrates, Socrates *had suffered from life!* And he also took his revenge for it—with that veiled, fearful, pious, and blasphemous phrase! Had even a Socrates to revenge himself? Was there a grain too little of magnanimity in his superabundant virtue? Ah, my friends! We must surpass even the Greeks!

341.

The Heaviest Burden.—What if a demon crept after thee into thy loneliest loneliness some day or night, and said to thee: "This life, as thou livest it at present, and hast lived it, thou must live it once more, and also innumerable times; and there will be nothing new in it, but every pain and every joy and every thought and every sigh, and all the unspeakably small and great in thy life must come to thee again, and all in the same series and sequence—and similarly this spider and this moonlight among the trees, and similarly this moment, and I myself. The eternal sand-glass of existence will ever be turned once more, and thou with it, thou speck of dust!"—Wouldst thou not throw thyself down and gnash thy teeth, and curse the demon that so spake? Or hast thou once experienced a tremendous moment in which thou wouldst answer him: "Thou art a God, and never did I hear anything so divine!" If that thought acquired power over thee as thou art, it would transform thee, and perhaps crush thee; the question with regard to all and everything: "Dost thou want this once more, and also for innumerable times?" would lie as the heaviest burden upon thy activity! Or, how wouldst thou have to become favourably inclined to thyself and to life, so as *to long for nothing more ardently* than for this last eternal sanctioning and sealing?—

342.

Incipit Tragœdia.—When Zarathustra was thirty years old, he left his home and the Lake of Urmi, and went into the mountains. There he enjoyed his spirit and his solitude, and for ten years did not weary of it. But at last his heart changed,—and rising one morning with the rosy dawn, he went before the sun and spake thus to it: "Thou great star! What would be thy happiness if thou hadst not those for whom thou shinest! For ten years hast thou climbed hither unto my cave: thou wouldst have wearied of thy light and of the journey, had it not been for me, mine eagle, and my serpent. But we awaited thee every morning, took from thee thine overflow, and blessed thee for it. Lo! I am weary of my wisdom, like the bee that hath gathered too much honey; I need hands outstretched to take it. I would fain bestow and distribute, until the wise have once more become joyous in their folly, and the poor happy in their riches. Therefore must I descend into the deep, as thou doest in the evening, when thou goest behind the sea and givest light also to the nether-world, thou most rich star! Like thee must I *go down*, as men say, to whom I shall descend. Bless me then, thou tranquil eye, that canst behold even the greatest happiness without envy! Bless the cup that is about to overflow, that the water may flow golden out of it, and carry everywhere the reflection of thy bliss! Lo! This cup is again going to empty itself, and Zarathustra is again going to be a man."—Thus began Zarathustra's down-going.

BOOK FIFTH

FEARLESS ONES

"Carcasse, tu trembles? Tu tremblerais bien davantage, tu savais, où je te mène." *Turenne.*

343.

What our Cheerfulness Signifies.—The most important of more recent events—that "God is dead," that the belief in the Christian God has become unworthy of belief—already begins to cast its first shadows over Europe. To the few at least whose eye, whose *suspecting* glance, is strong enough and subtle enough for this drama, some sun seems to have set, some old, profound confidence seems to have changed into doubt: our old world must seem to them daily more darksome, distrustful, strange and "old." In the main, however, one may say that the event itself is far too great, too remote, too much beyond most people's power of apprehension, for one to suppose that so much as the report of it could have *reached* them; not to speak of many who already knew *what* had taken place, and what must all collapse now that this belief had been undermined,—because so much was built upon it, so much rested on it, and had become one with it: for example, our entire European morality. This lengthy, vast and uninterrupted process of crumbling, destruction, ruin and overthrow which is now imminent: who has realised it sufficiently to-day to have to stand up as the teacher and herald of such a tremendous logic of terror, as the prophet of a period of gloom and eclipse, the like of which has probably never taken place on earth before?... Even we, the born riddle-readers, who wait as it were on the mountains posted 'twixt to-day and to-morrow, and engirt by their contradiction, we, the firstlings and premature children of the coming century, into whose sight especially the shadows which must forthwith envelop Europe *should* already have come—how is it that even we, without genuine sympathy for this period of gloom, contemplate its advent without any *personal* solicitude or fear? Are we still, perhaps, too much under the *immediate effects* of the event—and are these effects, especially as regards *ourselves,* perhaps the reverse of what was to be expected—not at all sad and depressing, but rather like a new and indescribable variety of light, happiness, relief, enlivenment, encouragement, and dawning day?... In fact, we philosophers and "free spirits" feel ourselves irradiated as by a new dawn by the report that the "old God is dead"; our hearts overflow with gratitude, astonishment, presentiment and expectation. At last the horizon seems open once more, granting even that it is not bright; our ships can at last put out to sea in face of every danger; every hazard is again permitted to the discerner; the sea, *our* sea, again lies open before us; perhaps never before did such an "open sea" exist.—

344.

To what Extent even We are still Pious.—It is said with good reason that convictions have no civic rights in the domain of science: it is only when a conviction voluntarily condescends to the modesty of an hypothesis, a preliminary standpoint for experiment, or a regulative fiction, that its access to the realm of knowledge, and a certain value therein, can be conceded,—always, however, with the restriction that it must remain under police supervision, under the police of our distrust.—Regarded more accurately, however, does not this imply that only when a conviction *ceases* to be a conviction can it obtain admission into science? Does not the discipline of the scientific spirit just commence when one no longer harbours any conviction?... It is probably so: only, it remains to be asked whether, *in order that this discipline may commence*, it is not necessary that there should already be a conviction, and in fact one so imperative and absolute, that it makes a sacrifice of all other convictions. One sees that science also rests on a belief: there is no science at all "without premises." The question whether *truth* is necessary, must not merely be affirmed beforehand, but must be affirmed to such an extent that the principle, belief, or conviction finds expression, that "there is *nothing more necessary* than truth, and in comparison with it everything else has only secondary value."—This absolute will to truth: what is it? Is it the will *not to allow ourselves to be deceived?* Is it the will *not to deceive?* For the will to truth could also be interpreted in this fashion, provided one included under the generalisation, "I will not deceive," the special case, "I will not deceive myself." But why not deceive? Why not allow oneself to be deceived?—Let it be noted that the reasons for the former eventuality belong to a category quite different from those for the latter: one does not want to be deceived oneself, under the supposition that it is injurious, dangerous, or fatal to be deceived,—in this sense science would be a prolonged process of caution, foresight and utility; against which, however, one might reasonably make objections. What? is not-wishing-to-be-deceived really less injurious, less dangerous, less fatal? What do you know of the character of existence in all its phases to be able to decide whether the greater advantage is on the side of absolute distrust, or of absolute trustfulness? In case, however, of both being necessary, much trusting *and* much distrusting, whence then should science derive the absolute belief, the conviction on which it rests, that truth is more important than anything else, even than every other conviction? This conviction could not have arisen if truth *and* untruth had both continually proved themselves to be useful: as is the case. Thus—the belief in science, which now undeniably exists, cannot have had its origin in such a utilitarian calculation, but rather *in spite of* the fact of the inutility and dangerousness of the "Will to truth," of "truth at all costs," being continually demonstrated. "At all costs": alas, we understand that sufficiently well, after having sacrificed and slaughtered one belief after another at this altar!—Consequently, "Will to truth" does *not* imply, "I will not allow myself to be deceived," but—there is no other alternative—"I will not deceive, not even myself": *and thus we have reached the realm of morality.* For, let one just ask oneself fairly: "Why wilt thou not deceive?" especially if it should seem—and it does seem—as if life were laid out with a view to appearance, I mean, with a view to error deceit, dissimulation, delusion, self-delusion; and when on the other hand it is a matter of fact that the great type of life has always manifested itself on the side of the most unscrupulous πολύτροποι. Such an intention might perhaps, to express it mildly, be a piece of Quixotism, a little enthusiastic craziness; it might also, however, be something worse, namely, a destructive principle, hostile to life... "Will to Truth,"—that might be a concealed Will to Death.—Thus the question Why is there science? leads back to the moral problem: *What in general is the purpose of morality,* if life, nature, and history are "non-moral"? There is no doubt that the conscientious man in the daring and extreme sense in which he is presupposed by the belief in science, *affirms thereby a world other than* that of life, nature, and history; and in so far as he affirms this "other world," what? must he not just thereby—deny its counterpart, this world, *our* world?... But what I have in view will now be understood, namely, that it is always a *metaphysical belief* on which our belief in science rests,—and that even we knowing ones of to-day, landless and anti-metaphysical, still take *our* fire from the conflagration kindled by a belief a millennium old, the Christian belief, which was also the belief of Plato, that God is truth, that the truth is divine... But what if this itself always becomes more untrustworthy, what if nothing any longer proves itself divine, except it be error, blindness, and falsehood;—what if God himself turns out to be our most persistent lie?—

345.

Morality as a Problem.—A defect in personality revenges itself everywhere: an enfeebled, lank, obliterated, self-disavowing and disowning personality is no longer fit for anything good—it is least of all fit for philosophy. "Selflessness" has no value either in heaven or on earth; the great problems all demand *great love,* and it is only the strong, well-rounded, secure spirits, those who have a solid basis, that are qualified for them. It makes the most material difference whether a thinker stands personally related to his problems, having his fate, his need, and even his highest happiness therein; or merely impersonally, that is to say, if he can only feel and grasp them with the tentacles of cold, prying thought. In the latter case I warrant that nothing comes of it: for the great problems, granting that they let themselves be grasped at all, do not let themselves be *held* by toads and weaklings: that has ever been their taste—a taste also which they share with all high-spirited women.—How is it that I have not yet met with any one, not even in books, who seems to have stood to morality in this position, as one who knew morality as a problem, and this problem as *his own* personal need, affliction, pleasure and passion? It is obvious that up to the present morality has not been a problem at all; it has rather been the very ground on which people have met after all distrust, dissension and contradiction, the hallowed place of peace, where thinkers could obtain rest even from themselves, could recover breath and revive. I see no one who has ventured to *criticise* the estimates of moral worth. I miss in this connection even the attempts of scientific curiosity, and the fastidious, groping imagination of psychologists and historians, which easily anticipates a problem and catches it on the wing, without rightly knowing what it catches. With difficulty I have discovered some scanty data for the purpose of furnishing a *history of the origin* of these feelings and estimates of value (which is something different from a criticism of them, and also something different from a history of ethical systems). In an individual case I have done everything to encourage the inclination and talent for this kind of history—in vain, as it would seem to me at present. There is little to be learned from those historians of morality (especially Englishmen): they themselves are usually, quite unsuspiciously, under the influence of a definite morality, and act unwittingly as its armour-bearers and followers—perhaps still repeating sincerely the popular superstition of Christian Europe, that the characteristic of moral action consists in abnegation, self-denial, self-sacrifice, or in fellow-feeling and fellow-suffering. The usual error in their premises is their insistence on a certain *consensus* among human beings, at least among civilised human beings, with regard to certain propositions of morality, from thence they conclude that these propositions are absolutely binding even upon you and me; or reversely, they come to the conclusion that *no* morality is binding, after the truth has dawned upon them that among different peoples moral valuations are *necessarily* different: both of which conclusions are equally childish follies. The error of the more subtle amongst them is that they discover and criticise the probably foolish opinions of a people about its own morality, or the opinions of mankind about human morality generally (they treat accordingly of its origin, its religious sanctions, the superstition of free will, and such matters), and they think that just by so doing they have criticised the morality itself. But the worth of a precept, "Thou shalt," is fundamentally different from and independent of such opinions about it, and must be distinguished from the weeds of error with which it has perhaps been overgrown: just as the worth of a medicine to a sick person is altogether independent of the question whether he has a scientific opinion about medicine, or merely thinks about it as an old wife would do. A morality could even have grown *out of* an error: but with this knowledge the problem of its worth would not even be touched.—Thus, no one hitherto has tested the *value* of that most celebrated of all medicines, called morality: for which purpose it is first of all necessary for one—*to call it in question.* Well, that is just our work.—

346.

Our Note of Interrogation.—But you don't understand it? As a matter of fact, an effort will be necessary in order to understand us. We seek for words; we seek perhaps also for ears. Who are we after all? If we wanted simply to call ourselves in older phraseology, atheists, unbelievers, or even immoralists, we should still be far from thinking ourselves designated thereby: we are all three in too late a phase for people generally to conceive, for *you,* my inquisitive friends, to be able to conceive, what is our state of mind under the circumstances. No! we have no longer the bitterness and passion of him who has broken loose, who has to make for himself a belief, a goal, and even a martyrdom out of his unbelief! We have become saturated with the conviction (and have grown cold and hard in it) that things are not at all divinely ordered in this world, nor even according to human standards do they go on rationally, mercifully, or justly: we know the fact that the world in which we live is ungodly, immoral, and "inhuman,"—we have far too long interpreted it to ourselves falsely and mendaciously, according to the wish and will of our veneration, that is to say, according to our *need.* For man is a venerating animal! But he is also a distrustful animal: and that the world is *not* worth what we believed it to be worth is about the surest thing our distrust has at last managed to grasp. So much distrust, so much philosophy! We take good care not to say that the world is of *less* value: it seems to us at present absolutely ridiculous when man claims to devise values *to surpass* the values of the actual world,—it is precisely from that point that we have retraced our steps; as from an extravagant error of human conceit and irrationality, which for a long period has not been recognised as such. This error had its last expression in modern Pessimism; an older and stronger manifestation in the teaching of Buddha; but Christianity also contains it, more dubiously, to be sure, and more ambiguously, but none the less seductive on that account. The whole attitude of "man *versus* the world," man as world-denying principle, man as the standard of the value of things, as judge of the world, who in the end puts existence itself on his scales and finds it too light—the monstrous impertinence of this attitude has dawned upon us as such, and has disgusted us,—we now laugh when we find, "Man *and* World" placed beside one another, separated by the sublime presumption of the little word "and"! But how is it? Have we not in our very laughing just made a further step in despising mankind? And consequently also in Pessimism, in despising the existence cognisable *by us?* Have we not just thereby awakened suspicion that there is an opposition between the world in which we have hitherto been at home with our venerations—for the sake of which we perhaps *endure* life—and another world *which we ourselves are:* an inexorable, radical, most profound suspicion concerning ourselves, which is continually getting us Europeans more annoyingly into its power, and could easily face the coming generation with the terrible alternative: Either do away with your venerations, or—*with yourselves!*" The latter would be Nihilism—but would not the former also be Nihilism? This is *our* note of interrogation.

347.

Believers and their Need of Belief.—How much *faith* a person requires in order to flourish, how much "fixed opinion" he requires which he does not wish to have shaken, because he *holds* himself thereby—is a measure of his power (or more plainly speaking, of his weakness). Most people in old Europe, as it seems to me, still need Christianity at present, and on that account it still finds belief. For such is man: a theological dogma might be refuted to him a thousand times,—provided, however, that he had need of it, he would again and again accept it as "true,"—according to the famous "proof of power" of which the Bible speaks. Some have still need of metaphysics; but also the impatient *longing for certainty* which at present discharges itself in scientific, positivist fashion among large numbers of the people, the longing by all means to get at something stable (while on account of the warmth of the longing the establishing of the certainty is more leisurely and negligently undertaken):—even this is still the longing for a hold, a support; in short, the *instinct of weakness*, which, while not actually creating religions, metaphysics, and convictions of all kinds, nevertheless—preserves them. In fact, around all these positivist systems there fume the vapours of a certain pessimistic gloom, something of weariness, fatalism, disillusionment, and fear of new disillusionment—or else manifest animosity, ill-humour, anarchic exasperation, and whatever there is of symptom or masquerade of the feeling of weakness. Even the readiness with which our cleverest contemporaries get lost in wretched corners and alleys, for example, in Vaterländerei (so I designate Jingoism, called *chauvinisme* in France, and "*deutsch*" in Germany), or in petty æsthetic creeds in the manner of Parisian *naturalisme* (which only brings into prominence and uncovers—*that* aspect of nature which excites simultaneously disgust and astonishment—they like at present to call this aspect *la vérité vraie*), or in Nihilism in the St Petersburg style (that is to say, in the *belief in unbelief*, even to martyrdom for it):—this shows always and above all the need of belief, support, backbone, and buttress... Belief is always most desired, most pressingly needed, where there is a lack of will: for the will, as emotion of command, is the distinguishing characteristic of sovereignty and power. That is to say, the less a person knows how to command, the more urgent is his desire for that; which commands, and commands sternly,—a God, a prince, a caste, a physician, a confessor, a dogma, a party conscience. From whence perhaps it could be inferred that the two world-religions, Buddhism and Christianity, might well have had the cause of their rise, and especially of their rapid extension, in an extraordinary *malady of the will* And in truth it has been so: both religions lighted upon a longing, monstrously exaggerated by malady of the will, for an imperative, a "Thou-shalt," a longing going the length of despair; both religions were teachers of fanaticism in times of slackness of will-power, and thereby offered to innumerable persons a support, a new possibility of exercising will, an enjoyment in willing. For in fact fanaticism is the sole "volitional strength" to which the weak and irresolute can be excited, as a sort of hypnotising of the entire sensory-intellectual system, in favour of the over-abundant nutrition (hypertrophy) of a particular point of view and a particular sentiment, which then dominates—the Christian calls it his *faith.* When a man arrives at the fundamental conviction that he *requires* to be commanded, he becomes "a believer." Reversely, one could imagine a delight and a power of self-determining, and a *freedom* of will, whereby a spirit could bid farewell to every belief, to every wish for certainty, accustomed as it would be to support itself on slender cords and possibilities, and to dance even on the verge of abysses. Such a spirit would be the *free spirit par excellence.*

348.

The Origin of the Learned.—The learned man in Europe grows out of all the different ranks and social conditions, like a plant requiring no specific soil: on that account he belongs essentially and involuntarily to the partisans of democratic thought. But this origin betrays itself. If one has trained one's glance to some extent to recognise in a learned book or scientific treatise the intellectual *idiosyncrasy* of the learned man—all of them have such idiosyncrasy,—and if we take it by surprise, we shall almost always get a glimpse behind it of the "antecedent history" of the learned man and his family, especially of the nature of their callings and occupations. Where the feeling finds expression, "That is at last proved, I am now done with it," it is commonly the ancestor in the blood and instincts of the learned man that approves of the "accomplished work" in the nook from which he sees things;—the belief in the proof is only an indication of what has been looked upon for ages by a laborious family as "good work." Take an example: the sons of registrars and office-clerks of every kind, whose main task has always been to arrange a variety of material, distribute it in drawers, and systematise it generally, evince, when they become learned men, an inclination to regard a problem as almost solved when they have systematised it There are philosophers who are at bottom nothing but systematising brains—the formal part of the paternal occupation has become its essence to them. The talent for classifications, for tables of categories, betrays something; it is not for nothing that a person is the child of his parents. The son of an advocate will also have to be an advocate as investigator: he seeks as a first consideration, to carry the point in his case, as a second consideration, he perhaps seeks to be in the right. One recognises the sons of Protestant clergymen and schoolmasters by the naïve assurance with which as learned men they already assume their case to be proved, when it has but been presented by them staunchly and warmly: they are thoroughly accustomed to people *believing* in them,—it belonged to their fathers' "trade"! A Jew, contrariwise, in accordance with his business surroundings and the past of his race, is least of all accustomed—to people believing him. Observe Jewish scholars with regard to this matter,—they all lay great stress on logic, that is to say, on *compelling* assent by means of reasons; they know that they must conquer thereby, even when race and class antipathy is against them, even where people are unwilling to believe them. For in fact, nothing is more democratic than logic: it knows no respect of persons, and takes even the crooked nose as straight. (In passing we may remark that in respect to logical thinking, in respect to *cleaner* intellectual habits, Europe is not a little indebted to the Jews; above all the Germans, as being a lamentably *déraisonnable* race, who, even at the present day, must always have their "heads washed"[12] in the first place. Wherever the Jews have attained to influence, they have taught to analyse more subtly, to argue more acutely, to write more clearly and purely: it has always been their problem to bring a people "to *raison.*")

349.

The Origin of the Learned once more.—To seek self-preservation merely, is the expression of a state of distress, or of limitation of the true, fundamental instinct of life, which aims at the *extension of power,* and with this in view often enough calls in question self-preservation and sacrifices it. It should be taken as symptomatic when individual philosophers, as for example, the consumptive Spinoza, have seen and have been obliged to see the principal feature of life precisely in the so-called self-preservative instinct:—they have just been men in states of distress. That our modern natural sciences have entangled themselves so much with Spinoza's dogma (finally and most grossly in Darwinism, with its inconceivably one-sided doctrine

---

[12]This poem is a parody of the "Chorus Mysticus" which concludes the second part of Goethe's "Faust." Bayard Taylor's translation of the passage in "Faust" runs as follows:—

of the "struggle for existence"—), is probably owing to the origin of most of the inquirers into nature: they belong in this respect to the people, their forefathers have been poor and humble persons, who knew too well by immediate experience the difficulty of making a living. Over the whole of English Darwinism there hovers something of the suffocating air of over-crowded England, something of the odour of humble people in need and in straits. But as an investigator of nature, a person ought to emerge from his paltry human nook: and in nature the state of distress does not *prevail*, but superfluity, even prodigality to the extent of folly. The struggle for existence is only an *exception*, a temporary restriction of the will to live; the struggle, be it great or small, turns everywhere on predominance, on increase and expansion, on power, in conformity to the will to power, which is just the will to live.

350.

In Honour of Homines Religiosi.—The struggle against the church is certainly (among other things—for it has a manifold significance) the struggle of the more ordinary, cheerful, confiding, superficial natures against the rule of the graver, profounder, more contemplative natures, that is to say, the more malign and suspicious men, who with long continued distrust in the worth of life, brood also over their own worth:—the ordinary instinct of the people, its sensual gaiety, its "good heart," revolts against them. The entire Roman Church rests on a Southern suspicion of the nature of man (always misunderstood in the North), a suspicion whereby the European South has succeeded, to the inheritance of the profound Orient—the mysterious, venerable Asia—and its contemplative spirit. Protestantism was a popular insurrection in favour of the simple, the respectable, the superficial (the North has always been more good-natured and more shallow than the South), but it was the French Revolution that first gave the sceptre wholly and solemnly into the hands of the "good man" (the sheep, the ass, the goose, and everything incurably shallow, bawling, and fit for the Bedlam of "modern ideas").

351.

In Honour of Priestly Natures.—I think that philosophers have always felt themselves very remote from that which the people (in all classes of society nowadays) take for wisdom: the prudent, bovine placidity, piety, and country-parson meekness, which lies in the meadow and *gazes at* life seriously and ruminatingly:—this is probably because philosophers have not had sufficiently the taste of the "people," or of the country-parson, for that kind of wisdom. Philosophers will also perhaps be the last to acknowledge that the people *should* understand something of that which lies furthest from them, something of the great *passion* of the thinker, who lives and must live continually in the storm-cloud of the highest problems and the heaviest responsibilities (consequently, not gazing at all, to say nothing of doing so indifferently, securely, objectively). The people venerate an entirely different type of men when on their part they form the ideal of a "sage," and they are a thousand times justified in rendering homage with the highest eulogies and honours to precisely that type of men—namely, the gentle, serious, simple, chaste, priestly natures and those related to them,—it is to them that the praise falls due in the popular veneration of wisdom. And to whom should the multitude have more reason to be grateful than to these men who pertain to its class and rise from its ranks, but are persons consecrated, chosen, and *sacrificed* for its good—they themselves believe themselves sacrificed to God,—before whom every one can pour forth his heart with impunity, by whom he can *get rid* of his secrets, cares, and worse things (for the man who "communicates himself" gets rid of himself, and he who has "confessed" forgets). Here there exists a great need: for sewers and pure cleansing waters are required also for spiritual filth, and rapid currents of love are needed, and strong, lowly, pure hearts, who qualify and sacrifice themselves for such service of the non-public health-department—for it *is* a sacrificing, the priest is, and continues to be, a human sacrifice... The people regard such sacrificed, silent, serious men of "faith" as "*wise*," that is to say, as men who have become sages, as "reliable" in relation to their own unreliability. Who would desire to deprive the people of that expression and that veneration?—But as is fair on the other side, among philosophers the priest also is still held to belong to the "people," and is *not* regarded as a sage, because, above all, they themselves do not believe in "sages," and they already scent "the people" in this very belief and superstition. It was *modesty* which invented in Greece the word "philosopher," and left to the play-actors of the spirit the superb arrogance of assuming the name "wise"—the modesty of such monsters of pride and self-glorification as Pythagoras and Plato.—

352.

Why we can hardly Dispense with Morality.—The naked man is generally an ignominious spectacle—I speak of us European males (and by no means of European females!). If the most joyous company at table suddenly found themselves stripped and divested of their garments through the trick of an enchanter, I believe that not only would the joyousness be gone and the strongest appetite lost;—it seems that we Europeans cannot at all dispense with the masquerade that is called clothing. But should not the disguise of "moral men," the screening under moral formulæ and notions of decency, the whole kindly concealment of our conduct under conceptions of duty, virtue, public sentiment, honourableness, and disinterestedness, have just as good reasons in support of it? Not that I mean hereby that human wickedness and baseness, in short, the evil wild beast in us, should be disguised; on the contrary, my idea is that it is precisely as *tame animals* that we are an ignominious spectacle and require moral disguising,—that the "inner man" in Europe is far from having enough of intrinsic evil "to let himself be seen" with it (to be *beautiful* with it). The European disguises himself *in morality* because he has become a sick, sickly, crippled animal, who has good reasons for being "tame," because he is almost an abortion, an imperfect, weak and clumsy thing... It is not the fierceness of the beast of prey that finds moral disguise necessary, but the gregarious animal, with its profound mediocrity, anxiety and ennui. *Morality dresses up the European*—let us acknowledge it!—in more distinguished, more important, more conspicuous guise—in "divine" guise—

353.

The Origin of Religions.—The real inventions of founders of religions are, on the one hand, to establish a definite mode of life and everyday custom, which operates as *disciplina voluntatis*, and at the same time does away with ennui; and on the other hand, to give to that very mode of life an *interpretation*, by virtue of which it appears illumined with the highest value; so that it henceforth becomes a good for which people struggle, and under certain circumstances lay down their lives. In truth, the second of these inventions is the more essential: the first, the mode of life, has usually been there already, side by side, however, with other modes of life, and still unconscious of the value which it embodies. The import, the originality of the founder of a religion, discloses itself usually in the fact that he *sees* the mode of life, *selects* it, and *divines* for the first time the purpose for which it can be used, how it can be interpreted. Jesus (or Paul) for example, found around him the life of the common people in the Roman province, a modest, virtuous, oppressed life: he interpreted it, he put the highest significance and value into it—and thereby the courage to despise every other mode of life, the calm fanaticism of the Moravians, the secret, subterranean self-confidence which goes on increasing, and is at last ready "to overcome the world" (that is to say, Rome, and the upper classes throughout the empire). Buddha, in like manner, found the same type of man,—he found it in fact dispersed among all the classes and social ranks of a people who were good and kind (and above all inoffensive), owing to indolence, and who likewise owing to indolence, lived abstemiously, almost without requirements. He understood that such a type of man, with all its *vis inertiæ*, had inevitably to glide into a belief which promises *to avoid* the return of earthly ill (that is to say, labour and activity generally),—this "understanding" was his genius. The founder of a religion possesses psychological infallibility in the knowledge of a definite, average type of souls, who have not yet *recognised* themselves as akin. It is he who brings them together: the founding of a religion, therefore, always becomes a long ceremony of recognition.—

354.

The "Genius of the Species."—The problem of consciousness (or more correctly: of becoming conscious of oneself) meets us only when we begin to perceive in what measure we could dispense with it: and it is at the beginning of this perception that we are now placed by physiology and zoology (which have thus required two centuries to overtake the hint thrown out in advance by Leibnitz). For we could in fact think, feel, will, and recollect, we could likewise "act" in every sense of the term, and nevertheless nothing of it all need necessarily "come into consciousness" (as one says metaphorically). The whole of life would be possible without its seeing itself as it were in a mirror: as in fact even at present the far greater part of our life still goes on without this mirroring,—and even our thinking, feeling, volitional life as well, however painful this statement may sound to an older philosopher. *What* then is *the purpose* of consciousness generally, when it is in the main *superfluous?*—Now it seems to me, if you will hear my answer and its perhaps extravagant supposition, that the subtlety and strength of consciousness are always in proportion to the *capacity for communication* of a man (or an animal), the capacity for communication in its turn being in proportion to the *necessity for communication:* the latter not to be understood as if precisely the individual himself who is master in the art of communicating and making known his necessities would at the same time have to be most dependent upon others for his necessities. It seems to me, however, to be so in relation to whole races and successions of generations: where necessity and need have long compelled men to communicate with their fellows and understand one another rapidly and subtly, a surplus of the power and art of communication is at last acquired as if it were a fortune which had gradually accumulated, and now waited for an heir to squander it prodigally (the so-called artists are these heirs, in like manner the orators, preachers, and authors: all of them men who come at the end of a long succession, "late-born" always, in the best sense of the word, and as has been said, *squanderers* by their very nature). Granted that this observation is correct, I may proceed further to the conjecture that *consciousness generally has only been developed under the pressure of the necessity for communication,*—that from the first it has been necessary and useful only between man and man (especially between those commanding and those obeying) and has only developed in proportion to its utility Consciousness is properly only a connecting network between man and man,—it is only as such that it has had to develop; the recluse and wild-beast species of men would not have needed it The very fact that our actions, thoughts, feelings and motions come within the range of our consciousness—at least a part of them—is the result of a terrible, prolonged "must" ruling man's destiny: as the most endangered animal he *needed* help and protection; he needed his fellows, he was obliged to express his distress, he had to know how to make himself understood—and for all this he needed "consciousness" first of all: he had to "know" himself what he lacked, to "know" how he felt, and to "know" what he thought. For, to repeat it once more, man, like every living creature, thinks unceasingly, but does not know it; the thinking which is becoming *conscious of itself* is only the smallest part thereof, we may say, the most superficial part, the worst part:—for this conscious thinking alone *is done in words, that is to say, in the symbols for communication,* by means of which the origin of consciousness is revealed. In short, the development of speech and the development of consciousness (not of reason, but of reason becoming self-conscious) go hand in hand. Let it be further accepted that it is not only speech that serves as a bridge between man and man, but also the looks, the pressure and the gestures; our becoming conscious of our sense impressions, our power of being able to fix them, and as it were to locate them outside of ourselves, has increased in proportion as the necessity has increased for communicating them to *others* by means of signs. The sign-inventing man is at the same time the man who is always more acutely self-conscious; it is only as a social animal that man has learned to become conscious of himself,—he is doing so still, and doing so more and more.—As is obvious, my idea is that consciousness does not properly belong to the individual existence of man, but rather to the social and gregarious nature in him; that, as follows therefrom, it is only in relation to communal and gregarious utility that it is finely developed; and that consequently each of us, in spite of the best intention of *understanding* himself as individually as possible, and of "knowing himself," will always just call into consciousness the non-individual in him, namely, his "averageness"; —that our thought itself is continuously as it were *outvoted* by the character of consciousness—by the imperious "genius of the species" therein—and is translated back into the perspective of the herd. Fundamentally our actions are in an incomparable manner altogether personal, unique and absolutely individual—there is no doubt about it; but as soon as we translate them into consciousness, they *do not appear so any longer* . . . . This is the proper phenomenalism and perspectivism as I understand it: the nature of *animal consciousness* involves the notion that the world of which we can become conscious is only a superficial and symbolic world, a generalised and vulgarised world;—that everything which becomes conscious *becomes* just thereby shallow, meagre, relatively stupid,—a generalisation, a symbol, a characteristic of the herd; that with the evolving of consciousness there is always combined a great, radical perversion, falsification, superficialisation, and generalisation. Finally, the growing consciousness is a danger, and whoever lives among the most conscious Europeans knows even that it is a disease. As may be conjectured, it is not the antithesis of subject and object with which I am here concerned: I leave that distinction to the epistemologists who have remained entangled in the toils of grammar (popular metaphysics). It is still less the antithesis of "thing in itself" and phenomenon, for we do not "know" enough to be entitled even *to make such a distinction*. Indeed, we have not any organ at all for *knowing*, or for "truth": we "know" (or believe, or fancy) just as much as may be *of use* in the interest of the human herd, the species; and even what is here called "usefulness" is ultimately only a belief, a fancy, and perhaps precisely the most fatal stupidity by which we shall one day be ruined.

355.

The Origin of our Conception of "Knowledge"—I take this explanation from the street. I heard one of the people saying that "he knew me," so I asked myself: What do the people really understand by knowledge? what do they want when they seek "knowledge"? Nothing more than that what is strange is to be traced back to something *known*. And we philosophers—have we really understood *anything more* by knowledge? The known, that is to say, what we are accustomed to so that we no longer marvel at it, the commonplace, any kind of rule to which we are habituated, all and everything in which we know ourselves to be at home:—what? is our need of knowing not just this need of the known? the will to discover in everything strange, unusual, or questionable, something which no longer disquiets us? Is it not possible that it should be the *instinct of fear* which enjoins upon us to know? Is it not possible that the rejoicing of the discerner should be just his rejoicing in the regained feeling of security?... One philosopher imagined the world "known" when he had traced it back to the "idea": alas, was it not because the idea was so known, so familiar to him? because he had so much less fear of the "idea"—Oh, this moderation of the discerners! let us but look at their principles, and at their solutions of the riddle of the world in this connection! When they again find aught in things, among things, or behind things that is unfortunately very well known to us, for example, our multiplication table, or our logic, or our willing and desiring, how happy they immediately are! For "what is known is understood": they are unanimous as to that. Even the most circumspect among them think that the known is at least *more easily understood* than the strange; that for example, it is methodically ordered to proceed outward from the "inner world," from "the facts of consciousness," because it is the world which is *better known to us!* Error of errors! The known is the accustomed, and the accustomed is the most difficult of all to "understand," that is to say, to perceive as a problem, to perceive as strange, distant, "outside of us."... The great certainty of the natural sciences in comparison with psychology and the criticism of the elements of consciousness—*unnatural* sciences, as one might almost be entitled to call them—rests precisely on the fact that they take *what is strange* as their object: while it is almost like something contradictory and absurd *to wish* to take generally what is not strange as an object...

356.

In what Manner Europe will always become "more Artistic."—Providing a living still enforces even in the present day (in our transition period when so much ceases to enforce) a definite *rôle* on almost all male Europeans, their so-called callings; some have the liberty, an apparent liberty, to choose this rôle themselves, but most have it chosen for them. The result is strange enough. Almost all Europeans confound themselves with their rôle when they advance in age; they themselves are the victims of their "good acting," they have forgotten how much chance, whim and arbitrariness swayed them when their "calling" was decided—and how many other rôles they *could* perhaps have played: for it is now too late! Looked at more closely, we see that their characters have actually *evolved* out of their rôle, nature out of art. There were ages in which people believed with unshaken confidence, yea, with piety, in their predestination for this very business, for that very mode of livelihood, and would not at all acknowledge chance, or the fortuitous rôle, or arbitrariness therein. Ranks, guilds, and hereditary trade privileges succeeded] with the help of this belief, in rearing those extraordinary broad towers of society which distinguished the Middle Ages, and of which at all events one thing remains to their credit: capacity for duration (and duration is a thing of the first rank on earth!). But there are ages entirely the reverse, the properly democratic ages, in which people tend to become more and more oblivious of this belief, and a sort of impudent conviction and quite contrary mode of viewing things comes to the front, the Athenian conviction which is first observed in the epoch of Pericles, the American conviction of the present day, which wants also more and more to become a European conviction: whereby the individual is convinced that he can do almost anything, that he *can play almost any rôle,* whereby everyone makes experiments with himself, improvises, tries anew, tries with delight, whereby all nature ceases and becomes art... The Greeks, having adopted this *rôle-creed*——an artist creed, if you will—underwent step by step, as is well known, a curious transformation, not in every respect worthy of imitation: *they became actual stage-players;* and as such they enchanted, they conquered all the world, and at last even the conqueror of the world, (for the *Græculus histrio* conquered Rome, and *not* Greek culture, as the naïve are accustomed to say...). What I fear, however, and what is at present obvious, if we desire to perceive it, is that we modern men are quite on the same road already; and whenever a man begins to discover in what respect he plays a rôle, and to what extent he *can* be a stage-player, he *becomes* a stage-player... A new flora and fauna of men thereupon springs up, which cannot grow in more stable, more restricted eras—or is left "at the bottom," under the ban and suspicion of infamy; thereupon the most interesting and insane periods of history always make their appearance, in which "stage-players," *all* kinds of stage-players, are the real masters. Precisely thereby another species of man is always more and more injured, and in the end made impossible: above all the great "architects"; the building power is now being paralysed; the courage that makes plans for the distant future is disheartened; there begins to be a lack of organising geniuses. Who is there who would now venture to undertake works for the completion of which millenniums would have to be *reckoned* upon? The fundamental belief is dying out, on the basis of which one could calculate, promise and anticipate the future in one's plan, and offer it as a sacrifice thereto, that in fact man has only value and significance in so far as he is *a stone in a great building;* for which purpose he has first of all to be *solid,* he has to be a "stone."... Above all, not a—stage-player! In short—alas! this fact will be hushed up for some considerable time to come!—that which from henceforth will no longer be built, and *can* no longer be built, is—a society in the old sense of the term; to build that structure everything is lacking, above all, the material. *None of us are any longer material for a society:* that is a truth which is seasonable at present! It seems to me a matter of indifference that meanwhile the most short-sighted, perhaps the most honest, and at any rate the noisiest species of men of the present day, our friends the Socialists, believe, hope, dream, and above all scream and scribble almost the opposite; in fact one already reads their watchword of the future-: "free society," on all tables and walls. Free society? Indeed! Indeed! But you know, gentlemen, sure enough whereof one builds it? Out of wooden iron! Out of the famous wooden iron! And not even out of wooden...

357.

The old Problem: "What is German?"—Let us count up apart the real acquisitions of philosophical thought for which we have to thank German intellects: are they in any allowable sense to be counted also to the credit of the whole race? Can we say that they are at the same time the work of the "German soul," or at least a symptom of it, in the sense in which we are accustomed to think, for example, of Plato's ideo-mania, his almost religious madness for form, as an event and an evidence of the "Greek soul"? Or would the reverse perhaps be true? Were they individually as much *exceptions* to the spirit of the race, as was, for example, Goethe's Paganism with a good conscience? Or as Bismarck's Macchiavelism was with a good conscience, his so-called "practical politics" in Germany? Did our philosophers perhaps even go counter to the *need* of the "German soul"? In short, were the German philosophers really philosophical *Germans*?—I call to mind three cases. Firstly, *Leibnitz's* incomparable insight—with which he obtained the advantage not only over Descartes, but over all who had philosophised up to his time,—that consciousness is only an accident of mental representation, and *not* its necessary and essential attribute; that consequently what we call consciousness only constitutes a state of our spiritual and psychical world (perhaps a morbid state), and is *far from being that world itself*:—is there anything German in this thought, the profundity of which has not as yet been exhausted? Is there reason to think that a person of the Latin race would not readily have stumbled on this reversal of the apparent?—for it is a reversal. Let us call to mind secondly, the immense note of interrogation which *Kant* wrote after the notion of causality. Not that he at all doubted its legitimacy, like Hume: on the contrary, he began cautiously to define the domain within which this notion has significance generally (we have not even yet got finished with the marking out of these limits). Let us take thirdly, the astonishing hit of *Hegel,* who stuck at no logical usage or fastidiousness when he ventured to teach that the conceptions of kinds develop *out of one another:* with which theory the thinkers in Europe were prepared for the last great scientific movement, for Darwinism—for without Hegel there would have been no Darwin. Is there anything German in this Hegelian innovation which first introduced the decisive conception of evolution into science?—Yes, without doubt we feel that there is something of ourselves "discovered" and divined in all three cases; we are thankful for it, and at the same time surprised; each of these three principles is a thoughtful piece of German self-confession, self-understanding, and self-knowledge. We feel with Leibnitz that "our inner world is far richer, ampler, and more concealed"; as Germans we are doubtful, like Kant, about the ultimate validity of scientific knowledge of nature, and in general about whatever *can* be known *causaliter*: the *knowable* as such now appears to us of *less* worth. We Germans should still have been Hegelians, even though there had never been a Hegel, inasmuch as we (in contradistinction to all Latin peoples) instinctively attribute to becoming, to evolution, a profounder significance and higher value than to that which "is"—we hardly believe at all in the validity of the concept "being." This is all the more the case because we are not inclined to concede to our human logic that it is logic in itself, that it is the only kind of logic (we should rather like, on the contrary, to convince ourselves that it is only a special case, and perhaps one of the strangest and most stupid).—A fourth question would be whether also *Schopenhauer* with his Pessimism, that is to say, the problem of *the worth of existence*, had to be a German. I think not. The event *after* which this problem was to be expected with certainty, so that an astronomer of the soul could have calculated the day and the hour for it—namely, the decay of the belief in the Christian God, the victory of scientific atheism,—is a universal European event, in which all races are to have their share of service and honour. On the contrary, it has to be ascribed precisely to the Germans—those with whom Schopenhauer was contemporary,—that they delayed this victory of atheism longest, and endangered it most. Hegel especially was its retarder *par excellence,* in virtue of the grandiose attempt which he made to persuade us at the very last of the divinity of existence, with the help of our sixth sense, "the historical sense." As philosopher, Schopenhauer was the *first* avowed and inflexible atheist we Germans have had: his hostility to Hegel had here its motive. The non-divinity of existence was regarded by him as something understood, palpable, indisputable; he always lost his philosophical composure and got into a passion when he saw anyone hesitate and beat about the bush here. It is at this point that his thorough uprightness of character comes in: unconditional, honest atheism is precisely the *preliminary condition* for his raising the problem, as a final and hardwon victory of the European conscience, as the most prolific act of two thousand years' discipline to truth, which in the end no longer tolerates the *lie* of the belief in a God... One sees what has really gained the victory over the Christian God—, Christian morality itself, the conception of veracity, taken ever more strictly, the confessional subtlety of the Christian conscience, translated and sublimated to the scientific conscience, to intellectual purity at any price. To look upon nature as if it were a proof of the goodness and care of a God; to interpret history in honour of a divine reason, as a constant testimony to a moral order in the world and a moral final purpose; to explain personal experiences as pious men have long enough explained them, as if everything were a dispensation or intimation of Providence, something planned and sent on behalf of the salvation of the soul: all that is now *past*, it has conscience *against* it, it is regarded by all the more acute consciences as disreputable and dishonourable, as mendaciousness, femininism, weakness, and cowardice,—by virtue of this severity, if by anything, we are *good* Europeans, the heirs of Europe's longest and bravest self-conquest. When we thus reject the Christian interpretation, and condemn its "significance" as a forgery, we are immediately confronted in a striking manner with the *Schopenhauerian* question: *Has existence then a significance at all?*—the question which will require a couple of centuries even to be completely heard in all its profundity. Schopenhauer's own answer to this question was—if I may be forgiven for saying so—a premature, juvenile reply, a mere compromise, a stoppage and sticking in the very same Christian-ascetic, moral perspectives, *the belief in which had got notice to quit* along with the belief in God... But he *raised* the question—as a good European, as we have said, and *not* as a German.—Or did the Germans prove at least by the way in which they seized on the Schopenhauerian question, their inner connection and relationship to him, their preparation for his problem, and their *need* of it? That there has been thinking and printing even in Germany since Schopenhauer's time on the problem raised by him,—it was late enough!—does not at all suffice to enable us to decide in favour of this closer relationship; one could, on the contrary, lay great stress on the peculiar *awkwardness* of this post-Schopenhauerian Pessimism—Germans evidently do not behave themselves here as in their element. I do not at all allude here to Eduard von Hartmann; on the contrary, my old suspicion is not vanished even at present that he is *too clever* for us; I mean to say that as arrant rogue from the very first, he did not perhaps make merry solely over German Pessimism—and that in the end he might probably "bequeathe" to them the truth as to how far a person could bamboozle the Germans themselves in the age of bubble companies. But further, are we perhaps to reckon to the honour of Germans, the old humming-top, Bahnsen, who all his life spun about with the greatest pleasure around his realistically dialectic misery and "personal ill-luck,"—was *that* German? (In passing I recommend his writings for the purpose for which I myself have used them, as anti-pessimistic fare, especially on account of his *elegantia psychologica*, which, it seems to me, could alleviate even the most consti-pated body and soul). Or would it be proper to count such dilettanti and old maids as the mawkish apostle of virginity, Mainländer, among the genuine Germans? After all he was probably a Jew (all Jews become mawkish when they moralise). Neither Bahnsen, nor Mainländer, nor even Eduard von Hartmann, give us a reliable grasp of the question whether the pessimism of Schopenhauer (his frightened glance into an undeified world, which has become stupid, blind, deranged and problematic, his *honourable* fright) was not only an exceptional case among Germans, but a *German* event: while everything else which stands in the foreground, like our valiant politics and our joyful Jingoism (which decidedly enough regards everything with reference to a principle sufficiently unphilosophical: *"Deutschland, Deutschland, über Alles"*[13] consequently *sub specie speciei*, namely, the German *species*), testifies very plainly to the contrary. No! The Germans of to-day are *not* pessimists! And Schopenhauer was a pessimist, I repeat it once more, as a good European, and *not* as a German.

358.

The Peasant Revolt of the Spirit.—We Europeans find ourselves in view of an immense world of ruins, where some things still tower aloft, while other objects stand mouldering and dismal, where most things however already lie on the ground, picturesque enough—where were there ever finer ruins?—overgrown with weeds, large and small. It is the Church which is this city of decay: we see the religious organisation of Christianity shaken to its deepest foundations. The belief in God is overthrown, the belief in the Christian ascetic ideal is now fighting its last fight. Such a long and solidly built work as Christianity—it was the last construction of the Romans!—could not of course be demolished..all at once; every sort of earthquake had to shake it, every sort of spirit which perforates, digs, gnaws and moulders had to assist in the work of destruction. But that which is strangest is that those who have exerted themselves most to retain and preserve Christianity, have been precisely those who did most to destroy it,—the Germans. It seems that the Germans do not understand the essence of a Church. Are they not spiritual enough, or not distrustful enough to do so? In any case the structure of the Church rests on a *southern* freedom and liberality of spirit, and similarly on a southern suspicion of nature, man, and spirit,—it rests on a knowledge of man an experience of man, entirely different from what the north has had. The Lutheran Reformation in all its length and breadth was the indignation of the simple against something "complicated." To speak cautiously, it was a coarse, honest misunderstanding, in which much is to be forgiven,—people did not understand the mode of expression of a *victorious* Church, and only saw corruption; they misunderstood the noble scepticism, the *luxury* of scepticism and toleration which every victorious, self-confident power permits... One overlooks the fact readily enough at present that as regards

---

[13]Translated by Miss M. D. Petre. Inserted by permission of the editor of the *Nation*, in which it appeared on April 17, 1909.

all cardinal questions concerning power Luther was badly endowed; he was fatally short-sighted, superficial and imprudent—and above all, as a man sprung from the people, he lacked all the hereditary qualities of a ruling caste, and all the instincts for power; so that his work, his intention to restore the work of the Romans, merely became involuntarily and unconsciously the commencement of a work of destruction. He unravelled, he tore asunder with honest rage, where the old spider had woven longest and most carefully. He gave the sacred books into the hands of everyone,—they thereby got at last into the hands of the philologists, that is to say, the annihilators of every belief based upon books. He demolished the conception of "the Church" in that he repudiated the belief in the inspiration of the Councils: for only under the supposition that the inspiring spirit which had founded the Church still lives in it, still builds it, still goes on building its house, does the conception of "the Church" retain its power. He gave back to the priest sexual intercourse: but three-fourths of the reverence of which the people (and above all the women of the people) are capable, rests on the belief that an exceptional man in this respect will also be an exceptional man in other respects. It is precisely here that the popular belief in something superhuman in man, in a miracle, in the saving God in man, has its most subtle and insidious advocate. After Luther had given a wife to the priest, he had *to take from him* auricular confession; that was psychologically right: but thereby he practically did away with the Christian priest himself, whose profoundest utility has ever consisted I in his being a sacred ear, a silent well, and a grave for secrets. "Every man his own priest"—behind such formulæ and their bucolic slyness, there was concealed in Luther the profoundest hatred of "higher men," and of the rule of "higher men," as the Church had conceived them. Luther disowned an ideal which he did not know how to attain, while he seemed to combat and detest the degeneration thereof. As a matter of fact, he, the impossible monk, repudiated the *rule* of the *homines religiosi*; he consequently brought about precisely the same thing within the ecclesiastical social order that he combated so impatiently in the civic order,—namely a "peasant insurrection."—As to all that grew out of his Reformation afterwards, good and bad, which can at present be almost counted up—who would be naïve enough to praise or blame Luther simply on account of these results? He is innocent of all; he knew not what he did. The art of making the European spirit shallower especially in the north, or more *good-natured*, if people would rather hear it designated by a moral expression, undoubtedly took a clever step in advance in the Lutheran Reformation; and similarly there grew out of it the mobility and disquietude of the spirit, its thirst for independence, its belief in the right to freedom, and its "naturalness." If people wish to ascribe to the Reformation in the last instance the merit of having prepared and favoured that which we at present honour as "modern science," they must of course add that it is also accessory to bringing about the degeneration of the modern scholar, with his lack of reverence, of shame and of profundity; and that it is also responsible for all naïve candour and plain-dealing in matters of knowledge, in short for the *plebeianism of the spirit* which is peculiar to the last two centuries, and from which even pessimism hitherto, has not in any way delivered us. "Modern ideas" also belong to this peasant insurrection of the north against the colder, more ambiguous, more suspicious spirit of the south, which has built itself its greatest monument in the Christian Church. Let us not forget in the end what a Church is, and especially in contrast to every "State": a Church is above all an authoritative organisation which secures to the *most spiritual* men the highest rank, and *believes* in the power of spirituality so far as to forbid all grosser appliances of authority. Through this alone the Church is under all circumstances a *nobler* institution than the State.—

359.

Vengeance on Intellect, and other Backgrounds of Morality.—Morality—where do you think it has its most dangerous and rancorous advocates?—There, for example, is an ill-constituted man, who does not possess enough of intellect to be able to take pleasure in it, and just enough of culture to be aware of the fact; bored, satiated, and a self-despiser; besides being cheated unfortunately by some hereditary property out of the last consolation, the "blessing of labour," the self-forgetfulness in the "day's work "; one who is thoroughly ashamed of his existence—perhaps also harbouring some vices,—and who on the other hand (by means of books to which he has no right, or more intellectual society than he can digest), cannot help vitiating himself more and more, and making himself vain and irritable: such a thoroughly poisoned man—for intellect becomes poison, culture becomes poison, possession becomes poison, solitude becomes poison, to such ill-constituted beings—gets at last into a habitual state of vengeance and inclination for vengeance... What do you think he finds necessary, absolutely necessary in order to give himself the appearance in his own eyes of superiority over more intellectual men, so as to give himself the delight of *perfect revenge*, at least in imagination? It is always *morality* that he requires, one may wager on it; always the big moral words, always the high-sounding words: justice, wisdom, holiness, virtue; always the Stoicism of gestures (how well Stoicism hides what one does *not* possess!); always the mantle of wise silence, of affability, of gentleness, and whatever else the idealist-mantle is called, in which the incurable self-despisers and also the incurably conceited walk about. Let me not be misunderstood: out of such born *enemies of the spirit* there arises now and then the rare specimen of humanity who is honoured by the people under the name of saint or sage: it is out of such men that there arise those prodigies of morality that make a noise, and make history,—St Augustine was one of these men. Fear of the intellect, vengeance on the intellect—Oh! how often have these powerfully impelling vices become the root of virtues! Yea, virtue *itself!*—And asking the question among ourselves, even the philosopher's pretension to wisdom, which has occasionally been made here and there on the earth, the maddest and most immodest of all pretensions,—has it not always been *above all* in India as well as in Greece, *a means of concealment?* Sometimes, perhaps, from the point of view of education which hallows so many lies, it is a tender regard for growing and evolving persons, for disciples who have often to be guarded against themselves by means of the belief in a person (by means of an error). In most cases, however, it is a means of concealment for a philosopher, behind which he seeks protection, owing to exhaustion, age, chilliness, or hardening; as a feeling of the approaching end, as the sagacity of the instinct which animals have before their death,—they go apart, remain at rest, choose solitude, creep into caves, become *wise*... What? Wisdom a means of concealment of the philosopher from—intellect?—

360.

Two Kinds of Causes which are Confounded.—It seems to me one of my most essential steps and advances that I have learned to distinguish the cause of an action generally from the cause of an action in a particular manner, say, in this direction, with this aim. The first kind of cause is a quantum of stored-up force, which waits to be used in some manner, for some purpose; the second kind of cause, on the contrary, is something quite unimportant in comparison with the first, an insignificant hazard for the most part, in conformity with which the quantum of force in question "discharges" itself in some unique and definite manner: the lucifer-match in relation to the barrel of gunpowder. Among those insignificant hazards and lucifer-matches I count all the so-called "aims," and similarly the still more so-called "occupations" of people: they are relatively optional, arbitrary, and almost indifferent in relation to the immense quantum of force which presses on, as we have said, to be used up in any way whatever. One generally looks at the matter in a different manner: one is accustomed to see the *impelling* force precisely in the aim (object, calling, &c.), according to a primeval error,—but it is only the *directing* force; the steersman and the steam have thereby been confounded. And yet it is not even always a steersman, the directing force... Is the "aim" the "purpose," not often enough only an extenuating pretext, an additional self-blinding of conceit, which does not wish it to be said that the ship *follows* the stream into which it has accidentally run? That it "wishes" to go that way, *because* it *must* go that way? That it has a direction, sure enough, but—not a steersman? We still require a criticism of the conception of "purpose."

361.

The Problem of the Actor—The problem of the actor has disquieted me the longest; I was uncertain (and am sometimes so still) whether one could not get at the dangerous conception of "artist"—a conception hitherto treated with unpardonable leniency—from this point of view. Falsity with a good conscience; delight in dissimulation breaking forth as power, pushing aside, overflowing, and sometimes extinguishing the so-called "character"; the inner longing to play a rôle, to assume a mask, to put on an *appearance;* a surplus of capacity for adaptations of every kind, which can no longer gratify themselves in the service of the nearest and narrowest utility: all that perhaps does not pertain *solely* to the actor in himself?... Such an instinct would develop most readily in families of the lower class of the people, who have had to pass their lives in absolute dependence, under shifting pressure and constraint, who (to accommodate themselves to their conditions, to adapt themselves always to new circumstances) had again and again to pass themselves off and represent themselves as different persons,—thus having gradually qualified themselves to adjust the mantle to *every* wind, thereby almost becoming the mantle itself, as masters of the embodied and incarnated art of eternally playing the game of hide and seek, which one calls *mimicry* among the animals:—until at last this ability, stored up from generation to generation, has become domineering, irrational and intractable, till as instinct it begins to command the other instincts, and begets the actor and "artist" (the buffoon, the pantaloon, the Jack-Pudding, the fool, and the clown in the first place, also the classical type of servant, Gil Blas: for in such types one has the precursors of the artist, and often enough even of the "genius"). Also under higher social conditions there grows under similar pressure a similar species of men: only the histrionic instinct is there for the most part held strictly in check by another instinct, for example, among "diplomatists";—for the rest, I should think that it would always be open to a good diplomatist to become a good actor on the stage, provided his dignity "allowed" it. As regards the *Jews,* however, the adaptable people *par excellence,* we should, in conformity to this line of thought, expect to see among them a world-wide historical institution at the very first, for the rearing of actors, a proper breeding-place for actors; and in fact the question is very pertinent just now: what good actor at present is *not*—a Jew? The Jew also, as a born literary man, as the actual ruler of the European press, exercises this power on the basis of his histrionic capacity: for the literary man is essentially an actor,—he plays the part of "expert," of "specialist."—Finally *women*. If we consider the whole history of women, are they not *obliged* first of all, and above all to be actresses? If we listen to doctors who have hypnotised women, or, finally, if we love them—and let ourselves be "hypnotised" by them—what is always divulged thereby? That they "give themselves airs," even when they—"give themselves." ... Woman is so artistic ...

362.

My Belief in the Virilising of Europe.—We owe it to Napoleon (and not at all to the French Revolution, which had in view the "fraternity" of the nations, and the florid interchange of good graces among people generally) that several warlike centuries, which have not had their like in past history, may now follow one another—in short, that we have entered upon *the classical age of war*, war at the same time scientific and popular, on the grandest scale (as regards means, talents and discipline), to which all coming millenniums will look back with envy and awe as a work of perfection:—for the national movement out of which this martial glory springs, is only the counter-*choc* against Napoleon, and would not have existed without him. To him, consequently, one will one day be able to attribute the fact that *man* in Europe has again got the upper hand of the merchant and the Philistine; perhaps even of "woman" also, who has become pampered owing to Christianity and the extravagant spirit of the eighteenth century, and still more owing to "modern ideas." Napoleon, who saw in modern ideas, and accordingly in civilisation, something like a personal enemy, has by this hostility proved himself one of the greatest continuators of the Renaissance: he has brought to the surface a whole block of the ancient character, the decisive block perhaps, the block of granite. And who knows but that this block of ancient character will in the end get the upper hand of the national movement, and will have to make itself in a *positive* sense the heir and continuator of Napoleon:—who, as one knows, wanted *one* Europe, which was to be *mistress of the world.*—

363.

How each Sex has its Prejudice about Love.—Notwithstanding all the concessions which I am inclined to make to the monogamie prejudice, I will never admit that we should speak of *equal* rights in the love of man and woman: there are no such equal rights. The reason is that man and woman understand something different by the term love,—and it belongs to the conditions of love in both sexes that the one sex does *not* presuppose the same feeling, the same conception of "love," in the other sex. What woman understands by love is clear enough: complete surrender (not merely devotion) of soul and body, without any motive, without any reservation, rather with shame and terror at the thought of a devotion restricted by clauses or associated with conditions. In this absence of conditions her love is precisely a *faith*: woman has no other.—Man, when he loves a woman, *wants* precisely this love from her; he is consequently, as regards himself, furthest removed from the prerequisites of feminine love; granted, however, that there should also be men to whom on their side the demand for complete devotion is not unfamiliar,—well, they are really—not men. A man who loves like a woman becomes thereby a slave; a woman, however, who loves like a woman becomes thereby a *more perfect* woman. ... The passion of woman in its unconditional renunciation of its own rights presupposes in fact that there does *not* exist on the other side an equal *pathos*, an equal desire for renunciation: for if both renounced themselves out of love, there would result—well, I don't know what, perhaps a *horror vacui?* Woman wants to be taken and accepted as a possession, she wishes to be merged in the conceptions of "possession" and "possessed"; consequently she wants one who *takes*, who does not offer and give himself away, but who reversely is rather to be made richer in "himself"—by the increase of power, happiness and faith which the woman herself gives to him. Woman gives herself, man takes her.—I do not think one will get over this natural contrast by any social contract, or with the very best will to do justice, however desirable it may be to avoid bringing the severe, frightful, enigmatical, and unmoral elements of this antagonism constantly before our eyes. For love, regarded as complete, great, and full, is nature, and as nature, is to all eternity something "unmoral."—*Fidelity* is accordingly included in woman's love, it follows from the definition thereof; with man fidelity *may* readily result in consequence of his love, perhaps as gratitude or idiosyncrasy of taste, and so-called elective affinity, but it does not belong to the *essence* of his love—and indeed so little, that one might almost be entitled to speak of a natural opposition between love and fidelity in man, whose love is just a desire to possess, and *not* a renunciation and giving away; the desire to possess, however, comes to an end every time with the possession... As a matter of fact it is the more subtle and jealous thirst for possession in a man (who is rarely and tardily convinced of having this "possession"), which makes his love continue; in that case it is even possible that his love may increase after the surrender,—he does not readily own that a woman has nothing more to "surrender" to him.—

364.

The Anchorite Speaks.—The art of associating with men rests essentially on one's skilfulness (which presupposes long exercise) in accepting a repast, in taking a repast, in the cuisine of which one has no confidence. Provided one comes to the table with the hunger of a wolf everything is easy "the worst society gives thee *experience*"— Mephistopheles says; but one has not always this wolf's-hunger when one needs it! Alas! how difficult are our fellow-men to digest! First principle: to stake one's courage as in a misfortune, to seize boldly, to admire oneself at the same time, to take one's repugnance between one's teeth, to cram down one's disgust. Second principle: to "improve" one's fellow-man, by praise for example, so that he may begin to sweat out his self-complacency; or to seize a tuft of his good or "interesting" qualities, and pull at it till one gets his whole virtue out, and can put him under the folds of it. Third principle: self-hypnotism. To fix one's eye on the object of one's intercourse as on a glass knob, until, ceasing to feel pleasure or pain thereat, one falls asleep unobserved, becomes rigid, and acquires a fixed pose: a household recipe used in married life and in friendship, well tested and prized as indispensable, but not yet scientifically formulated. Its proper name is—patience.—

365.

The Anchorite Speaks once more.—We also have intercourse with "men," we also modestly put on the clothes in which people know us (*as such,*) respect us and seek us; and we thereby mingle in society, that is to say, among the disguised who do not wish to be so called; we also do like a prudent masqueraders, and courteously dismiss all curiosity which has not reference merely to our "clothes" There are however other modes and artifices for "going about" among men and associating with them: for example, as a ghost,-which is very advisable when one wants to scare them, and get rid of them easily. An example: a person grasps at us, and is unable to seize us. That frightens him. Or we enter by a closed door. Or when the lights are extinguished. Or after we are dead The latter is the artifice of *posthumous* men *par excellence.* ("What?" said such a one once impatiently, "do you think we should delight in enduring this strangeness, coldness, death-stillness about us, all this subterranean, hidden, dim, undiscovered solitude, which is called life with us, and might just as well be called death, if we were not conscious of what *will arise* out of us,—and that only after our death shall we attain to *our* life and become living, ah! very living! we posthumous men!"—)

366.

At the Sight of a Learned Book.—We do not belong to those who only get their thoughts from books, or at the prompting of books,—it is our custom to think in the open air, walking, leaping, climbing, or dancing on lonesome mountains by preference, or close to the sea, where even the paths become thoughtful. Our first question concerning the value of a book, a man, or a piece of music is: Can it walk? or still better: Can it dance?... We seldom read; we do not read the worse for that—oh, how quickly we divine how a person has arrived at his thoughts:—if it is by sitting before an ink-bottle with compressed belly and head bent over the paper: oh, how quickly we are then done with his book! The constipated bowels betray themselves, one may wager on it, just as the atmosphere of the room, the ceiling of the room, the smallness of the room, betray themselves.—These were my feelings when closing a straightforward, learned book, thankful, very thankful, but also relieved... In the book of a learned man there is almost always something oppressive and oppressed: the "specialist" comes to light somewhere, his ardour, his seriousness, his wrath, his over-estimation of the nook in which he sits and spins, his hump—every specialist has his hump. A learned book also always mirrors a distorted soul: every trade distorts. Look at our friends again with whom we have spent our youth, after they have taken possession of their science: alas! how the reverse has always taken place! Alas! how they themselves are now for ever occupied and possessed by their science! Grown into their nook, crumpled into unrecognisability, constrained, deprived of their equilibrium, emaciated and angular everywhere, perfectly round only in one place,—we are moved and silent when we find them so. Every handicraft, granting even that it has a golden floor,[14] has also a leaden ceiling above it, which presses and presses on the soul, till it is pressed into a strange and distorted shape. There is nothing to alter here. We need not think that it is at all possible to obviate this disfigurement by any educational artifice whatever. Every kind of *perfection* is purchased at a high price on earth, where everything is perhaps purchased too dear; one is an expert in one's department at the price of being also a victim of one's department. But you want to have it otherwise—"more reasonable," above all more convenient—is it not so, my dear contemporaries? Very well! But then you will also immediately get something different: instead of the craftsman and expert, you will get the literary man, the versatile, "many-sided "littérateur, who to be sure lacks the hump—not taking account of the hump or bow which he makes before you as the shopman of the intellect and the "porter" of culture—, the

---

[14]Translated by Miss M. D. Petre. Inserted by permission of the editor of the *Nation*, in which it appeared on May 15, 1909.

littérateur, who *is* really nothing, but "represents" almost everything: he plays and "represents" the expert, he also takes it upon himself in all modesty *to see that he is* paid, honoured and celebrated in this position.—No, my learned friends! I bless you even on account of your humps! And also because like me you despise the littérateurs and parasites of culture! And because you do not know how to make merchandise of your intellect! And have so many opinions which cannot be expressed in money value! And because you do not represent anything which you *are* not! Because your sole desire is to become masters of your craft; because you reverence every kind of mastership and ability, and repudiate with the most relentless scorn everything of a make-believe, half-genuine, dressed-up, virtuoso, demagogic, histrionic nature in *litteris et artibus*—all that which does not convince you by its absolute *genuineness* of discipline and preparatory training, or cannot stand your test! (Even genius does not help a person to get over such a defect, however well it may be able to deceive with regard to it: one understands this if one has once looked closely at our most gifted painters and musicians,—who almost without exception, can artificially and supplementarily appropriate to themselves (by means of artful inventions of style, make-shifts, and even principles), the *appearance* of that genuineness, that solidity of training and culture; to be sure, without thereby deceiving themselves, without thereby imposing perpetual silence on their bad consciences. For you know of course that all great modern artists suffer from bad consciences?...)

367.

How one has to Distinguish first of all in Works of Art—Everything that is thought, versified, painted and composed, yea, even built and moulded, belongs either to monologic art, or to art before witnesses. Under the latter there is also to be included the apparently monologic art which involves the belief in God, the whole lyric of prayer; because for a pious man there is no solitude,—we, the godless, have been the first to devise this invention. I know of no profounder distinction in all the perspective of the artist than this: Whether he looks at his growing work of art (at "himself—") with the eye of the witness; or whether he "has forgotten the world," as is the essential thing in all monologic art,—it rests *on forgetting*, it is the music of forgetting.

368.

The Cynic Speaks.—My objections to Wagner's music are physiological objections. Why should I therefore begin by disguising them Under æsthetic formulæ? My "point" is that I can no longer breathe freely when this music begins to operate on me; my *foot* immediately becomes indignant at it and rebels: for what it needs is time, dance and march; it demands first of all from music the ecstasies which are in *good* walking, striding, leaping and dancing. But do not my stomach, my heart, my blood and my bowels also protest? Do I not become hoarse unawares under its influence? And then I ask myself what my body really *wants* from music generally. I believe it wants to have *relief:* so that all animal functions should be accelerated by means of light, bold, unfettered, self-assured rhythms; so that brazen, leaden life should be gilded by means of golden, good, tender harmonies. My melancholy would fain rest its head in the hiding-places and abysses of *perfection:* for this reason I need music. What do I care for the drama! What do I care for the spasms of its moral ecstasies, in which the "people" have their satisfaction! What do I care for the whole pantomimic hocus-pocus of the actor!... It will now be divined that I am essentially anti-theatrical at heart,—but Wagner on the contrary, was essentially a man of the stage and an actor, the most enthusiastic mummer-worshipper that has ever existed, even among musicians!... And let it be said in passing that if Wagner's theory was that "drama is the object, and music is only the means to it,"—his *practice* on the contrary from beginning to end has been to the effect that "attitude is the object, drama and even music can never be anything else but means to *this.*" Music as a means of elucidating, strengthening and intensifying dramatic poses and the actor's appeal to the senses, and Wagnerian drama only an opportunity for a number of dramatic attitudes! Wagner possessed, along with all other instincts, the dictatorial instinct of a great actor in all and everything, and as has been said, also as a musician.—I once made this clear with some trouble to a thorough-going Wagnerian, and I had reasons for adding:—"Do be a little more honest with yourself: we are not now in the theatre. In the theatre we are only honest in the mass; as individuals we lie, we belie even ourselves. We leave ourselves at home when we go to the theatre; we there renounce the right to our own tongue and choice, to our taste, and even to our courage as we possess it and practise it within our own four walls in relation to God and man. No one takes his finest taste in art into the theatre with him, not even the artist who works for the theatre: there one is people, public, herd, woman, Pharisee, voting animal, democrat, neighbour, and fellow-creature; there even the most personal conscience succumbs to the levelling charm of the 'great multitude'; there stupidity operates as wantonness and contagion; there the neighbour rules, there one *becomes* a neighbour..." (I have forgotten to mention what my enlightened Wagnerian answered to my physiological objections: "So the fact is that you are really not healthy enough for our music?"—)

369.

Juxtapositions in us.—Must we not acknowledge to ourselves, we artists, that there is a strange discrepancy in us; that on the one hand our taste, and on the other hand our creative power, keep apart in an extraordinary manner, continue apart, and have a separate growth;—I mean to say that they have entirely different gradations and *tempi* of age, youth, maturity, mellowness and rottenness? So that, for example, a musician could all his life create things which *contradicted* all that his ear and heart, spoilt for listening, prized, relished and preferred:—he would not even require to be aware of the contradiction! As an almost painfully regular experience shows, a person's taste can easily outgrow the taste of his power, even without the latter being thereby paralysed or checked in its productivity. The reverse, however, can also to some extent take place,—and it is to this especially that I should like to direct the attention of artists. A constant producer, a man who is a "mother" in the grand sense of the term, one who no longer knows or hears of anything except pregnancies and child-beds of his spirit, who has no time at all to reflect and make comparisons with regard to himself and his work, who is also no longer inclined to exercise his taste, but simply forgets it, letting it take its chance of standing, lying or falling,—perhaps such a man at last produces works *on which he is then quite unfit to pass a judgment:* so that he speaks and thinks foolishly about them and about himself. This seems to me almost the normal condition with fruitful artists,—nobody knows a child worse than its parents—and the rule applies even (to take an immense example) to the entire Greek world of poetry and art, which was never "conscious" of what it had done...

370.

What is Romanticism?—It will be remembered perhaps, at least among my friends, that at first I assailed the modern world with some gross errors and exaggerations, but at any rate with *hope* in my heart. I recognised—who knows from what personal experiences?—the philosophical pessimism of the nineteenth century as the symptom of a higher power of thought, a more daring courage and a more triumphant *plenitude* of life than had been characteristic of the eighteenth century, the age of Hume, Kant, Condillac, and the sensualists: so that the tragic view of things seemed to me the peculiar *luxury* of our culture, its most precious, noble, and dangerous mode of prodigality; but nevertheless, in view of its overflowing wealth, a *justifiable* luxury. In the same way I interpreted for myself German music as the expression of a Dionysian power in the German soul: I thought I heard in it the earthquake by means of which a primeval force that had been imprisoned for ages was finally finding vent—indifferent as to whether all that usually calls itself culture was thereby made to totter. It is obvious that I then misunderstood what constitutes the veritable character both of philosophical pessimism and of German music,—namely, their *Romanticism*. What is Romanticism? Every art and every philosophy may be regarded as a healing and helping appliance in the service of growing, struggling life: they always presuppose suffering and sufferers. But there are two kinds of sufferers: on the one hand those that suffer from *overflowing vitality*, who need Dionysian art, and require a tragic view and insight into life; and on the other hand those who suffer from *reduced vitality*, who seek repose, quietness, calm seas, and deliverance from themselves through art or knowledge, or else intoxication, spasm, bewilderment and madness. All Romanticism in art and knowledge responds to the twofold craving of the *latter;* to them Schopenhauer as well as Wagner responded (and responds),—to name those most celebrated and decided romanticists, who were then *misunderstood* by me (*not* however to their disadvantage, as may be reasonably conceded to me). The being richest in overflowing vitality, the Dionysian God and man, may not only allow himself the spectacle of the horrible and questionable, but even the fearful deed itself, and all the luxury of destruction, disorganisation and negation. With him evil, senselessness and ugliness seem as it were licensed, in consequence of the overflowing plenitude of procreative, fructifying power, which can convert every desert into a luxuriant orchard. Conversely, the greatest sufferer, the man poorest in vitality, would have most need of mildness, peace and kindliness in thought and action: he would need, if possible, a God who is specially the God of the sick, a "Saviour"; similarly he would have need of logic, the abstract intelligibility of existence—for logic soothes and gives confidence;—in short he would need a certain warm, fear-dispelling narrowness and imprisonment within optimistic horizons. In this manner I gradually began to understand Epicurus, the opposite of a Dionysian pessimist;—in a similar manner also the "Christian," who in fact is only a type of Epicurean, and like him essentially a romanticist:—and my vision has always become keener in tracing that most difficult and insidious of all forms of *retrospective inference*, in which, most mistakes have been made—the inference from the work to its author from the deed to its doer, from the ideal to him who *needs* it, from every mode of thinking and valuing to the imperative *want* behind it.—In regard to all æsthetic values I now avail myself of this radical distinction: I ask in every single case, "Has hunger or superfluity become creative here?" At the outset another distinction might seem to recommend itself more—it is far more conspicuous,—namely, to have in view whether the desire for rigidity, for perpetuation, for *being* is the cause of the creating, or the desire for destruction, for change, for the new, for the future—for *becoming*. But when looked at more carefully, both these kinds of desire prove themselves ambiguous, and are explicable precisely according to the before-mentioned, and, as it seems to me, rightly preferred scheme. The desire for *destruction*, change and becoming, may be the expression of overflowing power, pregnant with futurity (my *terminus* for this is of course the word "Dionysian"); but it may also be the hatred of the ill-constituted, destitute and unfortunate, which destroys, and *must* destroy, because the enduring, yea, all that endures, in fact all being, excites and provokes it. To understand this emotion we have but to look closely at our anarchists. The will to *perpetuation* requires equally a double interpretation. It may on the one hand proceed from gratitude and love:—art of this origin will always be an art of apotheosis, perhaps dithyrambic, as with Rubens, mocking divinely, as with Hafiz, or clear and kind-hearted as with Goethe, and spreading a Homeric brightness and glory over everything (in this case I speak of *Apollonian* art). It may also, however, be the tyrannical will of a sorely-suffering, struggling or tortured being, who would like to stamp his most personal, individual and narrow characteristics, the very idiosyncrasy of his suffering, as an obligatory law and constraint on others; who, as it were, takes revenge on all things, in that he imprints, enforces and brands *his* image, the image of *his* torture, upon them. The latter is *romantic pessimism* in its most extreme form, whether it be as Schopenhauerian will-philosophy, or as Wagnerian music:—romantic pessimism, the last *great* event in the destiny of our civilisation. (That there *may be* quite a different kind of pessimism, a classical pessimism—this presentiment and vision belongs to me, as something inseparable from me, as my *proprium* and *ipsissimum;* only that the word "classical" is repugnant to my ears, it has become far too worn, too indefinite and indistinguishable. I call that pessimism of the future,—for it is coming! I see it coming!—*Dionysian* pessimism.)

371.

We Unintelligible Ones.—Have we ever complained among ourselves of being misunderstood, misjudged, and confounded with others; of being calumniated, misheard, and not heard? That is just our lot—alas, for a long time yet! say, to be modest, until 1901—, it is also our distinction; we should not have sufficient respect for ourselves if we wished it otherwise. People confound us with others—the reason of it is that we ourselves grow, we change continually, we cast off old bark, we still slough every spring, we always become younger, higher, stronger, as men of the future, we thrust our roots always more powerfully into the deep—into evil—, while at the same time we embrace the heavens ever more lovingly, more extensively, and suck in their light ever more eagerly with all our branches and leaves. We grow like trees—that is difficult to understand, like all life!—not in one place, but everywhere, not in one direction only, but upwards and outwards, as well as inwards and downwards. At the same time our force shoots forth in stem, branches, and roots; we are really no longer free to do anything separately, or to *be* anything separately... Such is our lot, as we have said: we grow in *height*; and even should it be our calamity—for we dwell ever closer to the lightning!—well, we honour it none the less on that account; it is that which we do not wish to share with others, which we do not wish to bestow upon others, the fate of all elevation, *our* fate...

372.

Why we are not Idealists.—Formerly philosophers were afraid of the senses: have we, perhaps, been far too forgetful of this fear? We are at present all of us sensualists, we representatives of the present and of the future in philosophy,—*not* according to theory, however, but in *praxis*, in practice... Those former philosophers, on the contrary, thought that the senses lured them out of *their* world, the cold realm of "ideas," to a dangerous southern island, where they were afraid that their philosopher-virtues would melt away like snow in the sun. "Wax in the ears," was then almost a condition of philosophising; a genuine philosopher no longer listened to life, in so far as life is music, he *denied* the music of life—it is an old philosophical superstition that all music is Sirens' music.—Now we should be inclined at the present day to judge precisely in the opposite manner (which in itself might be just as false), and to regard *ideas*, with their cold, anæmic appearance, and not even in spite of this appearance, as worse seducers than the senses. They have always lived on the "blood" of the philosopher, they always consumed his senses, and indeed, if you will believe me, his "heart" as well. Those old philosophers were heartless: philosophising was always a species of vampirism. At the sight of such figures even as Spinoza, do you not feel a profoundly enigmatical and disquieting sort of impression? Do you not see the drama which is here performed, the constantly *increasing pallor*—, the spiritualisation always more ideally displayed? Do you not imagine some long-concealed blood-sucker in the background, which makes its beginning with the senses, and in the end retains or leaves behind nothing but bones and their rattling?—I mean categories, formulæ, and *words*(for you will pardon me in saying that what *remains* of Spinoza, *amor intellectualis dei*, is rattling and nothing more! What is *amor*, what is *deus*, when they have lost every drop of blood?...) *In summa:* all philosophical idealism has hitherto been something like a disease, where it has not been, as in the case of Plato, the prudence of superabundant and dangerous healthfulness, the fear of *overpowerful* senses, and the wisdom of a wise Socratic.—Perhaps, is it the case that we moderns are merely not sufficiently sound *to require* Plato's idealism? And we do not fear the senses because——

373.

"Science" as Prejudice.—It follows from the laws of class distinction that the learned, in so far as they belong to the intellectual middle-class, are debarred from getting even a sight of the really *great* problems and notes of interrogation. Besides, their courage, and similarly their outlook, does not reach so far,—and above all, their need, which makes them investigators, their innate anticipation and desire that things should be constituted *in such and such a way*, their fears and hopes are too soon quieted and set at rest. For example, that which makes the pedantic English-man, Herbert Spencer, so enthusiastic in his way, and impels him to draw a line of hope, a horizon of desirability, the final reconciliation of "egoism and altruism" of which he dreams,—that almost causes nausea to people like us:—a humanity with such Spencerian perspectives as ultimate perspectives would seem to us deserving of contempt, of extermination! But the *fact* that something has to be taken by him as his highest hope, which is regarded, and may well be regarded, by others merely as a distasteful possibility, is a note of interrogation which Spencer could not have foreseen... It is just the same with the belief with which at present so many ma-terialistic natural-scientists are content, the belief in a world which is supposed to have its equivalent and measure in human thinking and human valuations, a "world of truth" at which we might be able ultimately to arrive with the help of our insignificant, four-cornered human reason! What? do we actually wish to have existence debased in that fashion to a ready-reckoner exercise and calculation for stay-at-home mathematicians? We should not, above all, seek to divest existence of its *ambiguous* character: *good* taste forbids it, gentlemen, the taste of reverence for everything that goes beyond your horizon! That a world-interpretation is alone right by which *you* maintain your position, by which investigation and work can go on scientifically in *your* sense (you really mean *mechanically?*), an interpretation which acknowledges numbering, calculating, weighing, seeing and handling, and nothing more—such an idea is a piece of grossness and naïvety, provided it is not lunacy and idiocy. Would the reverse not be quite probable, that the most superficial and external characters of existence—its most apparent quality, its outside, its embodi-ment—should let themselves be apprehended first? perhaps alone allow themselves to be apprehended? A "scientific" interpretation of the world as you understand it might consequently still be one of the *stupidest*, that is to say, the most destitute of

significance, of all possible world-interpretations—I say this in confidence to my friends the Mechanicians, who to-day like to hobnob with philosophers, and absolutely believe that mechanics is the teaching of the first and last laws upon which, as upon a ground-floor, all existence must be built. But an essentially mechanical world would be an essentially *meaningless* world! Supposing we valued the *worth* of a music with reference to how much it could be counted, calculated, or formulated —how absurd such a "scientific" estimate of music would be! What would one have apprehended, understood, or discerned in it! Nothing, absolutely nothing of what is really "music" in it!...

374.

Our new "Infinite"—How far the perspective character of existence extends, or whether it have any other character at all, whether an existence without explanation, without "sense" does not just become "nonsense," whether, on the other hand, all existence is not essentially an *explaining* existence—these questions, as is right and proper, cannot be determined even by the most diligent and severely conscientious analysis and self-examination of the intellect, because in this analysis the human intellect cannot avoid seeing itself in its perspective forms, and *only* in them. We cannot see round our corner: it is hopeless curiosity to want to know what other modes of intellect and perspective there *might* be: for example, whether any kind of being could perceive time backwards, or alternately forwards and backwards (by which another direction of life and another conception of cause and effect would be given). But I think that we are to-day at least far from the ludicrous immodesty of decreeing from our nook that there *can* only be legitimate perspectives from that nook. The world, on the contrary, has once more become "infinite" to us: in so far we cannot dismiss the possibility that it *contains infinite interpretations.* Once more the great horror seizes us—but who would desire forthwith to deify once more *this* monster of an unknown world in the old fashion? And perhaps worship *the* unknown thing as *the* "unknown person" in future? Ah! there are too many *ungodly* possibilities of interpretation comprised in this unknown, too much devilment, stupidity and folly of interpretation,—our own human, all too human interpretation itself, which we know...

375.

Why we Seem to be Epicureans.—We are cautious, we modern men, with regard to final convictions, our distrust lies in wait for the enchantments and tricks of conscience involved in every strong belief, in every absolute Yea and Nay: how is this explained? Perhaps one may see in it a good deal of the caution of the "burnt child," of the disillusioned idealist; but one may also see in it another and better element, the joyful curiosity of a former lingerer in a corner, who has been brought to despair by his nook, and now luxuriates and revels in its antithesis, in the unbounded, in the "open air in itself." Thus there is developed an almost Epicurean inclination for knowledge, which does not readily lose sight of the questionable character of things; likewise also a repugnance to pompous moral phrases and attitudes, a taste that repudiates all coarse, square contrasts, and is proudly conscious of its habitual reserve. For *this too* constitutes our pride, this easy tightening of the reins in our headlong impulse after certainty, this self-control of the rider in his most furious riding: for now, as of old, we have mad, fiery steeds under us, and if we delay, it is certainly least of all the danger which causes us to delay...

376.

Our Slow Periods.—It is thus that artists feel, and all men of "works," the maternal species of men: they always believe at every chapter of their life—a work always makes a chapter—that they have now reached the goal itself; they would always patiently accept death with the feeling: "we are ripe for it." This is not the expression of exhaustion,—but rather that of a certain autumnal sunniness and mildness, which the work itself, the maturing of the work, always leaves behind in its originator. Then the *tempo* of life slows down—turns thick and flows with honey—into long pauses, into the belief in *the* long pause...

377.

We Homeless Ones.—Among the Europeans of to-day there are not lacking those who may call themselves homeless ones in a way which is at once a distinction and an honour; it is by them that my secret wisdom and *gaya scienza* is especially to be laid to heart! For their lot is hard, their hope uncertain; it is a clever feat to devise consolation for them. But what good does it do! We children of the future, how *could* we be at home in the present? We are unfavourable to all ideals which could make us feel at home in this frail, broken-down, transition period; and as regards the "realities" thereof, we do not believe in their *endurance.* The ice which still carries has become very thin: the thawing wind blows; we ourselves, the homeless ones, are an agency that breaks the ice, and the other too thin "realities."... We "preserve" nothing, nor would we return to any past age; we are not at all "liberal," we do not labour for "progress," we do not need first to stop our ears to the song of the market-place and the sirens of the future—their song of "equal rights," "free society," "no longer either lords or slaves," does not allure us! We do not by any means think it desirable that the kingdom of righteousness and peace should be established on earth (because under any circumstances it would be the kingdom of the profoundest mediocrity and Chinaism); we rejoice in all men, who like ourselves love danger, war and adventure, who do not make compromises, nor let themselves be captured, conciliated and stunted; we count ourselves among the conquerors; we ponder over the need of a new order of things, even of a new slavery—for every strengthening and elevation of the type "man" also involves a new form of slavery. Is it not obvious that with all this we must feel ill at ease in an age which claims the honour of being the most humane, gentle and just that the sun has ever seen? What a pity that at the mere mention of these fine words, the thoughts at the bottom of our hearts are all the more unpleasant, that we see therein only the expression—or the masquerade—of profound weakening, exhaustion, age, and declining power! What can it matter to us with what kind of tinsel an invalid decks out his weakness? He may parade it as his *virtue;* there is no doubt whatever that weakness makes people gentle, alas, so gentle, so just, so inoffensive, so "humane"!—The "religion of pity," to which people would like to persuade us—yes, we know sufficiently well the hysterical little men and women who need this religion at present as a cloak and adornment! We are no humanitarians; we should not dare to speak of our "love of mankind"; for that, a person of our stamp is not enough of an actor! Or not sufficiently Saint-Simonist, not sufficiently French. A person must have been affected with a *Gallic* excess of erotic susceptibility and amorous impatience even to approach mankind honourably with his lewdness... Mankind! Was there ever a more hideous old woman among all old women (unless perhaps it were "the Truth": a question for philosophers)? No, we do not love Mankind! On the other hand, how-ever, we are not nearly "German" enough (in the sense in which the word "German" is current at present) to advocate nationalism and race-hatred, or take delight in the national heart-itch and blood-poisoning, on account of which the nations of Europe are at present bounded off and secluded from one another as if by quarantines. We are too unprejudiced for that, too perverse, too fastidious; also too well-informed, and too much "travelled." We prefer much rather to live on mountains, apart and "out of season," in past or coming centuries, in order merely to spare ourselves the silent rage to which we know we should be condemned as witnesses of a system of politics which makes the German nation barren by making it vain, and which is a *petty* system besides:—will it not be necessary for this system to plant itself between two mortal hatreds, lest its own creation should immediately collapse? Will it not *be obliged* to desire the perpetuation of the petty-state system of Europe?... We homeless ones are too diverse and mixed in race and descent for "modern men," and are consequently little tempted to participate in the falsified racial self-admiration and lewdness which at present display themselves in Germany, as signs of German sentiment, and which strike one as doubly false and unbecoming in the people with the "historical sense." We are, in a word—and it shall be our word of honour!—*good Europeans*, the heirs of Europe, the rich, over-wealthy heirs, but too deeply obligated heirs of millenniums of European thought. As such, we have also outgrown Christianity, and are disinclined to it—and just because we have grown *out of* it, because our forefathers were Christians uncompromising in their Christian integrity, who willingly sacrificed possessions and positions, blood and country, for the sake of their belief. We—do the same. For what, then? For our unbelief? For all sorts of unbelief? Nay, you know better than that, my friends! The hidden *Yea* in you is stronger than all the Nays and Perhapses, of which you and your age are sick; and when you are obliged to put out to sea, you emigrants, it is—once more a *faith* which urges you thereto!...

378.

"And once more Grow Clear."—We, the generous and rich in spirit, who stand at the sides of the streets like open fountains and would hinder no one from drinking from us: we do not know, alas! how to defend ourselves when we should like to do so; we have no means of preventing ourselves being made *turbid* and dark,—we have no means of preventing the age in which we live casting its "up-to-date rubbish" into us, or of hindering filthy birds throwing their excrement, the boys their trash, and fatigued resting travellers their misery, great and small, into us. But we do as we have always done: we take whatever is cast into us down into our depths—for we are deep, we do not forget—*and once more grow clear*...

379.

The Fool's Interruption.—It is not a misanthrope who has written this book: the hatred of men costs too dear to-day. To hate as they formerly hated *man*, in the fashion of Timon, completely, without qualification, with all the heart, from the pure *love* of hatred—for that purpose one would have to renounce contempt:—and how much refined pleasure, how much patience, how much benevolence even, do we owe to contempt! Moreover we are thereby the "elect of God": refined contempt is our taste and privilege, our art, our virtue perhaps, we, the most modern amongst the moderns!... Hatred, on the contrary, makes equal, it puts men face to face, in hatred there is honour; finally, in hatred there is *fear*, quite a large amount of fear. We fearless ones, however, we, the most intellectual men of the period, know our advantage well enough to live without fear as the most intellectual persons of this age. People will not easily behead us, shut us up, or banish us; they will not even ban or burn our books. The age loves intellect, it loves us, and needs us, even when we have to give it to understand that we are artists in despising; that all intercourse with men is something of a horror to us; that with all our gentleness, patience, humanity and courteousness, we cannot persuade our nose to abandon its prejudice against the proximity of man; that we love nature the more, the less humanly things are done by her, and that we love art *when* it is the flight of the artist from man, or the raillery of the artist at man, or the raillery of the artist at himself...

380.

"The Wanderer" Speaks.—In order for once to get a glimpse of our European morality from a distance, in order to compare it with other earlier or future moralities, one must do as the traveller who wants to know the height of the towers of a city: for that purpose he *leaves* the city. "Thoughts concerning moral prejudices," if they are not to be prejudices concerning prejudices, presuppose a position *outside of* morality, some sort of world beyond good and evil, to which one must ascend, climb, or fly—and in the given case at any rate, a position beyond *our* good and evil, an emancipation from all "Europe," understood as a sum of inviolable valuations which have become part and parcel of our flesh and blood. That one does *want* to get outside, or aloft, is perhaps a sort of madness, a peculiar, unreasonable "thou must"—for even we thinkers have our idiosyncrasies of "unfree will"—: the question is whether one *can* really get there. That may depend on manifold conditions: in the main it is a question of how light or how heavy we are, the problem of our "specific gravity." One must be *very light* in order to impel one's will to knowledge to such a distance, and as it were beyond one's age, in order to create eyes for oneself for the survey of millenniums, and a pure heaven in these eyes besides! One must have freed oneself from many things by which we Europeans of to-day are oppressed, hindered, held down, and made heavy. The man of such a "Beyond," who wants to get even in sight of the highest standards of worth of his age, must first of all "surmount" this age in himself—it is the test of his power—and consequently not only his age, but also his past aversion and opposition *to* his age, his suffering *caused by* his age, his unseasonableness, his Romanticism...

381.

The Question of Intelligibility.—One not only wants to be understood when one writes, but also—quite as certainly—*not* to be understood. It is by no means an objection to a book when someone finds it unintelligible: perhaps this might just have been the intention of its author,—perhaps he did not *want* to be understood by "anyone." A distinguished intellect and taste, when it wants to communicate its thoughts, always selects its hearers; by selecting them, it at the same time closes its barriers against "the others." It is there that all the more refined laws of style have their origin: they at the same time keep off, they create distance, they prevent "access" (intelligibility, as we have said,)—while they open the ears of those who are acoustically related to them. And to say it between ourselves and with reference to my own case,—I do not desire that either my ignorance, or the vivacity of my temperament, should prevent me being understood by *you*, my friends: I certainly do not desire that my vivacity should have that effect, however much it may impel me to arrive quickly at an object, in order to arrive at it at all. For I think it is best to do with profound problems as with a cold bath—quickly in, quickly out. That one does not thereby get into the depths, that one does not get deep enough *down*—is a superstition of the hydrophobic, the enemies of cold water; they speak without experience. Oh! the great cold makes one quick!—And let me ask by the way: Is it a fact that a thing has been misunderstood and unrecognised when it has only been touched upon in passing, glanced at, flashed at? Must one absolutely sit upon it in the first place? Must one have brooded on it as on an egg? *Diu noctuque incubando*, as Newton said of himself? At least there are truths of a peculiar shyness and ticklishness which one can only get hold of suddenly, and in no other way,—which one must either *take by surprise*, or leave alone... Finally, my brevity has still another value: on those questions which pre-occupy me, I must say a great deal briefly, in order that it may be heard yet more briefly. For as immoralist, one has to take care lest one ruins innocence, I mean the asses and old maids of both sexes, who get nothing from life but their innocence; moreover my writings are meant to fill them with enthusiasm, to elevate them, to encourage them in virtue. I should be at a loss to know of anything more amusing than to see enthusiastic old asses and maids moved by the sweet feelings of virtue: and "that have I seen"—spake Zarathustra. So much with respect to brevity; the matter stands worse as regards my ignorance, of which I make no secret to myself. There are hours in which I am ashamed of it; to be sure there are likewise hours in which I am ashamed of this shame. Perhaps we philosophers, all of us, are badly placed at present with regard to knowledge: science is growing, the most learned of us are on the point of discovering that we know too little. But it would be worse still if it were otherwise,—if we knew too much; our duty is and remains first of all, not to get into confusion about ourselves. We *are* different from the learned; although it cannot be denied that amongst other things we are also learned. We have different needs, a different growth, a different digestion: we need more, we need also less. There is no formula as to how much an intellect needs for its nourishment; if, however, its taste be in the direction of independence, rapid coming and going, travelling, and perhaps adventure for which only the swiftest are qualified, it prefers rather to live free on poor fare, than to be unfree and plethoric. Not fat, but the greatest suppleness and power is what a good dancer wishes from his nourishment,—and I know not what the spirit of a philosopher would like better than to be a good dancer. For the dance is his ideal, and also his art, in the end likewise his sole piety, his "divine service.". . .

382.

Great Healthiness.—We, the new, the nameless, the hard-to-understand, we firstlings of a yet untried future—we require for a new end also a new means, namely, a new healthiness, stronger, sharper, tougher, bolder and merrier than any healthiness hitherto. He whose soul longs to experience the whole range of hitherto recognised values and desirabilities, and to circumnavigate all the coasts of this ideal "Mediterranean Sea," who, from the adventures of his most personal experience, wants to know how it feels to be a conqueror and discoverer of the ideal—as likewise how it is with the artist, the saint, the legislator, the sage, the scholar, the devotee, the prophet, and the godly Nonconformist of the old style:—requires one thing above all for that purpose, *great healthiness*—such healthiness as one not only possesses, but also constantly acquires and must acquire, because one continually sacrifices it again, and must sacrifice it!—And now, after having been long on the way in this fashion, we Argonauts of the ideal, who are more courageous perhaps than prudent, and often enough shipwrecked and brought to grief, nevertheless, as said above, healthier than people would like to admit, dangerously healthy, always healthy again,—it would seem, as if in recompense for it all, that we have a still undiscovered country before us, the boundaries of which no one has yet seen, a beyond to all countries and corners of the ideal known hitherto, a world so over-rich in the beautiful, the strange, the questionable, the frightful, and the divine, that our curiosity as well as our thirst for possession thereof, have got out of hand—alas! that nothing will now any longer satisfy us! How could we still be content with *the man of the present day* after such peeps, and with such a craving in our conscience and consciousness? What a pity; but it is unavoidable that we should look on the worthiest aims and hopes of the man of the present day with ill-concealed amusement, and perhaps should no longer look at them. Another ideal runs on before us, a strange, tempting ideal, full of danger, to which we should not like to persuade any one, because we do not so readily acknowledge any one's *right thereto*: the ideal of a spirit who plays naïvely (that is to say involuntarily and from overflowing abundance and power) with everything that has hitherto been called holy, good, inviolable, divine; to whom the loftiest conception which the people have reasonably made their measure of value, would already imply danger, ruin, abasement, or at least relaxation, blindness, or temporary self-forgetfulness; the ideal of a humanly superhuman welfare and benevolence, which may often enough appear *inhuman,* for example, when put by the side of all past seriousness on earth, and in comparison with all past solemnities in bearing, word, tone, look, morality and pursuit, as their truest involuntary parody,—but with which, nevertheless, perhaps *the great seriousness* only commences, the proper interrogation mark is set up, the fate of the soul changes, the hour-hand moves, and tragedy *begins...*

383.

Epilogue.—-But while I slowly, slowly finish the painting of this sombre interrogation-mark, and am still inclined to remind my readers of the virtues of right reading—oh, what forgotten and unknown virtues—it comes to pass that the wickedest, merriest, gnome-like laughter resounds around me: the spirits of my book themselves pounce upon me, pull me by the ears, and call me to order. "We cannot endure it any longer," they shout to me, "away, away with this raven-black music. Is it not clear morning round about us? And green, soft ground and turf, the domain of the dance? Was there ever a better hour in which to be joyful? Who will sing us a song, a morning song, so sunny, so light and so fledged that it will *not* scare the tantrums,—but will rather invite them to take part in the singing and dancing. And better a simple rustic bagpipe than such weird sounds, such toad-croakings, grave-voices and marmot-pipings, with which you have hitherto regaled us in your wilderness, Mr Anchorite and Musician of the Future! No! Not such tones! But let us strike up something more agreeable and more joyful!"—You would like to have it so, my impatient friends? Well! Who would not willingly accede to your wishes? My bagpipe is waiting, and my voice also—it may sound a little hoarse; take it as it is! don't forget we are in the mountains! But what you will hear is at least new; and if you do not understand it, if you misunderstand the *minstrel,* what does it matter! That—has always been "The Minstrel's Curse."[15] So much the more distinctly can you hear his music and melody, so much the better also can you—dance to his piping. *Would you like* to do that?...

---

[15] Title of the well-known poem of Uhland.—TR.

APPENDIX

SONGS OF PRINCE FREE-AS-A-BIRD

TO GOETHE.[16]

"The Undecaying"
Is but thy label,
God the betraying
Is poets' fable.
Our aims all are thwarted
By the World-wheel's blind roll:
"Doom," says the downhearted,
"Sport," says the fool.
The World-sport, all-ruling,
Mingles false with true:
The Eternally Fooling
Makes us play, too!
THE POET'S CALL.
As 'neath a shady tree I sat
After long toil to take my pleasure,
I heard a tapping "pit-a-pat"
Beat prettily in rhythmic measure.
Tho' first I scowled, my face set hard,
The sound at length my sense entrapping
Forced me to speak like any bard,
And keep true time unto the tapping.
As I made verses, never stopping,
Each syllable the bird went after,
Keeping in time with dainty hopping!
I burst into unmeasured laughter!
What, you a poet? You a poet?
Can your brains truly so addled be?
"Yes, yes, good sir, you are a poet,"
Chirped out the pecker, mocking me.
What doth me to these woods entice?

---

[16]This poem is a parody of the "Chorus Mysticus" which concludes the second part of Goethe's "Faust." Bayard Taylor's translation of the passage in "Faust" runs as follows:—

The chance to give some thief a trouncing?
A saw, an image? Ha, in a trice
My rhyme is on it, swiftly pouncing!
All things that creep or crawl the poet
Weaves in his word-loom cunningly.
"Yes, yes, good sir, you are a poet,"
Chirped out the pecker, mocking me.
Like to an arrow, methinks, a verse is,
See how it quivers, pricks and smarts
When shot full straight (no tender mercies!)
Into the reptile's nobler parts!
Wretches, you die at the hand of the poet,
Or stagger like men that have drunk too free.
"Yes, yes, good sir, you are a poet,"
Chirped out the pecker, mocking me.
So they go hurrying, stanzas malign,
Drunken words—what a clattering, banging!—
Till the whole company, line on line,
All on the rhythmic chain are hanging.
Has he really a cruel heart, your poet?
Are there fiends who rejoice, the slaughter to see
"Yes, yes, good sir, you are a poet,"
Chirped out the pecker, mocking me.
So you jest at me, bird, with your scornful graces?
So sore indeed is the plight of my head?
And my heart, you say, in yet sorrier case is?
Beware! for my wrath is a thing to dread!
Yet e'en in the hour of his wrath the poet
Rhymes you and sings with the selfsame glee.
"Yes, yes, good sir, you are a poet,"
Chirped out the pecker, mocking me.
IN THE SOUTH.[17]
I swing on a bough, and rest
My tired limbs in a nest,

---

[17]Translated by Miss M. D. Petre. Inserted by permission of the editor of the *Nation,* in which it appeared on April 17, 1909.

In the rocking home of a bird,
Wherein I perch as his guest,
In the South!
I gaze on the ocean asleep,
On the purple sail of a boat;
On the harbour and tower steep,
On the rocks that stand out of the deep,
In the South!
For I could no longer stay,
To crawl in slow German way;
So I called to the birds, bade the wind
Lift me up and bear me away
To the South!
No reasons for me, if you please;
Their end is too dull and too plain;
But a pair of wings and a breeze,
With courage and health and ease,
And games that chase disease
From the South!
Wise thoughts can move without sound,
But I've songs that I can't sing alone;
So birdies, pray gather around,
And listen to what I have found
In the South!
. . . .
"You are merry lovers and false and gay,
"In frolics and sport you pass the day;
"Whilst in the North, I shudder to say,
"I worshipped a woman, hideous and gray,
"Her name was Truth, so I heard them say,
"But I left her there and I flew away
"To the South!"
BEPPA THE PIOUS.
While beauty in my face is,
Be piety my care,
For God, you know, loves lasses,

And, more than all, the fair.
And if yon hapless monkling
Is fain with me to live,
Like many another monkling,
God surely will forgive.
No grey old priestly devil,
But, young, with cheeks aflame—
Who e'en when sick with revel,
Can jealous be and blame.
To greybeards I'm a stranger,
And he, too, hates the old:
Of God, the world-arranger,
The wisdom here behold!
The Church has ken of living,
And tests by heart and face.
To me she'll be forgiving!
Who will not show me grace?
I lisp with pretty halting,
I curtsey, bid "good day,"
And with the fresh defaulting
I wash the old away!
Praise be this man-God's guerdon,
Who loves all maidens fair,
And his own heart can pardon
The sin he planted there.
While beauty in my face is,
With piety I'll stand,
When age has killed my graces,
Let Satan claim my hand!
THE BOAT OF MYSTERY.
Yester-eve, when all things slept—
Scarce a breeze to stir the lane—
I a restless vigil kept,
Nor from pillows sleep could gain,
Nor from poppies nor—most sure
Of opiates—a conscience pure.

Thoughts of rest I 'gan forswear,
Rose and walked along the strand,
Found, in warm and moonlit air,
Man and boat upon the sand,
Drowsy both, and drowsily
Did the boat put out to sea.
Passed an hour or two perchance,
Or a year? then thought and sense
Vanished in the engulfing trance
Of a vast Indifference.
Fathomless, abysses dread
Opened—then the vision fled.
Morning came: becalmed, the boat
Rested on the purple flood:
"What had happened?" every throat
Shrieked the question: "was there—
Blood?"
Naught had happened! On the swell
We had slumbered, oh, so well!
AN AVOWAL OF LOVE
(*during which, however, the poet fell into a pit*).
Oh marvel! there he flies
Cleaving the sky with wings unmoved—what force
Impels him, bids him rise,
What curb restrains him? Where's his goal, his course?
Like stars and time eterne
He liveth now in heights that life forswore,
Nor envy's self doth spurn:
A lofty flight were't, e'en to see him soar!
Oh albatross, great bird,
Speeding me upward ever through the blue!
I thought of her, was stirred
To tears unending—yea, I love her true!
SONG OF A THEOCRITEAN GOATHERD.
Here I lie, my bowels sore,
Hosts of bugs advancing,

Yonder lights and romp and roar!
What's that sound? They're dancing!
At this instant, so she prated,
Stealthily she'd meet me:
Like a faithful dog I've waited,
Not a sign to greet me!
She promised, made the cross-sign, too,
Could her vows be hollow?
Or runs she after all that woo,
Like the goats I follow?
Whence your silken gown, my maid?
Ah, you'd fain be haughty,
Yet perchance you've proved a jade
With some satyr naughty!
Waiting long, the lovelorn wight
Is filled with rage and poison:
Even so on sultry night
Toadstools grow in foison.
Pinching sore, in devil's mood,
Love doth plague my crupper:
Truly I can eat no food:
Farewell, onion-supper!
Seaward sinks the moon away,
The stars are wan, and flare not:
Dawn approaches, gloomy, grey,
Let Death come! I care not!
"SOULS THAT LACK DETERMINATION."
Souls that lack determination
Rouse my wrath to white-hot flame!
All their glory's but vexation,
All their praise but self-contempt and shame!
Since I baffle their advances,
Will not clutch their leading-string,
They would wither me with glances
Bitter-sweet, with hopeless envy sting.
Let them with fell curses shiver,

Curl their lip the livelong day!
Seek me as they will, forever
Helplessly their eyes shall go astray!
THE FOOL'S DILEMMA.
Ah, what I wrote on board and wall
With foolish heart, in foolish scrawl,
I meant but for their decoration!
Yet say you, "Fools' abomination!
Both board and wall require purgation,
And let no trace our eyes appal!"
Well, I will help you, as I can,
For sponge and broom are my vocation
As critic and as waterman.
But when the finished work I scan,
I'm glad to see each learned owl
With "wisdom" board and wall defoul.
RIMUS REMEDIUM
(*or a Consolation to Sick Poets*).
From thy moist lips,
O Time, thou witch, beslavering me,
Hour upon hour too slowly drips
In vain—I cry, in frenzy's fit,
"A curse upon that yawning pit,
A curse upon Eternity!"
The world's of brass,
A fiery bullock, deaf to wail:
Pain's dagger pierces my cuirass,
Wingéd, and writes upon my bone:
"Bowels and heart the world hath none,
Why scourge her sins with anger's flail?"
Pour poppies now,
Pour venom, Fever, on my brain!
Too long you test my hand and brow:
What ask you? "What—reward is paid?"
A malediction on you, jade,
And your disdain!

No, I retract,
'Tis cold—I hear the rain importune—
Fever, I'll soften, show my tact:
Here's gold—a coin—see it gleam!
Shall I with blessings on you beam,
Call you "good fortune"?
The door opes wide,
And raindrops on my bed are scattered,
The light's blown out—woes multiplied!
He that hath not an hundred rhymes,
I'll wager, in these dolorous times
We'd see him shattered!
MY BLISS.
Once more, St Mark, thy pigeons meet my gaze,
The Square lies still, in slumbering morning mood:
In soft, cool air I fashion idle lays,
Speeding them skyward like a pigeon's brood:
And then recall my minions
To tie fresh rhymes upon their willing pinions.
My bliss! My bliss!
Calm heavenly roof of azure silkiness,
Guarding with shimmering haze yon house divine!
Thee, house, I love, fear—envy, I'll confess,
And gladly would suck out that soul of thine!
"Should I give back the prize?"
Ask not, great pasture-ground for human eyes!
My bliss! My bliss!
Stern belfry, rising as with lion's leap
Sheer from the soil in easy victory,
That fill'st the Square with peal resounding, deep
Wert thou in French that Square's "accent aigu"?
Were I for ages set
In earth like thee, I know what silk-meshed net——
My bliss! My bliss!
Hence, music! First let darker shadows come,
And grow, and merge into brown, mellow night!

Tis early for your pealing, ere the dome
Sparkle in roseate glory, gold-bedight
While yet 'tis day, there's time
For strolling, lonely muttering, forging rhyme—
My bliss! My bliss!
COLUMBUS REDIVIVUS.
Thither I'll travel, that's my notion,
I'll trust myself, my grip,
Where opens wide and blue the ocean
I'll ply my Genoa ship.
New things on new the world unfolds me,
Time, space with noonday die:
Alone thy monstrous eye beholds me,
Awful Infinity!
SILS-MARIA.
Here sat I waiting, waiting, but for naught!
Beyond all good and evil—now by light wrought
To joy, now by dark shadows—all was leisure,
All lake, all noon, all time sans aim, sans measure.
Then one, dear friend, was swiftly changed to twain,
And Zarathustra left my teeming brain. . .
A DANCING SONG TO THE MISTRAL WIND.[18]
Wildly rushing, clouds outleaping,
Care-destroying, Heaven sweeping,
Mistral wind, thou art my friend!
Surely 'twas one womb did bear us,
Surely 'twas one fate did pair us,
Fellows for a common end.
From the crags I gaily greet you,
Running fast I come to meet you,
Dancing while you pipe and sing.
How you bound across the ocean,
Unimpeded, free in motion,
Swifter than with boat or wing!

---

[18]Translated by Miss M. D. Petre. Inserted by permission of the editor of the *Nation*, in which it appeared on May 15, 1909.

Through my dreams your whistle sounded,
Down the rocky stairs I bounded
To the golden ocean wall;
Saw you hasten, swift and glorious,
Like a river, strong, victorious,
Tumbling in a waterfall.
Saw you rushing over Heaven,
With your steeds so wildly driven,
Saw the car in which you flew;
Saw the lash that wheeled and quivered,
While the hand that held it shivered,
Urging on the steeds anew.
Saw you from your chariot swinging,
So that swifter downward springing
Like an arrow you might go
Straight into the deep abysses,
As a sunbeam falls and kisses
Roses in the morning glow.
Dance, oh! dance on all the edges,
Wave-crests, cliffs and mountain ledges,
Ever finding dances new!
Let our knowledge be our gladness,
Let our art be sport and madness,
All that's joyful shall be true!
Let us snatch from every bower,
As we pass, the fairest flower,
With some leaves to make a crown;
Then, like minstrels gaily dancing,
Saint and witch together prancing,
Let us foot it up and down.
Those who come must move as; quickly
As the wind—we'll have no sickly,
Crippled, withered, in our crew.;
Off with hypocrites and preachers,
Proper folk and prosy teachers,
Sweep them from our heaven blue.

Sweep away all sad grimaces,
Whirl the dust into the faces
Of the dismal sick and cold!
Hunt them from our breezy places,
Not for them the wind that braces,
But for men of visage bold.
Off with those who spoil earth's gladness,
Blow away all clouds of sadness,
Till our heaven clear we see;
Let me hold thy hand, best fellow,
Till my joy like tempest bellow!
Freest thou of spirits free!
When thou partest, take a token
Of the joy thou hast awoken,
Take our wreath and fling it far;
Toss it up and catch it never,
Whirl it on before thee ever,
Till it reach the farthest star.
"All things transitory
But as symbols are sent,
Earth's insufficiency
Here grows to Event:
The Indescribable
Here it is done:
The Woman-Soul leadeth us
Upward and on!"

Made in the USA
Monee, IL
03 February 2024

52851777R20121